D1381182

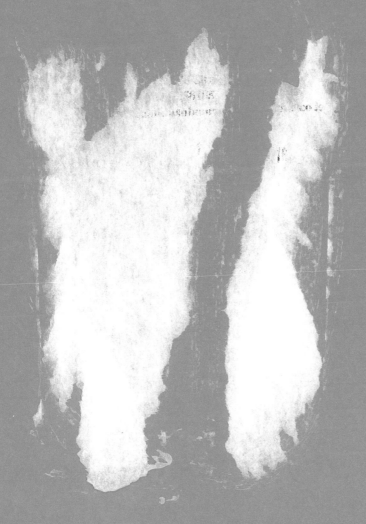

# MYSTERIES
## OF PLANET EARTH

AN ENCYCLOPEDIA OF THE INEXPLICABLE

Dedication
To my good friend William M. Rebsamen, the Audubon of crytozoology

THIS IS A CARLTON BOOK

Text © Dr Karl P. N. Shuker 1999
Design © Carlton Books Limited, 1999

This edition published by Carlton Books Limited, 1999

A CIP catalogue for this book is available from the British Library.

ISBN 1 85868 679 2

Design and editorial: Andy Jones, Barry Sutcliffe and Deborah Martin
Project Editor: Camilla MacWhannell
Project Art Direction: Tim Brown and Phil Scott
Picture Research: Lorna Ainger

Printed in Dubai

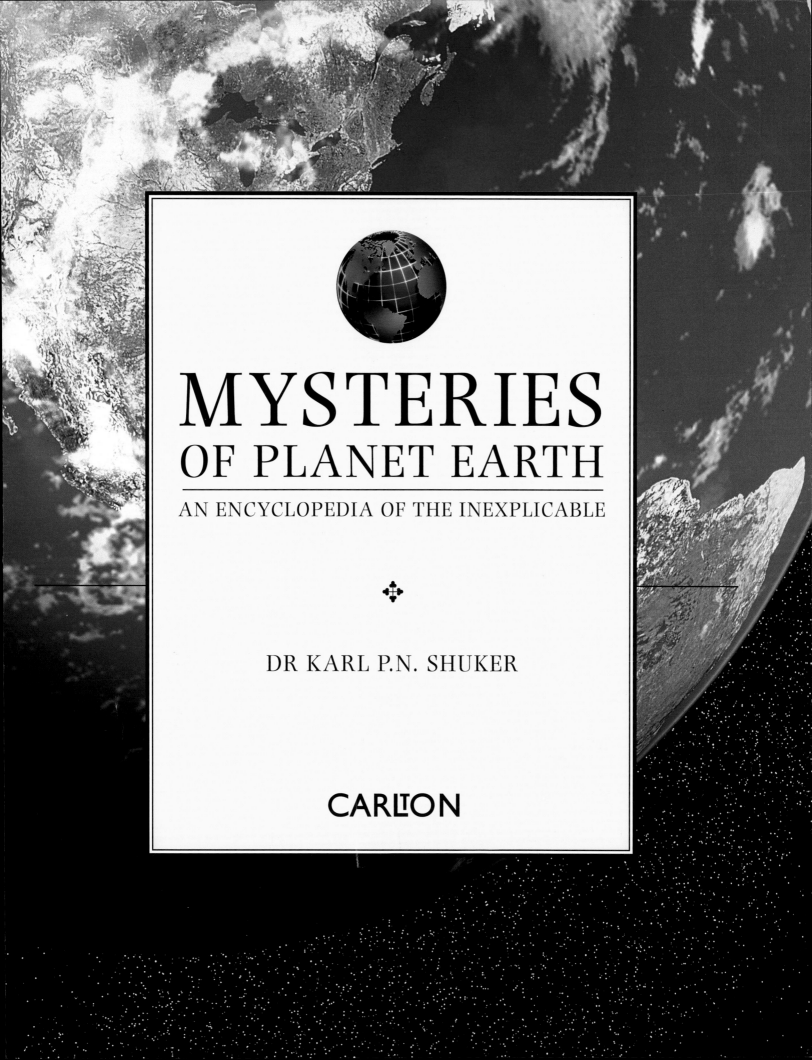

# MYSTERIES
## OF PLANET EARTH

### AN ENCYCLOPEDIA OF THE INEXPLICABLE

DR KARL P.N. SHUKER

**CARLTON**

# CONTENTS

# INTRODUCTION

## AN ISLAND OF INEXPLICABILIA

*I do not know what I may appear to the world, but to myself I seem to have been only a boy playing on the sea-shore, and diverting myself in now and then finding a smoother pebble or a prettier shell than ordinary, whilst the great ocean of truth lay all undiscovered before me.*

Sir Isaac Newton (quoted in Brewster's
Memoirs of Newton, 1855, vol. ii, ch. 27)

Notwithstanding every advance made by science since Newton spoke those words almost three hundred years ago, humanity's continuing efforts to elucidate the great ocean of truth have scarcely rippled its dark, shadow-dappled surface, let alone penetrated its opaque and fathomless depths. In the triple century that has succeeded the age of Newton's pioneering discoveries, we may have uncovered a few more pebbles smoother than those previously collected, or a

*This photograph taken by Louise Whipps shows the strange "globster" she discovered on the shore of Benbecula – see page 90.*

few more shells prettier than those seen before, but that is all. Our planet is a realm still replete with mystery, an island of inexplicabilia drifting passively upon the ever-trembling currents of time that emanate from the greatest undivined secret of all, which we call the universe for want of a better name or definition, and it is sheer folly to profess otherwise.

Inevitably, therefore, countless books dealing with a wide range of mysterious phenomena have appeared over the years – a trend which, nurtured as it is by our species' primeval fascination with the unknown and unexplained, shows no sign of abating. Unfortunately, however, such books all too frequently concentrate upon the more famous or generalized examples of inexplicabilia, at the expense of an extraordinary wealth of additional cases that are much more specific and far less familiar – but certainly no less interesting. Accordingly, these books normally suffer from an unavoidable (but often extensive) duplication of data and accompanying illustrative material.

In stark contrast, this present book of mine purposefully focuses its attention upon a

veritable treasure trove of hitherto little-publicized yet compellingly strange, thoroughly fascinating mysteries of every kind, but all directly linked with planet Earth. (Sorry, but UFOs, aliens, lost solar planets, mysteries of Outer Space, and other ostensibly extraterrestrial enigmas will have to wait for a future book!) Many have not previously been documented at all, or have until now been confined to obscure, relatively inaccessible journals or specialist publications, and thus have never been featured before in a mainstream popular-format book. Moreover, as I can read several European languages, I have also been able to include a number of very remarkable subjects previously documented only in foreign-language works.

Faced with the daunting task of instating a measure of order and conformity upon this eclectic corpus of inexplicabilia, I have divided its contents into three sections, dealing respectively with the natural world, the supernatural world, and the vanished world. Each of these sections is then subdivided into two chapters, thus yielding six in total.

*Dr Karl Shuker with a model of a giant octopus – a mystery from the ocean's depths.*

Subjects surveyed in the natural world's section include a unique array of hitherto-obscure but truly outstanding mystery beasts relevant to the fledgling investigative science of cryptozoology; a diverse assortment of mystifying anomalies in the fields of animal behaviour and morphology; controversial flora of many kinds; and some very bizarre geological and meteorological oddities; as well as a captivating selection of unexpected aerial and aquatic phenomena, all well deserving of mainstream attention.

The supernatural world's section contains a spine-chilling phantasmagoria of incorporeal incongruities, and other paranormal entities of the weird but very wonderful variety; exceptional psychic facilities and phenomena seemingly transcending current frameworks of knowledge; plus an astounding array of religious wonders and marvels from around the world that continue to defy rational, scientific elucidation.

The vanished world's section unfurls mysteries from (or in some manner linked to) the distant past and bygone ages. These include mystifying artefacts or constructions whose very existence indicates that some civilizations possessed certain facets of knowledge far earlier in time than present-day science is currently willing to accept; evidence that several regions of the world were visited by ancient voyagers long before their "official" dates of discovery; and the exciting prospect that certain famous figures, creatures or events in mythology and folklore may actually have a firm basis in reality.

In addition, as with all of my books, this present work contains an informative bibliography of publications that can be consulted by readers wishing to pursue further any of the subjects documented here. Equally significant are its illustrations, which include a large number of top-quality, full-colour pictures that have never previously appeared in any book.

Notable among these are the beautiful artwork and full-colour paintings by William M. Rebsamen, emphatically establishing himself as America's finest cryptozoological artist; by England's own Philippa Foster, whose passionate interest in our planet's inexplicabilia radiates forth from all of her sumptuous illustrations; and by Sweden's Richard Svensson, whose dramatic line drawings vividly animate eyewitness descriptions of bizarre entities.

The sceptics and cynics of this world have little patience with mysteries. They choose to see only what they can comprehend – in their eyes, therefore, our planet has few if any surprises still to offer. Conversely, after reading this latest book of mine, I hope that you may feel able to share, as I do, the view eloquently expressed by naturalist Loren Eiseley in his book *The Unexpected Universe* (1964): "Things get odder on this planet, not less so".

# MYSTERIES OF THE
# NATURAL
# WORLD

*Nature is no great mother who has borne us. She is our own creation. It is in our brain that she quickens to life. Things are because we see them, and what we see and how we see it depends on the arts that have influenced us. To look at a thing is very different from seeing a thing.*

Oscar Wilde, *The Decay of Lying*

THERE IS NO PHYSICAL DEMARCATION BETWEEN WHAT IS NATURAL AND WHAT IS UNNATURAL IN THE REAL WORLD: SUCH DISCRIMINATION EXISTS ONLY IN THE HUMAN MIND, IN HUMAN PERCEPTION. WHAT SHOULD OR SHOULD NOT EXIST, WHAT CAN AND CANNOT OCCUR, DEPENDS ENTIRELY UPON THE PREVAILING CONSENSUS OF OPINION, SCIENTIFIC OR OTHERWISE, AT ANY GIVEN MOMENT IN TIME OR LOCALITY IN SPACE. ALL OF THE CASES CONSIDERED IN THIS SECTION HAVE BEEN DEEMED CONTENTIOUS BY SCIENCE; TOMORROW, HOWEVER, THEY MAY ALL BECOME ACCEPTABLE. YET WHEN AND IF THEY DO, THEY WILL NOT HAVE CHANGED IN ANY WAY; ALL THAT WILL HAVE SHIFTED IS THE METAPHORICAL MARKER SEPARATING THE INCLUDED FROM THE EXCLUDED WITHIN THE SPECTRUM OF CONTEMPORARY SCIENTIFIC COMPREHENSION.

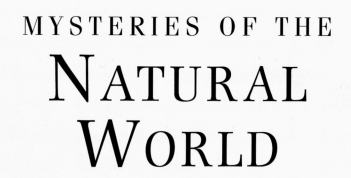

## CHAPTER ONE

## A LESSON IN UNNATURAL HISTORY

# NATURE

## THY NAME IS CAPRICE

NOT ALL MYSTERIOUS, UNEXPECTED CREATURES ARE LIKELY TO BE NEW SPECIES. SOME OF THE MOST
CONTROVERSIAL AND CONTRADICTORY ANIMALS ON RECORD ASSUREDLY REPRESENT BIZARRE,
HITHERTO-UNDOCUMENTED MUTANTS OF SPECIES ALREADY KNOWN TO SCIENCE — AS EXEMPLIFIED BY
THE FOLLOWING MENAGERIE OF DECIDEDLY EXOTIC ZOOLOGICAL CAPRICES AND CURIOSITIES.

## WHITHER THE WOOLLY CHEETAH?

In 1877, a most unusual male cheetah from Beaufort West in South Africa arrived at London Zoo. Although only a subadult, it was larger in overall size than the three fully mature specimens of normal cheetahs already housed here, but its body appeared thicker, with shorter, stouter limbs. Equally distinctive was its fur, which was much more dense and woolly

*The woolly cheetah – rare mutant, now extinct?*

than in ordinary cheetahs, especially on its neck, ears, and tail. Moreover, instead of sporting the normal cheetah's familiar black polka-dot spots, this odd specimen's fur, whose background colour was pale isabelline (greyish-yellow), was mottled with tiny dark fulvous (tawny) blotches.

As a result of its singular appearance, Philip Sclater, secretary of the Zoological Society of London, opined that it may represent a discrete species, and dubbed it *Felis lanea*, the woolly cheetah. By the end of the 1800s, at

least two further specimens, also from Beaufort West, had been recorded, but with no modern-day records, this feline enigma seems to have become extinct. As to its zoological identity, some researchers have speculated that it may have comprised an erythristic (i.e. abnormally red) mutant of the normal cheetah. Conversely, in 1978, world-renowned cat geneticist Roy Robinson postulated that it might well have been a chinchilla albino – that is, a cheetah equivalent of the famous white tigers of Rewa and white lions of Timbavati.

## THE MYSTERY OF BREVET'S BLACK TAPIRS

Another colour-confused mystery beast that has actually been exhibited at one time or another in a major zoo is the nowadays largely forgotten *brevetianus* variety of Malayan tapir. Largest of the four living tapir species and the only Old World species, the Malayan tapir *Tapirus indicus* is further distinguished by its striking "saddle" of white, encompassing much of its torso and haunches; its three New World relatives are all uniformly dark. Naturally, therefore, zoologists were nonplussed when one of the adult Malayan tapirs sent to Rotterdam Zoo in spring 1924 from Sumatra proved to be entirely black, with no saddle.

According to Dr K. Kuiper of Rotterdam Zoo, there were no previous records of all-black Malayan tapirs, and not even Captain K. Brevet (of the Royal Dutch-Indian Army), from whom the tapirs had been received, had ever heard tell of such creatures before. Despite this, the Rotterdam specimen, a male, confirmed that at least one could (and did) exist – and when, just a few months later, Brevet sent two juvenile Malayan tapirs to the zoo, one of these matured into a second all-black individual.

Yet although they were evidently Malayan tapirs, what was their precise identity, taxonomically speaking? Both specimens had been captured within the Babat district in the low-lying plains of Palembang, a district where the familiar white-backed form also exists – thereby eliminating any possibility that they constituted a morphologically distinctive geographical subspecies. And as these two mystifying individuals were both from this same region, with no reports of any all-black tapirs elsewhere, Kuiper also deemed it unlikely that they were merely the product of a simple genetic mutation – i.e. a melanistic (all-black) variant that could appear anywhere and at any time within any population of white-backed specimens (like black panthers within populations of spotted leopards).

Accordingly, Kuiper looked upon them as representatives of a newly emerging variety, not replacing the white-backed version in any specific area (and hence not a subspecies), but nonetheless possessing a specific geographical distribution. In 1926, he formally christened his newly categorized variety *Tapirus indicus* var. *brevetianus*, in honour of its discoverer.

However, it now seems much more plausible that this all-black form was nothing more than a melanistic mutant after all, because no further *brevetianus* specimens have

*The Malayan tapir normally has a large area of white hair over its back, as seen here.*

*Even zebra-horse hybrids, such as this specimen, are normally striped.*

distinctively decorated with rows of white spots and thin white dashes.

As commented upon in 1981 by Dr J.B.L. Bard within a *Journal of Theoretical Biology* paper dealing with mammalian coat patterns, this eyecatching oddity offers proof for believing that zebras are black animals with white stripes, rather than white animals with black stripes. For as Bard noted: "It is only possible to understand the pattern [of the spotted zebra] if the white stripes had failed to form properly and that therefore the 'default' colour is black. The role of the striping mechanism is thus to inhibit natural pigment formation rather than to stimulate it."

## THE SEPIA PANDAS OF QINLING

Another famously black-and-white mammal is the giant panda *Ailuropoda melanoleuca*, but in recent years several brown-and-white specimens have unexpectedly appeared, all within the Qinling Mountains of China's Shaanxi Province. During the 1980s, a female

ever been documented. And both of the Rotterdam individuals died before any matings with white-backed specimens could take place, thereby denying science the opportunity of investigating the genetic basis of their uniformly dark colouration. Even so, their preserved remains at the Leiden Museum of Natural History bear silent witness to their erstwhile existence, and to the tantalizing prospect that at some stage in the future, their kind will reappear, reviving the *brevetianus* zoogeographical paradox – the presence of all-black tapirs in the Old World.

## A SPOTTED ZEBRA

If an all-black Malayan tapir seems paradoxical, then how much more so a zebra with spots? Remarkably, however, spotted zebras have occasionally been reported. Probably the most famous specimen, pictured in London's *Daily*

*Mirror* newspaper on 3 January 1968, was observed in a herd of normal plains zebras *Equus burchelli* roaming northern Zambia's Rukwa Valley. Instead of exhibiting the familiar zebra patterning of white stripes, its body was

*An anomalous spotted zebra in a herd of normal zebras in Rukwa Valley, Zambia.*

*One of China's strange sepia-tinted pandas.*

sepia-shaded specimen was captured by biologist Pan Wenshi and exhibited at Xi'an Zoo, where on 31 August 1989 she gave birth to what seemed to be a normal male black-and-white cub, christened Bao Bei. Four months later, however, zoo staff were startled to see that his fur was changing colour, its black portions eventually becoming brown. As the Qinling panda population is both isolated and small, this brown-and-white mutant form may have arisen through inbreeding, rendering visible the effect of a mutant gene normally suppressed.

## HOW GREEN WERE MY POLAR BEARS

Green polar bears, conversely, are another matter entirely. Not surprisingly, during summer 1978 San Diego Zoo in California became somewhat perturbed when three of its adult polar bears inexplicably turned green! Anticipating that this bizarre colouration was merely due to algae from the bears' pool attaching to their fur (hence paralleling the presence of algae upon the fur of sloths), staff took some hair samples and had them examined microscopically, but no algal presence was detected – externally, that is. Remarkably,

however, algae had penetrated the hollow medullae of many of the wide, stiff guard hairs of the bears' outer pelage, and hence were growing *inside* their fur!

## THE NONAPUS OF ZAKYNTHOS

An octopus is called an octopus because it has eight limbs – which is why the specimen captured by amateur underwater fisherman Gregory Pissas off the coast of the Ionian island of Zakynthos in April 1987 was truly a contradiction in terms. Scorning its species' defining octet of tentacles, this exceptionally endowed specimen boasted nine – a veritable nonapus! After briefly achieving showbusiness stardom on the TV show "3 On The Air", however, the world's only-known nine-tentacled octopus ended its days as a prized museum specimen.

## HORNING IN ON THE UNICORN SNAILS

As for unicorn snails, such creatures really do occur too – albeit very rarely. Two notable specimens, both Roman (edible) snails *Helix pomatia* and discovered in France, were documented in 1959 by E. Fischer-Piette within the *Journal de Conchyliologie*. Whereas normal snails possess a pair of long, laterally sited stalks with a single eye at the tip of each stalk, each of these molluscan monoceri sported just a single centrally located stalk with two eyes borne side by side at its tip. This condition recalls the better-known teratological phenomenon of cyclopia, reported from many vertebrate species, even man, in which a single central eye develops instead of the normal pair of lateral eyes. This is usually of genetic origin, but it can be externally induced in young fishes and amphibian larvae if they are reared in water containing high concentrations of magnesium chloride or lithium chloride.

*Looking almost like a moss-covered branch, the fur of this three-toed sloth is coloured by algae.*

# THE LIGHT
# FANTASTIC

BIOLUMINESCENCE IS THE EMISSION OF LIGHT BY CERTAIN LIFE FORMS. THESE INCLUDE MANY KNOWN SPECIES OF BACTERIA, FUNGI, PROTOZOANS, INVERTEBRATES, AND FISHES, BUT THERE ARE ALSO SEVERAL CONTROVERSIAL EXAMPLES, INCLUDING SOME THAT MAY BE SPECIES STILL UNDESCRIBED BY SCIENCE.

### SEEING RED IN SERAM

One evening in June 1986, for instance, while working on the small eastern Indonesian island of Seram (Ceram) for the VSO, tropical agriculturalist Tyson Hughes spied some very eyecatching, unidentified fishes in a river. They resembled mudskippers in general size and shape, but unlike all known species of mudskipper these curious fishes emitted a bright, pulsating red light. Hughes earnestly attempted to catch one, but failed to do so.

*Mudskippers climb a stem – in their normal colours!*

### THE FROG WITH THE LUMINOUS NOSE

While visiting an animal fair at Newton Abbot in Devon, England, in June 1997, local mystery beast investigator Jonathan Downes noticed a cage containing some tree frogs, reputedly from northern Cameroon in western Africa and priced at £25 per frog. Downes was intrigued by these creatures, which each bore a blue spot on its snout, because he could not identify their species. He was even more so when informed by their vendor that the blue spot on their snout glowed in the dark, possibly to attract insects as prey.

Nevertheless, Downes felt that £25 was too expensive a sum, and so resisted the temptation to buy one – a decision that he would soon bitterly regret. For when he later described these curious frogs to various herpetological colleagues, he discovered that there is no species of frog known to science that can glow. Hence he had missed the opportunity to purchase a specimen of what might not only be a completely unknown species, but also exhibit a talent unique even among the world's considerably varied array of frogs.

## THE GLOWING LIZARD OF TRINIDAD

There is no formally accepted species of bioluminescent lizard either, which is why the little-known saga of Trinidad's glowing tejid is so noteworthy. It began in March 1937, when animal-collecting zoologist Ivan T. Sanderson was visiting Mount Aripo in Trinidad. While

*Left: A painting of Trinidad's luminescent lizard shows its curious glowing portholes.*

*A specimen of Sloane's viperfish, showing its bioluminescent markings.*

capturing some crabs in a series of dark subterranean pools, he suddenly spied a faint light in a crevice beneath a ledge. The light promptly went out, so Sanderson flashed his torch into the crevice, and was very surprised to find a small lizard. When he attempted to capture it, instead of running out of the crevice the lizard merely turned its head away, but as it did so, Sanderson was startled to see both of its flanks briefly lighting up "... like the portholes on a ship". It repeated this unexpected performance when he finally succeeded in capturing it, glowing brightly with a pale greenish hue likened by Sanderson to the glow produced by a luminous watch's hands and figures.

As science was unaware of any bioluminescent lizards, Sanderson was thrilled by his discovery, which he subsequently documented in his book *Caribbean Treasure* (1939). Except for its glowing ability, however, the lizard, a male, was quite nondescript – sporting a sharp muzzle, short legs, long tail, dark brown upperparts, and rosy salmon-pink underparts (becoming yellow under its head) surfaced with large rectangular plate-like scales.

Its only distinctive features were its body's lateral eyespots or "portholes" – a series of large circular black blots running from the neck to the groin on both flanks. For each of these blots contained a vivid white bead-like spot and were the source of the lizard's mysterious luminescence. By conducting a series of basic experiments, such as subjecting the lizard alternately to conditions of hot and cold, and moist and dry, gently tickling it, blowing a loud whistle at it, and exposing it to flashes of bright light, Sanderson revealed that it produced its light in response to sudden emotional disturbance (as with the loud whistle, sudden winds and flashes of light), rather than through actual physical reactions. He also noted that its light was brightest when first emitted following a period of quiescence, and especially so after it had previously been subjected to intense illumination.

Sanderson shipped his mystifying lizard to Europe, where it was studied by fellow zoologist H.W. Parker, who identified it as a known but exceedingly rare species of tejid, called *Proctoporus* (=*Oreosaurus*) *shrevei* – hitherto represented in scientific collections only by a single preserved adult female, and one preserved juvenile. Hence this was the first male on record, and no one had previously suspected that the species might be bioluminescent.

While in Trinidad, meanwhile, Sanderson obtained another seven specimens, which were also examined in preserved form by Parker, who published his findings in 1939 within the zoological journal of London's Linnaean Society. He revealed that only male specimens possessed the "porthole" markings, and that in every "porthole" the epidermis of the white bead at the centre was less than half the thickness of the epidermis of the black ring encircling it, and was transparent – lacking any form of pigment. In other words, each "porthole" quite literally constituted a circular, black-edged window.

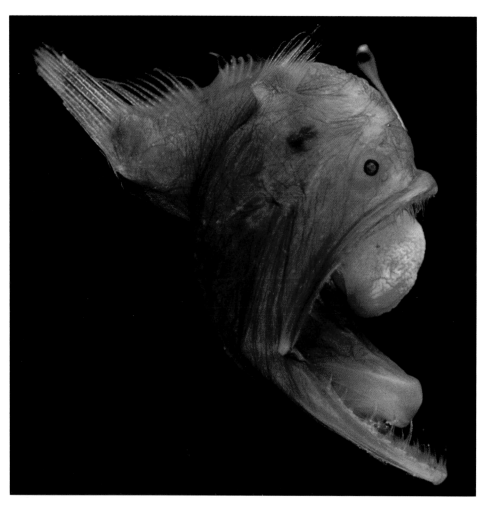

*The deep sea anglerfish uses its luminescence to attract prey.*

Still unexplained, however, was the mechanism by which the "portholes" produced their glow. Parker had been unable to find any associated nerve endings or an increased blood supply, thus eliminating the likelihood that they were directly connected with the sensory or circulatory systems. Nor had he located any ducts connecting these "portholes" with the exterior, or any complex lenses or reflecting structures.

Whatever they were, therefore, these "portholes" were clearly very simple in structure, and Parker offered three possible explanations for their luminosity. In life, the "portholes" may contain some substance that glows either when it breaks down (the principle of bioluminescence in various fishes), or when

exposed to light (as with the paint used in luminous watches). The third option is that the transparent central beads of the "portholes" are underlain with reflective tissue. A fourth possibility, that the "portholes" contain glowing bacteria which create their luminosity, can be rejected, because Parker did not report the presence of any bacteria within them.

Several other zoologists subsequently followed up Parker's work, by monitoring specimens of *P. shrevei* and various related tejids to see whether any of theirs glowed – but none of them did. Consequently, when in 1960 they reported their own negative findings with *P. achlyens* from Venezuela and *Neusticurus ecpleopus ocellatus* (both of which possess "porthole" markings), American biologists

Dr Willard Roth and Carl Gans rejected Sanderson's claim that *P. shrevei* was bioluminescent.

Yet Sanderson was a competent zoologist, and Parker's histological studies convinced him that the "portholes" were genuine luminous organs. So who is correct? After all, if, for instance, *P. shrevei* is the only bioluminescent species, any comparative studies conducted with related species are worthless. Yet except for Sanderson, only one zoologist actually investigated bioluminescence with this particular species – and he may simply not have stimulated his specimens sufficiently for them to light up.

Only further, detailed studies are likely to solve this riddle conclusively. However, that option is severely hampered by the great rarity of *P. shrevei*. Moreover, as discovered by a colleague of American cryptozoologist Chad Arment when pursuing the glowing lizard during a visit to Trinidad in late 1998, during the six decades since Sanderson was there the terrain visited by him has changed out of all recognition. Hence it was impossible to relocate the place where Sanderson collected his first specimen. In short, there may not be any light at the end of the tunnel of investigation into Trinidad's reputedly luminous lizard after all.

## FLUORESCENT FLORA

Another still-unexplained phenomenon is the extraordinary occurrence, discussed by several naturalists during the nineteenth century, of sparks and flame-like flashes of light unexpectedly emitted by certain plants. Those most commonly associated with this bizarre enigma are species such as marigolds and geraniums, which possess red, orange or yellow flowers.

In 1843, the following account of an observation with common marigolds, penned by Richard Dowden, appeared in Part 2 of that year's *Report of the British Association*:

*This circumstance was noticed on the 4th of August, 1842, at eight p.m., after a week of very dry warm weather; four persons observed the phaenomenon [sic]; by shading off the declining daylight, a gold-coloured lambent light appeared to play from petal to petal of the flower, so as to make a more or less interrupted corona round its disk. It seemed as if this emanation grew less vivid as the light declined; it was not examined in darkness, which omission will be supplied on a future occasion. It may be here added, in the view to facilitate any other observer who may give attention to this phaenomenon, that the double marigold is the best flower to experiment on, as the single flower "goeth to sleep with the sun," and has not the disk exposed for investigation.*

In 1882, *Scientific American* published a short note on this same subject by Louis Crie:

*In living vegetables emissions of light have been observed in a dozen phaenogamous plants and in some fifteen cryptogamous ones. The phosphorescence of the flowers of Pyrethrum [Chrysanthemum] inodorum, Polyanthes [sic – Polianthes] (tuberose), and the Pandani has been known for a long time. Haggren and Crome were the first to discover such luminous emanations from the Indian cross and marigold, and a few years ago I myself was permitted to observe, during a summer storm, a phosphorescent light emitted from the flowers of a nasturtium (Tropoeolum [sic – Tropaeolum] majus) cultivated in a garden at Sarthe.*

Several reports concerning light-emitting flowers appeared during the 1880s in the English periodical *Knowledge*. These revealed that one early eyewitness had been none other than the daughter of Carolus Linnaeus, the father of modern botanical and zoological

classification, who witnessed this phenomenon while gazing at some garden flowers one summer twilight in 1762. A later eyewitness, a Mr S. Ingham, reported his sighting in *Knowledge* in 1883:

*A short time ago, I was picking out some annuals on a flower-bed, on which some geraniums were already planted, when I was surprised to see flashes of light coming from a truss of geranium flowers. At first I thought it was imagination, but my wife and a friend who were present also saw them. Time was about 9 p.m., and the atmosphere clear. There were other geraniums of a different colour on the same bed, but there was no effect on them. The particular geranium was a Tom Thumb.*

*Is this at all common? I have never seen or read of it before.*

In fact, eleven years earlier a tome published by Simpkin, Marshall, & Co., entitled *Lessons in Physical Science*, had included the following comments regarding this curious matter:

*To the same source – electricity – we probably owe the light which, at certain seasons, and at certain times of the day,*

*issues from a number of yellow or orange-coloured flowers, such as the marigold, the sunflower, and the orange-lily ... similar phenomena have been witnessed by several naturalists. Flashes, more or less brilliant, have been seen to dart in rapid succession from the same flower. At other times the tiny flame-jets have followed one another at intervals of several minutes.*

The concept of flowers releasing visible discharges of electricity is undeniably somewhat dramatic. A less radical alternative, perhaps, is that this curious optical effect may be caused by the reflection of sunlight by petals of certain colours acting as miniature mirrors (thus explaining why the effect lessens as daylight declines).

Whatever the answer, however, it is certainly true today that light-emitting flowers have become one of the forgotten phenomena of botany, ignored – if indeed even known about – by contemporary researchers. Yet they were once known, and witnessed, by naturalists. Surely, therefore, it is time for a new generation to rediscover these excluded enigmas, and extract their long-hidden secrets. After all, as succinctly pointed out by Fortean writer Mark Chorvinsky regarding this subject: "There are a lot of marigolds and geraniums out there".

*The bright orange petals of marigolds have been known to emit flashes of light.*

# CROSSBREEDING CONTROVERSY

COUNTLESS FULLY AUTHENTICATED CASES TESTIFY THAT CLOSELY RELATED ANIMAL SPECIES SOMETIMES
MATE SUCCESSFULLY WITH ONE ANOTHER, YIELDING HYBRID PROGENY. ALSO ON FILE, HOWEVER, ARE
REPORTS OF CERTAIN HIGHLY CONTROVERSIAL HYBRIDS – SUPPOSEDLY RESULTING FROM
CROSSBREEDING BETWEEN PAIRS OF ANIMAL SPECIES GENERALLY CONSIDERED TO BE TOO DISTANTLY
RELATED TO YIELD VIABLE OFFSPRING.

## UNMASKING THE JUMAR

Take, for instance, the jumar – purportedly the product of an illicit liaison between a horse and a cow. The birth of such a creature would require a successful mating between species from two entirely discrete taxonomic orders of hoofed mammal – Perissodactyla (odd-

*A lion-tiger hybrid.*

toed ungulates, which include horses) and Artiodactyla (even-toed ungulates, which include cattle) – whose respective members are far too dissimilar genetically to yield viable offspring.

Yet there are many cases of supposed jumars on record, dating back at least as far as 1546, when documented by the physician/ mathematician Jerome Cardan. It seemed to gain its name from the famous bestiary compiler

Conrad Gesner; in the first volume of his great work *Historia Animalium* (1551), he wrote about a creature resulting "... from a she-ass and a bull, which as I hear is met with at Gratianopolis, and is called the jumar in French".

Referring to the jumar in *Magiae Naturalis* (1558), Neapolitan physicist Giovanni Battista della Porta stated: "I myself saw at Ferraria, certain beasts in the shape of a Mule, but they had a Bull's head, and two great knobs instead of horns: they also had a Bull's eyes, and were exceedingly stomackful, and their colour was black ... I have heard, that in France, they be common: but I could see none there, though I have passed through the whole country."

Throughout the seventeenth century, scholars readily accepted the jumar's reality, but during the eighteenth century scepticism grew, voiced in particular by the eminent French zoologist George de Buffon in his *Histoire Naturelle*. Buffon oversaw the dissection of two supposed jumars, one from the Pyrenees, the other from Dauphiné, but found no trace of bovine characters in either specimen.

The same outcome was obtained from the dissection of two jumars at the instigation of Cardinal Delle Lanze. They were nothing more than small, stunted mules, just like other jumars subsequently examined. Experiments striving to induce matings between stallions and cows, and between bulls and mares, were wholly unsuccessful too. And so, by the end of the 1700s this impossible hybrid had finally been exposed and expunged.

Exit the jumar.

## CUINO – HOGGING THE CRYPTOZOOLOGICAL LIMELIGHT

Accepted by some writers until much more recently than the jumar, yet scarcely less improbable, was the cuino – claimed to be a hybrid of sheep and pig, and widely met with in the Mexican state of Oaxaca. At the turn of the nineteenth century, a highly esteemed American journal called the *Breeder's Gazette* published a detailed article concerning the cuino, in which it stated that this remarkable crossbreed results from matings between sows and polled (dehorned) rams of the typical long-legged, light-bodied Mexican sheep.

In a somewhat contradictory account, the article claimed that the cuino has: "... the form and all the characteristics of the pigs, but he is entirely different from his dam; he is round-

ribbed and blocky, his short legs cannot take him far away from his sty, and his snout is too short to root. His head is not unlike that of the Berkshire. His body is covered with long thick curly hair, not soft enough to be called wool, but which, nevertheless, he takes from his sire. His colour is black, white, black and white or brown and white."

In 1900, this and various similar accounts, including one concerning Brazilian cuinos, came to the attention of W.B. Tegetmeier of London's Zoological Society, who duly denounced the cuino's crossbred identity in a series of communications within *The Field*. The matter was finally resolved in 1902, when he received a cuino skull from a Mexican correspondent.

To quote Tegetmeier's response:

*I was very glad to receive the skull, but, as I anticipated, it has no hybrid character about it whatever. It is purely and simply the skull of a pig. Without stopping to enter into such details as the character of the orbit, or the articulation of the lower jaw, which are utterly distinct in the sheep and in the pig, I need only call attention to the teeth in the fore part of the upper jaw. These are present as in the pig, and perfectly developed, whereas in the sheep, as every anatomist knows, the fore part of the jaw is utterly destitute of teeth, there being only a horny pad against which the lower incisors act. No zoologist could for a moment regard the skull as showing the slightest trace of ovine structure. In order to obtain corroboration of these facts I exhibited the skull at the last meeting of the Zoological Society, and its true character was recognised by every anatomist and zoologist present who noticed it.*

Farewell the cuino.

## KOOLOOKAMBA – MAKING A CHUMP OF A CHIMP?

Whereas the jumar and the cuino were controversial because of their blatant unlikeliness, the koolookamba has been controversial because of its tantalising

*A question mark hangs over the koolookamba: could it be a chimpanzee x gorilla hybrid?*

plausibility. That this perplexing African ape exists is not in question – several specimens have been displayed in captivity.

These include probably the most famous koolookamba of all – a large aggressive female called Mafuca, brought from Gabon's Loango Coast and exhibited at Dresden Zoo during the 1870s. There was also Johanna, displayed in the late 1800s at the Barnum Bailey World Show after four years at Lisbon Zoo; as well as Minnie and Sevim, two adult females present during the 1980s in the chimpanzee colony belonging to Holloman Air Force Base at Alamagordo, New Mexico.

What is in question is whether, as suggested by eminent zoologist Dr Richard Lydekker, German game hunter Hugo von Koppenfels, and a number of other experienced authorities, it constitutes a bona fide hybrid between the chimpanzee and the gorilla.

Although these two species of great ape are closely related, hybridization between them has never been proven – which is why Mafuca attracted such attention from zoologists. Whereas the most conservative voices opined that she was merely an unusual chimpanzee, her wide nose, fairly small ears, heavy brows and powerful, projecting jaws persuaded certain others to classify her as a small gorilla. There were also some who felt sure that she represented a separate third species, distinct from both the chimpanzee and the gorilla (in 1967, primatologist Professor W.C. Osman Hill leaned a little toward this viewpoint by designating the koolookamba as a separate subspecies of chimpanzee, naming it *Pan troglodytes koolokamba*). And there were those who echoed Lydekker's belief that she was a hybrid.

DNA analyses conducted with blood and tissue samples from a koolookamba should ultimately bring this longstanding controversy to a satisfactory conclusion. In the meantime, as pointed out by American anthropologist Dr Brian Shea and gorilla expert Don Cousins,

individuals displaying the koolookamba's distinctive morphology arise spasmodically in totally separate populations of chimpanzees. This indicates that the koolookamba is merely the product of a chance assemblage of chimpanzee genes, rather than a segregated form that breeds true – or a chimpanzee x gorilla hybrid.

Having said that, there does seem to be a link between koolookamba occurrence and montane habitat. And as its distinguishing features happen to be much the same as those that delineate eastern mountain gorillas from western lowland gorillas, could the koolookamba therefore prove to be an incipient mountain-favouring race of chimpanzee?

## SERVING UP SOME SERVICALS

Although many different feline hybrids have been recorded over the years, not a single case of crossbreeding between the big-eared, black-blotched serval *Felis serval* and the sandy-furred, lynx-like caracal *Felis caracal* had ever been documented – until a certain highly unexpected interspecific mating took place that remains unique even today.

*Cute and cuddly – and also unique: this servical kitten is a cross between a serval and a caracal.*

In 1993, I learnt from Dr Warren D. Thomas that when he had been director of Los Angeles Zoo a few years earlier, a male serval and a female caracal had been maintained together during an educational programme there. To the zoo staff's surprise, the caracal became pregnant, giving birth to the world's first-recorded litter of serval x caracal hybrids, four in number and duly nicknamed servicals. As seen from the photo included here, these delightfully appealing kittens combined their caracal mother's sandy, unpatterned fur with their serval father's huge ears (but tipped with long tufts of hair typical of caracals). Sadly, two of the servicals died within 10 days after their birth, but the other two survived, and at the age of 8 months they were given away by the zoo to a local animal sanctuary.

## KRAUSE, THE FIRST FERTILE MULE

Equally unexpected is a fertile mule. These male donkey x female horse hybrids are, after all, celebrated for being not only stubborn but also barren (because mules have 63 chromosomes, whereas horses have 64, and donkeys have only 62). All that changed, however, on 6 July 1984, when Krause, a female mule living on Bill and Oneta Sylvester's farm at Champion, Nebraska, was seen with a newborn male foal, later named Blue Moon, standing beside her. Tissue samples were duly taken from Krause and Blue Moon, and subjected to cytogenetic analysis by a scientific team led by Dr Oliver Ryder from San Diego Zoo. In a 1985 *Journal of Heredity* paper, Ryder *et al.* confirmed that both animals were mules and that Blue Moon was indeed Krause's offspring (the father proved to be a donkey called Chester).

Nor was that the end of the saga. In November 1987, Krause did it again, giving birth to a second male foal, sired by Chester and dubbed White Lightning. In just 40 months, Krause had refuted the age-old belief that mules were invariably infertile, and gave a new dimension of meaning to the sayings "Once in a blue moon" and "Lightning never strikes twice"!

## "NOT ONE OF GOD'S CREATIONS"

"The geep – half goat, half sheep – is not one of God's creations. It could not occur naturally. It was made by scientists in Cambridge seven years ago." This is how a BBC2 TV science programme from 1988 described one of the most anomalous animals ever seen.

Notwithstanding the perennial plethora of unconfirmed tabloid reports, attempts to crossbreed the domestic goat *Capra hircus* with the domestic sheep *Ovis aries* and obtain viable hybrid offspring have not been successful. In 1984, however, the world learnt that these two species had at last been united, but via a truly remarkable method

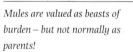

*Mules are valued as beasts of burden – but not normally as parents!*

*The "geep" was created from a mixture of cells from a goat embryo and a sheep embryo, hence its distinctive appearance.*

that was very different indeed from straightforward hybridization.

As documented in a *Nature* paper by Drs Carole B. Fehilly, S.M. Willadsen, and Elizabeth M. Tucker from the ARC Institute of Animal Physiology in Cambridge, England, early-stage goat embryos had been artificially combined with early-stage sheep embryos, and the resulting composite embryos, termed chimaeras, had then been implanted into surrogate parent sheep in order to develop and mature like normal sheep embryos. The creatures that were eventually born, however, were certainly not normal sheep, or goats – instead, they were both, yet neither. Their entire bodies (even their blood constituents) were composed of a mixture of goat cells and sheep cells, a situation mirrored externally too – because their pelage consisted of portions of hairy goat fur alongside portions of woolly sheep fleece, and their horns were goat-like in construction but spiralled like sheep horns. Their dual nature also inspired the media to coin a catchy name for these chimaeras – "geep".

# MYSTERIES FROM THE
# GREEN WORLD

BENEATH ITS INNOCUOUS VEIL OF VIRIDIAN QUIESCENCE, THE BOTANICAL KINGDOM ABOUNDS IN ANOMALOUS FORMS AND PHENOMENA AS MYSTIFYING AS ANYTHING REPORTED FROM ITS ANIMALIAN COUNTERPART.

## A SHOCKING POKEWEED

The pokeweeds and other members of the genus *Phytolacca* are best known for the medicinal properties of their roots, and the dyes

*The rich colours of the pokeweed belie the electrical shocks some of its kind administer.*

obtained from their berries. However, the aptly named *Phytolacca electrica* would appear to have a much more unexpected talent.

In 1877, the journal *Scientific American* referred to an extraordinary article by an author called Levy concerning this species, which had lately appeared in a German periodical,

*Hamburger Garten-und Blumenzeitung*, and provided the following summary of its data:

*The curious fact about this plant is its strongly marked electro-magnetic properties. On breaking off a twig a sensation is produced in the hand like that*

given by a Ruhmkorff induction coil. This sensation was so marked that he [Levy] began to experiment with a small compass. The compass began to be affected by it at a distance of seven or eight paces. The needle vibrated on approaching nearer to it, and finally began to revolve rapidly. On receding, the phenomena were repeated in reversed order. In the soil where this plant grew, there was not a trace of iron or other magnetic metal, like nickel or cobalt, and there is no doubt that the plant itself possesses these peculiar properties. The strength of the phenomena varied with the time of day. During the night it is almost nothing, and reaches its maximum about two o'clock in the afternoon. When the weather is stormy the energy increases still more, and when it rains the plant appears withered. Levy also states that he never saw any insects or birds on or about this electrical plant.

Despite its considerable curiosity value, I have not uncovered any further references to this species' electrical activity. However, American Fortean writer/investigator Mark Chorvinsky revealed in a short *Fate* account from November 1996 that he had lately been contacted by a lady concerning a strange plant that grew in her backyard, and which gave her a mild electric shock whenever she touched it. Interestingly, as with Levy's *P. electrica* report, the strength of the electric shock varied in relation to the time of day. Chorvinsky speculated that the answer may involve some form of high-voltage ground charge, but as he correctly pointed out, such a phenomenon would be expected to affect more than just one plant within a given locality.

## RAIN TREES AND WEEPING TREES

I have several reports on file of mystifying plants that allegedly "weep" considerable quantities of liquid, so much so that they are locally referred to as rain trees. Some owe more to legend than

Froghopper larva, commonly known as "cuckoo-spit" – the insect may also be responsible for the "rain" from certain trees.

The rain apparently produced by the rain tree has a more prosaic origin.

any mysterious life process, such as the famous Peruvian Andes rain tree. According to travellers' tales, the leaves of this extraordinary tree are able to condense atmospheric moisture in appreciable quantities and precipitate it in the form of rain, lending this species to use as an efficient irrigator if planted in dry, arid terrain.

The reality, however, is rather different. Some plants exhibit a physiological phenomenon known as guttation (especially at night or in foggy or cloudy weather, when the air's relative humidity is highest): that is, moisture drawn up from the roots of plants often passes via transpiration into the surrounding atmosphere, which, if eventually saturated with moisture and if the continuing supply of moisture to the plants' roots is extensive, will result in the exudation of liquid drops, sometimes in considerable quantities. Needless to say, however, this process can only occur in moist localities, not in dry ones as claimed for the rain tree.

There is a second, rather more bizarre but fully confirmed explanation for reports of rain trees or weeping trees. One such example is the Zimbabwe rain tree *Lonchocarpus domingensis*, as recently witnessed by Harare resident Cynthia Hind, who was startled to experience what seemed like a heavy shower of rain while driving through an avenue of these eyecatching yellow-flowered trees in her home city, even though the sky above was cloudless. Taking a sample twig from one of the trees, she consulted botanist Soul Shava at Harare's Botanical Gardens, where she learnt the true identity of the "rain". A tiny species of homopteran bug called a froghopper

*The green cicada is another possible source of "rain".*

attaches itself in vast numbers to this species of tree, rapidly ingesting great quantities of its sap, and concomitantly excreting with comparable speed copious quantities of water that fall to the ground in a veritable shower.

Nor is this an isolated example. In 1988, a 17-year-old pine tree whose leaves wept profuse quantities of watery liquid in the Chinese coastal village of Xinfu became the object of reverential worship by people from near and far, who came to imbibe its "tears", convinced that this so-called "tree of the gods" possessed healing properties and brought good fortune. Tragically for the tree, this good fortune evidently did not extend to itself, because when scientists examined it and revealed that its tears were actually the exudation from countless minute insects, the local police swiftly felled it in order to annihilate the insect infestation.

Similarly, with regard to the cow tamarind tree *Pithecellobium saman*, the species most commonly claimed to be the mysterious Peruvian Andes rain tree, the nineteenth-century South American explorer Spruce recorded the following telling observation:

*I first witnessed the phenomenon in September, 1855, when residing at Tarapoto. I had gone one morning at daybreak, with two assistants, into the adjacent wooded hills to botanize. A little after seven o'clock we came under a lowish spreading tree, from which with a perfectly clear sky overhead a smart rain was falling. A glance upward showed a multitude of cicadas [homopteran insects closely related to froghoppers] sucking the juices of the tender young branches and leaves, and squirting forth slender streams of limpid fluid.*

Quaint folklore is hardly a satisfactory substitute for scientific wisdom. Nevertheless, I cannot avoid preferring the poetic if wholly fictitious image of a tree weeping tears of sorrow down upon those who pass beneath its mournful branches to the prosaic yet botanically factual concept of being soaked by a tree raining down copious quantities of insect urine!

## BLEEDING TREES

Even more curious than weeping trees are bleeding trees. Take, for instance, the bleeding yew, estimated to be over 700 years old, growing in the sixth-century churchyard of St Brynach at Nevern, near Newport in Pembrokeshire, Wales. For several decades, a red blood-like substance has been continually oozing forth from a natural gash in its trunk, roughly 7 feet (2 metres) from the ground. Local legend claims that it is the blood of a medieval monk, hanged in the churchyard for a crime that he did not

*The famous "bleeding" yew tree in the churchyard at Nevern, west Wales.*

commit. Science, conversely, in the shape of Derek Patch from the Forestry Commission, contends that it is more likely to be rainwater which becomes trapped in a hollow, creating a reddish decay of the wood, and is thence stained red as it oozes back out again.

A eucalyptus tree felled near the Madagascan village of Ambohibao on 19 June 1984 unnervingly spurted forth gushes of red blood-like liquid as soon as the first strike of the axe made contact with its trunk. This macabre event incited the villagers to worship it, especially as it stood in a sacred site referred to locally as "the tomb of the sorcerers". When samples of the tree's "blood" were scientifically analysed, however, it was suggested that the red pigment was most probably a water-soluble flavonoid known as an anthocyanin.

## A ROSE IS A ROSE IS A ROSE ... ISN'T IT?

Freaks and sports of nature are not limited to the animal kingdom. Commonly reported botanical equivalents include four-leaved clovers, witches' brooms (abnormal, closely grouped, many-branched outgrowths occurring on many species of tree and shrub), and fasciated flower heads (aberrantly flattened, excessively expanded). Every so often, however, a truly outstanding, inexplicable example arises – and the Kronenbourg rose grown by Leeds gardener Jan Kubas during summer 1997 certainly falls into this highly select category.

Ever since he bought the bush 30 years earlier, all of Kubas's Kronenbourgs had been blood-red, but one of its collection of 1997 blooms constituted a very special exception. As if a line had been drawn down the middle of its flower head, all of the petals to the left of centre were red, and all of the petals to the right of centre were white.

As suggested by the Royal National Rose Society, the most reasonable explanation is that a long-suppressed gene from the original briar had suddenly been activated. Nevertheless, the reason why such a mutation should only now have occurred on this bush, and the mysterious mechanism by which it had created a perfect half-white, half-red rose, rather than simply a red rose interspersed with a few white petals (or vice versa), remain unrevealed.

## THE ZILPHION ENIGMA

As with animal species bred as livestock, it is rare indeed for a species of foodplant to become extinct, especially if it has proved popular – which is why the apparent disappearance of zilphion remains one of the great botanical enigmas of the age.

Today, few people will even have heard of zilphion, yet it was once an extremely familiar plant in great demand during Greek and Roman times, and was even depicted on various Didrachmai coins from classical Cyrene (a former Greek colony in Cyrenaica, eastern Libya). Its popularity was due to its great versatility, for whereas its stem and young shoots were tasty to eat, its sap and roots could be condensed into a special syrup, called laserpitium. Not surprisingly, such a well-favoured plant earned great riches for the many merchants who shipped it to Europe across the Mediterranean from its native North African homeland where it grew wild, particularly in Syria, according to Pliny the Elder.

Perhaps it was its overwhelming popularity that proved to be zilphion's undoing. Certainly it would seem that its wild population could not sustain the greed of the merchants, for it became ever rarer. Indeed, by the fourth century AD zilphion was completely unknown.

Utilizing a few ancient descriptions and depictions, modern-day botanists have sought to identify its species, nominating the umbellifer *Ferula assafoetida* or the Gargan death carrot *Thapsia garganica* among others, but none of the suggestions offered is very satisfactory.

During my own zilphion researches, however, I uncovered some tantalizing clues. When written in its original Greek form, the name "zilphion" begins not with the letter zeta ("z"), but with sigma ("s"). Technically, therefore, it should really be written as silphion. And it just so happens that the common name of *Ferula narthex*, a close relative of the above-mentioned *F. assafoetida*, is the very similar-sounding silphium. Moreover, according to George Usher's authoritative *A Dictionary of Plants Used By Man* (1974), silphium was indeed known to the Romans and Greeks, as well as to the ancient Egyptians. So could it be that zilphion and silphium are indeed one and the same plant? Not if Pliny the Elder's documentation is correct, for whereas he and other early chroniclers claimed that zilphion grew wild in North Africa, Usher reveals that silphium is native to Baltisthan – a mountainous region of northern Kashmir between the Karakoram Mountains and the Himalayas, also called Little Tibet.

Unless this major geographical discrepancy can somehow be reconciled, for the forseeable future zilphion seems destined to remain yet another mystery of the green world.

*The Kronenbourg rose startled the botanical world with this aberrant flower head.*

# OLIVER
## AND COMPANY

THERE ARE MANY MYSTERY ANIMALS ON FILE THAT ARE FAR LESS FAMOUS THAN NESSIE AND THE
BIGFOOT, BUT ARE CERTAINLY NO LESS STRANGE OR MYSTERIOUS, AS REVEALED HERE

## A KNOBBLY NEWCOMER TO CRYPTOZOOLOGY

A prime example is the very peculiar feline beast said to inhabit the tiny isles of Alor and Solor in Indonesia's Lesser Sundas chain. British cryptozoological researcher Debbie Martyr has gathered from local tribespeople what little information is currently on file regarding this obscure creature (during her continuing pursuit of Sumatra's elusive man-beast, the orang pendek). This reveals that it is

*The veo could be a giant, undiscovered, species of pangolin (scaly anteater).*

the size of a typical domestic cat, but is instantly differentiated from all known felids by virtue of the pair of short but conspicuous horn-like knobs projecting from its forehead.

## SCALING THE HEIGHTS OF MAMMALIAN MYSTERY ON RINTJA

Another sparsely publicized mystery beast of the Lesser Sundas is the veo, reported from the small island of Rintja. As revealed in French traveller Pierre Pfeiffer's book *Bivouacs à Borneo* (1963), and supplemented more recently by information passed on from Rintja natives to

Czech cryptozoologist Dr Jaroslav Mares by an Indonesian friend called Uning, the veo is as large as a horse, with huge claws, and a long head. Its body is covered dorsally and laterally with large overlapping scales, but it has hair upon its head, throat, belly, lower legs and the end of its tail. During the daytime this formidable creature remains concealed in the island's mountains, but at night it comes down to the mangrove coasts, and lives upon ants and termites, plus any small marine creatures that it discovers stranded upon the beach by the tide. The local hunters take pains to avoid the veo, because if threatened it will rear up on to its haunches and lash out savagely with the deadly claws on its forepaws.

Except for its enormous size, the veo's description readily recalls the pangolins (scaly anteaters), which inhabit Africa and Asia, but do not attain anything remotely approaching the veo's dimensions. During the Pleistocene epoch (2 million to 10,000 years ago), however, a gigantic pangolin, *Manis palaeojavanicus*, over 8 feet (2.5 metres) long, did exist on nearby Java and Borneo. Perhaps this supposedly vanished giant, or a modern-day descendant, still survives on Rintja.

## OLIVER – A CHIMP OFF THE OLD BLOCK AFTER ALL

The veo's identity may remain unresolved, but one long-running cryptozoological saga of taxonomic controversy that *has* finally been brought to a satisfactory conclusion involves the notoriously mystifying chimpanzee-like primate known as Oliver.

Housed since 1996 at a Texan animal sanctuary called Primarily Primates, his bald head, upright bipedal gait, and strangely human behaviour earned him a starring role in newspaper headlines and television shows worldwide, especially during the mid-1970s, when he was owned by New York attorney Michael Miller. Throughout the past 20 years, speculation has raged concerning this enigmatic ape's identity – with suggestions ranging from a freak chimpanzee to an unknown species, or even a hybrid of chimpanzee and human.

After conducting mitochondrial DNA sequence analyses and chromosomal studies with tissue samples obtained from Oliver and various other primates, however, in 1998 a team of American geneticists featuring Drs John Ely from Texas's Trinity University and Charleen Moore from Texas University's Health Science Center published their findings in the *American Journal of Physical Anthropology*. Their paper revealed that Oliver has a normal cell karyotype

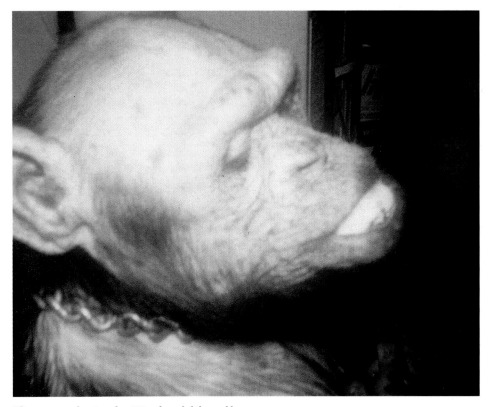

*Oliver, an ape who starred on TV and puzzled the world.*

(the appearance, number and arrangement of chromosomes within an individual's cells) for the common chimpanzee *Pan troglodytes*. Furthermore, genetically speaking, he closely resembles a specimen of this species known to have originated from Gabon in western Africa, thus indicating that this is Oliver's likely place of origin too – as I speculated back in 1993 within *Man and Beast*, a cryptozoological compendium.

## FLIGHTLESS BUT FLEET-FOOTED – THE ELUSIVE KOAO

It is not every day that a celebrity has a close encounter with a mystery beast, but that is precisely what happened in 1937 during a visit by world-famous explorer-navigator Thor Heyerdahl to Hiva Oa – principal member of the Marquesas, a group of French Polynesian islands in the South Pacific. While journeying through one of its rugged mountain forests, he and a native guide unexpectedly came upon a strange, seemingly wingless bird roughly the size of a long-legged gull. Instantly, this odd-

looking bird fled away, swiftly plunging into a natural tunnel formed from the dense overhanging ferns, and was not seen by them again.

Heyerdahl's guide informed him that this was a koao, which, as he had just seen, is exceedingly fleet-footed and hence quite impossible to capture. Other accounts of the koao also exist, including that of French explorer Francis Mazière, who recorded in 1956 that this flightless bird does have wings, but only very small, vestigial ones. However, in total size it is as large as a cockerel, its plumage is a handsome purplish-blue, and its beak is yellow, as are its long legs. This description recalls New Zealand's famously resurrected takahe *Porphyrio* (=*Notornis*) *mantelli* – a hefty flightless relative of moorhens dismissed as extinct until sensationally rediscovered on South Island in 1948. Indeed, the only principal difference is that its beak and legs are coral-pink, not yellow. Could the koao be a related species?

Tantalizingly, some thousand-year-old

*The flightless koao, often glimpsed but never captured.*

bones of a hitherto-unknown, ostensibly demised relative of the takahe, *Porphyrio paepae*, were actually unearthed on Hiva Oa in 1988, by Dr David W. Steadman from the New York State Museum, leading some cryptozoologists to speculate that this species may be one and the same as the mysterious koao. Only when someone succeeds in capturing a koao, however, can this theory finally be tested.

## WAS THE IZCUINTLIPOTZOTLI A CANINE QUASIMODO?

Tragically, it may be too late to secure a specimen of another still-unidentified creature – Mexico's unpronounceable izcuintlipotzotli – because it has not been reported for more than 150 years. This bizarre beast first came to attention in 1780, courtesy of a tome entitled *Historia Antigua de Mexico* ("Mexico's Ancient History"), penned by Jesuit priest Father Francisco Javier Clavijero, a highly respected New World scholar. Inhabiting the Tarascan region of Michoacán in western Mexico, the

izcuintlipotzotli was the size of a maltese terrier, with a small, wolf-like head, extremely short neck, lumpy muzzle and small pendant ears. Strangely, its forelimbs were notably shorter than the hindlimbs, its skin was mottled with black, brown and white spots, and – most striking of all – a grotesque hump (but possibly fatty rather than bony in composition) extended the entire length of its back, from its shoulders to its haunches. Indeed, part of its name, "potzotli", translates as "hunchback".

So singular was its appearance that some zoologists questioned the accepted belief that the izcuintlipotzotli was a breed of dog (albeit an emphatically homely one), even speculating that it may be some exotic species of rodent! However, the few known engravings of it that exist suggest that this idiosyncratic entity was even less like a rodent than a dog. Whatever it was, however, the izcuintlipotzotli is no more. What appears to be the last documented mention of such a creature occurred in 1843, within Frances Calderón de la Barca's book *Life*

*in Mexico*, noting a dead specimen that she saw hanging from a hook near the door of an inn in the valley of Guajimalco. I am not aware of any preserved museum specimens either.

## DIGGING UP THE EARTH HOUND

In 1994, actor Stephen McHattie starred as a cryptozoological biker (sounds familiar?) in the movie *The Dark*, seeking a mysterious creature that inhabited graveyards and devoured corpses, which ultimately proved to be a hitherto-unknown species of archaic rat. However, they do say that fact is even stranger than fiction, and if *The Dark* is the fiction, then the following item may prove to be the fact.

I was fascinated to read recently about a truly weird mystery beast called the earth hound or yard pig, which reputedly inhabits graveyards in Banffshire, north-east Scotland, burrowing among corpses and devouring them. My source of information regarding this eerie, sinister creature, referred to locally at least as long ago as the 1880s, is an article by Alexander Fenton and cryptozoological chronicler David Heppell that appeared in the volume of *Scottish Studies* for 1992–93, and contains the following data.

According to one account in a letter from 1917 by a Mr A. Smith (now in the archives of the Department of Natural History of the National Museums of Scotland), about 50 years earlier a gardener had turned up an earth hound "... in its nest when ploughing in the haughs [alluvial flats]". After killing it when it bit and cut his boot, he took its carcase home:

*It was brown in colour somewhat like a rat, but had a long head like a dog's – (hound's), and a tail bushier than a rat's, but he could not say how bushy. Their nests were from time to time turned up by the plough, but the animals themselves were very rarely seen, reputed to frequent churchyards. This was in the immediate*

*The izcuintlipotzotli – unprepossessing and unidentified.*

guinea-pig's, noticeable white "tusks" (incisors?) and very prominent pig-like nostrils. As recently as April 1990, while in Keith, Banffshire, Alexander Fenton was told about earth hounds by a friend there, who stated that they were between a rat and a rabbit, lived in graveyards and forced their way inside buried coffins.

It seems scarcely credible that a distinctive species of ferret-sized mammal could elude scientific detection in modern-day Scotland, and this country's folklore is renowned for its fanciful fauna. Yet reports of the earth hound and its unsavoury behaviour are remarkably consistent, and far more mundane than one might expect if dealing with a fabled beast of legend. So how can we explain the earth hound – a macabre myth or a troubling truth?

*neighbourhood of a churchyard which was eventually disused owing to the firm belief that it was infested with earth-hunds [sic]. They invariably lived in the immediate neighbourhood of water, and their nests were in haughs.*

A second eyewitness of this same specimen of earth hound described it to A. Smith as:

*... being something between a rat and a weasel, and about the size of a ferret, head very like that of a dog, and I think he said the tail was not very long. At a casual glance it would be mistaken for a rat, but was quite unlike on close examination.*

Another earth hound, reputedly killed around 1915 near Mastrick, close to a churchyard, after being turned up by a plough, was said to resemble a dark rat in size and colour, but had mole-like feet, a tail only about half as long as a rat's, a long head somewhat similar to a

*The sinister earth hound may yet be flushed out of the dark.*

# BLUE
## IS THE COLOUR ...

WHILE ON VACATION IN MOROCCO DURING 1981, HERTFORDSHIRE-BASED BROADCASTER ANNA GRAYSON, A QUALIFIED GEOLOGIST, SPOTTED A VERY UNUSUAL ITEM ON A MARKET TRADER'S STALL. AS LARGE AS TWO FISTS, IT WAS A PYRAMIDAL CHUNK OF VIVID SKY-BLUE ROCK, WHICH THE TRADER CLAIMED TO BE LAPIS LAZULI.

Grayson, however, doubted this, but nonetheless assumed that it was simply a compound of copper. Pleased to have found such an attractive souvenir of her holiday, she promptly purchased the rock and brought it back home, where, for the next 15 years, this caerulean curiosity remained as one of her prized possessions. As time went by, however, Grayson became ever more curious as to whether it really was merely of cuprous composition, or whether it may be something more unusual.

Finally, in 1995, Grayson decided to resolve the issue of her blue rock's precise geological nature once and for all, and took it for formal identification to London's Natural History Museum – where, to everyone's amazement, it defied all attempts to classify it. Nor was this the only surprise. When researchers rotated it through 90° while viewing it through filtered polarized light, this mineralogical chameleon abruptly changed colour, transforming from brilliant blue to rich purple – and when rotated a second time, it became transparent! The explanation for these polychromatic metamorphoses lay in its distinctive atomic structure, which enabled it to absorb different frequencies (i.e. colours) of the visible spectrum of electromagnetic radiation at different angles. Eschewing any copper-based influence for its intense blue hue, Grayson's geological enigma was found to contain silicon, aluminium, calcium, magnesium, iron and oxygen as its principal constituent elements.

A year later, as widely documented in media reports during March 1996, the museum's associate keeper of mineralogy, Dr Gordon Cressey, publicly announced: "This is like nothing seen before and it's very exciting. It shows the earth still holds mysteries."

And so it seemed – until news of what had begun to be dubbed "graysonite" reached the ears of Dr Mohammed Bensaid, from the Moroccan Ministry of Mines. In September 1996, Bensaid exposed "graysonite" as aerinite – an exceedingly obscure, rarely spied mineral present in Morocco's Rif Mountains. Indeed, even London's Natural History Museum has only four specimens, which had not been seen before by recent researchers because they had been tucked away unnoticed in a drawer marked "P" – for "Problems"!

Nevertheless, spectacular, hitherto-unknown types of mineral are still discovered from time to time. A year after Grayson's bewildering blue rock hit the headlines, Russian scientists announced the discovery in the Ural Mountains of a layer of a totally new mineral, characterized visually by its charismatic light blue colouration, which, in honour of the late Princess of Wales, they have since christened dianite. And two decades earlier, a beautiful new type of deep violet mineral was discovered by uranium prospectors on the banks of Siberia's River Charo; this unexpected find was subsequently named charoite.

Left: *The very rare mineral known as aerinite, found in the Rif Mountains of Morocco.*
Above: *The dramatic colour of charoite recalls the purple transformation of Anna Grayson's enigmatic rock.*

# Beware the
# Trees
# of Terror!

In this current book's predecessor, "The Unexplained: An Illustrated Guide to the World's Natural and Paranormal Mysteries" (1996), I documented several giant carnivorous plants whose existence has been reported, but so far never confirmed, from various regions of the world. My files on such entities also include accounts of certain additional examples.

## Brazilian Devil Tree

In *Secret Cities of Old South America* (1952), Harold T. Wilkins reported two particularly monstrous forms from Brazil. One, said to exist in the Mato Grosso and known aptly as the octopod or devil tree, is claimed by the local Indians to be

*Known as the blood vine, this sinister-looking plant seems intent on strangling its host.*

as big as a willow, but its true stature is not readily perceived – until it is too late. This is because the devil tree's branches are normally concealed deep in the surrounding undergrowth or beneath the soil. Should an unsuspecting creature, or human, stumble over them, however, they reputedly draw themselves stealthily out of their hiding place and grasp their hapless victim within their ever-tightening coil-like tendrils.

Although such a tree may sound far too fanciful to be real, its dark romance was sufficient to entice Captain Thomas W.H. Sarll away from his home in Middlesex, England, during summer 1932 and into the Amazon jungle's verdant depths, in a valiant bid to discover, uproot and return home with a living specimen of this tendrilled terror! As I have been unable to uncover any news of this singular expedition's outcome, however, I can only assume that Sarll's search was unsuccessful – or proved too successful for his own good!

## STRICTLY FOR THE BIRDS

Wilkins's second Brazilian carnivorous mystery plant is also equipped with tentacular tendrils. Happily, however, its preferred prey does not include humans, which are, in any case, readily warned of its presence by the vile stink of rotting flesh suffusing from it (reminiscent, therefore, of the world's largest flower, Sumatra's *Rafflesia*, which exudes a similar stench to attract flies, which act as its pollinators). Instead, it entices small birds, lured by its sweet-tasting berries, to alight upon its branches. As soon as this happens, however, the unfortunate birds are seized by its tendrils, pressed firmly against the tree's trunk, and held

in place there by specialized sucker-like structures, until their fragile bodies are crushed. During this grisly process, the birds' blood is absorbed by the suckers, after which their dry, shattered corpses are released, falling to the ground.

Interestingly, as I noted in *The Unexplained*, a very similar plant, sporting blood-absorbing suckered branches, has been reported from Mexico's Sierra Madre, where it is referred to as the snake-tree by locals, on account of its constricting tendrils; and a comparable version has also been described from the environs of Lake Nicaragua.

## MADAGASCAN MYSTERIES AND THE SLUMBER OF DEATH

In *The Unexplained*, I documented the alleged Madagascan man-eating tree too, known locally

as the tepe, and reputedly encountered in the 1800s by a mysterious explorer, Carl Liche. As I noted, however, most scientists believe that both the tree and Liche are fictitious.

Nevertheless, rumours have continued to emerge from this vast island. Moreover, Czech explorer Ivan Mackerle was eager to uncover more after learning that a former British army officer called L. Hearst had spent four months in Madagascar during 1935 and had taken photos of unknown trees under which were skeletons of large animals. According to Mackerle's researches, Hearst's photos were later published, but discounted as hoaxes by scientists. This reaction incensed Hearst, who duly planned a second Madagascan expedition but died under mysterious circumstances. Although he has not succeeded in uncovering where these photos were supposedly published,

*The vile-smelling* Rafflesia *is among the world's more bizarre plants.*

Above: *A depiction of the fabled man-eating plant featured in* The Day of the Triffids, *1963.* Opposite: *Madagascar's verdant terrain may yet yield some botanical surprises.*

Mackerle had become intrigued enough to lead a month-long expedition to Madagascar during 1998, in search of the truth. In a letter to me of 21 September 1998, he described his findings as follows, which make interesting reading:

*We had taken a Malagasy guide and interpreter with us, who lives in Prague and knows Czech. And so we could speak with the natives about mysteries. We had travelled all over the country, mainly in the south region. It is interesting, but no-one had known anything about the man-eating tree. Neither people in town (botanists, journalists, etc.) nor natives. They had heard only about pitcher plants. Natives know killer trees but no man-eating ones. The story of Karl [sic] Liche is unknown there. We spoke with many botanists. I could not believe it, because I had supposed that it was a widespread legend there. But killer trees are also very interesting. Many of them are little-known or unknown to science. We found the killer tree "kumanga", which is poisonous when it has flowers. We took gas-masks for protecting ourselves, but the tree did not blossom at that time. We had seen a*

*skeleton of a dead bird and a dead turtle under the tree. The tree grows only in one place in Madagascar and it is rare today. It was difficult to find it. There are other dangerous trees in the country, but no cannibal tree. One of them is "andrindritra" (Harpagophytum grandidiere), which can tie you up in its long branches with little hooks, or "lumbiru" (Cryptostegia madagascariensis). Natives are afraid of it and believe that when you sleep under this plant you will never wake up ... The leaves of the tree kumanga could be poisonous. Natives told us that this tree kills their cattle eating the leaves and drinking water near the tree, and so they burn out this tree.*

Mundanely, the tying-up talents of the andrindritra (also called the grapple plant) owe more to local legend than to botanical believability – as does the malign soporific association of the lumbiru, in reality a species of vine from which a type of latex can be extracted.

Worth noting here is that Harold T. Wilkins's book also referred to a sinister sleep-associated climbing plant, one that was allegedly known to the Indians inhabiting the

dense Chaco forest on the border of Bolivia and Argentina as *el juy-juy*. According to Wilkins:

*The plant is one of great beauty and seductiveness and is said to exhale a soporific perfume which sends to sleep men or large animals unlucky enough to seek its shade, in the noonday and siesta hours when the denizens of the forest are silent. Once the victim has sunk into a drugged sleep, the floral canopy overhead sends down masses of lovely blossoms, each flower of which is armed with a powerful sucker, which draws from the body all its blood and juices, leaving not even a fragment to tempt the vulture to shoot down from the skies to gorge on a bare skeleton.*

A mesmerizingly gruesome jungle legend, possibly, but as an authentic mystery plant this floral vampire is no more plausible a prospect than Wilkins's octopod tree.

Conversely, if Ivan Mackerle's claim regarding still-unknown species of "killer" (i.e. poisonous) trees existing in Madagascar is correct, then even though it does not appear after all to have a man-eating tree this huge Indian Ocean island may still hold some significant surprises in store for future botanists.

# OOPS, IT'S AN O-O-P!

ANIMALS APPEARING WHERE THEY SHOULD NOT BE FOUND, ZOOGEOGRAPHICALLY, ARE POPULARLY TERMED OUT-OF-PLACE ANIMALS — OR O-O-PS, FOR SHORT. MANY ARE EXOTIC SPECIES THAT HAVE ESCAPED FROM CAPTIVITY IN REGIONS FAR FROM THEIR NATIVE DOMAIN. SOMETIMES THEY MERELY COMPRISE A SINGLE SPECIMEN OR TWO; IN OTHER INSTANCES, THE ESCAPEES HAVE ESTABLISHED A THRIVING POPULATION.

## BARKING UP THE WRONG ISLAND

One of the most unexpected o-o-p cases features the black-tailed prairie dog *Cynomys ludovicianus*. This barking ground squirrel is native to North America, but after a number escaped from a country park on the Isle of Wight in southern England when it closed down, they rapidly multiplied, yielding 250–400 specimens by the

*Black-tailed prairie dogs – are they set to overrun the Isle of Wight?*

early 1990s. Attempts to snare them have largely failed, as they are very intelligent, and it is feared that this New World interloper may overrun the entire island.

## CAUGHT GOLDEN-HANDED

Another unusual rodent colonization occurred at Cap d'Antibes, southern France, in the early 1980s, featuring what appears to be a subspecies of *Calliosciurus flavimanus hendeei* – an Asian squirrel with distinctive golden-coloured paws. Scientists assumed that the

harsh 1984–85 winter would wipe out the population, but the colony tenaciously persisted, and would probably have expanded its range into other coastal areas, had it not been prevented by the dense intervening city centre.

## EUROPE'S OTHER WILD MONKEYS

It is commonly but erroneously assumed that the only monkeys living wild anywhere in Europe are the famous Barbary apes (in reality a species of macaque monkey) on Gibraltar. Less well known, however, is that since the 1970s, a colony of anubis baboons has been established in the wild in Cadiz, a province of Spain. They originated from a mass escape of 60 baboons from the Auto Safari Andaluz safari park in 1972. Forty were soon killed by hunters, but, quite remarkably, the remaining ones survived unnoticed, until finally discovered by a team of environmentalists as recently as 1992.

## BEWARE THE WOLVERINE, MY SON ...

Even more baffling, because they are presently still officially unconfirmed, are reports of wolverines on the prowl in Britain. As large as a small bear, with a characteristic yellow-fawn horizontal band across each flank, and a thick bushy tail, the wolverine *Gulo gulo* is the world's largest species of weasel, and has a reputation for ferocity and enormous strength. Supposedly confined to the montane forests of northern Eurasia and North America, this formidable creature has lately been nominated as the identity of several mystifying beasts allegedly encountered in Wales and the West Country.

One of the most significant sightings, made by highly experienced Exmoor naturalist Trevor Beer and his assistant Endymion in early January 1994 while walking their dog, featured what would indeed seem to be a couple of wolverines, running along a disused railway line near South Molton, on Exmoor's edge.

Spied at a distance of only 40 yards or so away, both of these mystery beasts were bear-like in general shape, 3–4 feet (about 1 metre) long, and noisy, with a very thickset body, a long bushy tail, and dense dark brown fur, banded by a paler horizontal stripe on each flank – a perfect description of the wolverine. When one of them turned round to face their dog, Trevor quickly called the dog back and placed it on a leash, after which the two creatures moved off.

In summer 1994, while travelling through Devon, London photographer Joanne Crowther saw the dead body of a strange beast lying beside the road at Wembworthy. Thinking nothing of it, she did not collect it, or even photograph it; only later, when describing its appearance to some naturalists, did she (and they) realize that it must have been a wolverine.

Sceptics of the wolverine identity for such creatures note that this species has not been widely maintained in British zoos for a number of years, so where could any have escaped from? Instead, they favour a badger, possibly one with muddy fur, or even a rare erythristic (abnormally red) specimen. However, as Trevor Beer is very familiar with badgers, he is hardly likely not to recognize a pair when viewed at such close range, and he has speculated that wolverine specimens may have escaped from fur farms.

## DOWN AND OUT, IN OUTBACK FARM AND ASHDOWN FOREST

Also unexplained is the canine mystery beast of Outback Farm, adjoining Ashdown Forest in East Sussex, reported in spring 1971 by farmer Alistair Whitley. After finding a number of strange footprints nearby, Whitley had several sightings of a "very heavy strong dog with fierce eyes and round pricked ears, yellowish in colour splotched with darker marks", lying in the fields, watching his sheep. Finally, in October 1971 Whitley shot the creature, which vanished into

*Normally found in montane forests, could the wolverine be the mystery beast of Exmoor?*

the forest and was not reported again. Based upon hair samples, spoor and his descriptions, according to Whitley the Natural History Museum in London identified his unwelcome speckled visitor as a spotted hyaena *Crocuta crocuta*. Yet there had been no spotted hyaena escapes from zoos, and it is not a species normally kept even as an exotic pet. Consequently, zoological historian Clinton Keeling deems it likelier that the animal was a Cape hunting dog *Lycaon pictus*, which corresponds well with Whitley's description. Whatever its identity, however, its origin and ultimate fate have never been established.

## WHERE TO SPOT A SPOTTED LION

Equally enigmatic are reports of diminutive, heavily spotted, sparsely maned lions frequenting the dense, high-altitude forests of Kenya's Aberdare Mountains – a highly unexpected habitat for lions. The native people, however, are familiar with this o-o-p cat form, which they call the marozi and readily distinguish from leopards and normal lions. There is even a pair of marozi skins, retained at London's Natural History Museum, from a male and female shot during the early 1930s by Aberdares farmer Michael Trent. These have been dismissed by some authorities as mere freaks. Conversely, veteran cryptozoologist Dr Bernard Heuvelmans considers that the marozi constitutes a valid taxonomic race of lion specifically modified for a montane, forest-dwelling existence, and notes that similar felids have been reported from other mountain ranges across East and Central Africa.

## ENCOUNTERING THE SNOW EELS

Snow eels are controversial o-o-p mini-beasts occasionally encountered wriggling on the surface of snow, much to the surprise of their bemused observers. A classic snow-eel report is that of Dr Israel Russell, who witnessed the

*The marozi is smaller than a normal lion and has a distinctive spotted coat.*

snow-eel phenomenon on Alaska's Malaspina Glacier in 1891. In a report later published by the American periodical *Natural History*, Russell stated: "In the early morning before the sunlight touched the snow its surface was literally covered with small, slim black worms, about an inch long, and having a remarkably snake-like appearance. These creatures were wiggling over the snow in thousands, but as soon as the sun rose and made its warmth felt they disappeared beneath the surface. They are not seen when the temperature is above freezing." Although specimens of snow eels have been formally examined, scientists have failed to agree upon their identity. Some favour small enchytraeid earthworms, which are certainly able to survive very cold temperatures; others believe them to be insect larvae. In truth, it is likely that both animal types are involved (and perhaps others too), i.e. that snow worms do not constitute a single species or taxonomic group of animal.

## A BIG ONE BULLOCKY DOWN UNDER

Australia is renowned as a land of strange animals. During the early 1800s, however, reports emanated from here of a creature bizarre even by that island continent's

zoological standards. The somewhat tragic history of this enigmatic, still-unexplained, yet nowadays long-forgotten entity was recalled in E. Lloyd's *A Visit to the Antipodes* (1846) as follows:

*I have to record a tradition that exists among the white people in the north country, with reference to an animal that sometimes appears, much to their alarm. This is no other than a camel. It is said, amongst the other wise things done by the sanguine people that first settled the land, that one gentleman, arguing from the natural dryness of the climate, that it was a country similar to the Zahara [sic], or Great Desert, and required animals of the same powers of endurance to travel over it, resolved upon doing nothing less than importing a camel, from which he anticipated reaping a fortune. However, calamitously, the camel, after its arrival in the colony, got lost, or ran away into the bush, and for a long time afterwards was never heard of. It is however stated, that he appeared to some shepherds, while tending their flocks, and who were not a little surprised, not to say amazed, at the unlooked-for visitation.*

*The dromedary may have been introduced into Australia earlier in the nineteenth century than realized.*

*The blacks, in terror, fled at his approach, exclaiming, "big one bullocky! big one bullocky!" It is likewise stated, that the forlorn camel, for a long time roamed through the country, like the wandering Jew,*

*seeking society but finding none; sometimes appearing unintentionally and unexpectedly to shepherds and black fellows, and being innocently the cause of great alarm, until at last another outcast left the realms of social intercourse, and cast himself upon his own energies. This was a harmless donkey, one of three which had found their way into this province. Having strayed from his sphere, like a comet, he took an orbit of his own, exceedingly eccentric, until the two forlorn and wandering planets came within the reach of each other's attraction, and were brought into contact, the result of which is, that they now roam the forest together, alike forsaken, and irrevocably lost.*

This sad little episode was no doubt repeated many times thereafter too, with dromedaries imported Down Under for desert exploration ultimately escaping (or being deliberately released), because today there are small naturalized herds of these one-humped camels in many parts of Australia. What makes Lloyd's account so noteworthy is that according to official records, the first camels imported into Australia (all dromedaries) did not arrive until 1840, and their whereabouts were fully documented until beyond 1846 (the publication date of Lloyd's book). Moreover, the first major importations did not occur until 1860. Yet his account makes clear that the camel reported by Lloyd had been roaming the deserts Down Under long before the 1840s – so who was its original owner, and when exactly had it been imported into Australia? Unless this episode is a hoax, or unless there are even earlier records still awaiting disclosure, it would appear that this bewildering "big one bullocky" was the very first dromedary ever to set hoof in the Antipodes. Little wonder, then, that it elicited such consternation among its astonished aboriginal observers.

*Alaska's frozen landscape provides a home for snow eels.*

# THERAPEUTIC ANIMALS

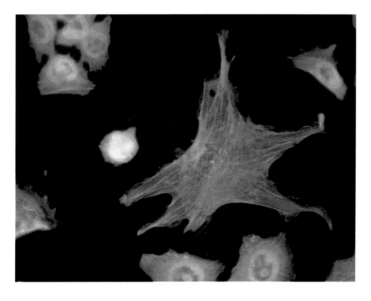

OVER A CENTURY AGO, FLORENCE NIGHTINGALE RECORDED IN HER DIARY THAT THE PRESENCE OF A PET WAS BENEFICIAL TO THE RECOVERY OF ITS OWNER. TODAY, NUMEROUS CASES ARE ON FILE TESTIFYING TO THE OFTEN EXTRAORDINARY THERAPEUTIC EFFECTS OF ANIMALS UPON HUMAN HEALTH. SOME CAN BE EASILY EXPLAINED; OTHERS, SUCH AS THE SELECTION PRESENTED HERE, ARE DECIDEDLY LESS COMPREHENSIBLE.

## CANINE PREDICTION OF EPILEPTIC SEIZURES AND DIABETIC COMAS

Once dismissed as fantasy by the medical profession, it is widely accepted nowadays that some pet dogs possess the uncanny ability to detect an oncoming epileptic fit or diabetic coma in their owners – often considerably before it actually takes place.

*A micrograph of melanoma cancer cells and fibroblasts of the type detected by George.*

A recent media-publicized example is Chad, a golden retriever owned by eleven-year-old epileptic Richard Beale from Erdington in Birmingham, England. Before any visible symptoms occur, the normally placid Chad begins to bark wildly and runs to Richard's mother, Ruth, alerting her that her son is about to have a seizure. This canine early warning system enables his parents to take all necessary precautions in order to prevent Richard from injuring himself during the seizure – an unpleasant, all-too-frequent reality before Chad

was bought by the Beales as a pet for Richard in 1995.

Epileptic Tony Brown-Griffin from Tunbridge Wells, Kent, is similarly protected from seizure-induced injury by her pet border collie, Rupert, who is so attuned to his owner's impending seizures that he can actually detect which type of seizure Tony is about to experience. In the case of an absence seizure, he will suddenly stop whatever he is doing and sit at her feet 3–5 minutes before it begins. And in the case of a tonic-chlonic seizure, he begins to bark in a distinctive, urgent manner, up to 45 minutes prior to its onset.

Several theories have been aired to explain such remarkable canine prescience in relation to epilepsy. The British Epilepsy Association states that the dogs are detecting a high-pitched sound and an exceedingly faint odour, both of which are emitted by an epileptic up to half an hour before the onset of a seizure. Researchers claim that the sound is linked to abnormal electrical impulses occurring in the epileptic's brain prior to a seizure, but they have yet to discover the source of the strange associated odour. Humans, like other living organisms, are surrounded by a magnetic field created by the body's electrical activity, and in the opinion of animal psychologist Roger Mugford, dogs can accurately detect changes in this magnetic field that occur with an epileptic prior to the start of a seizure.

Whatever the precise nature of the mechanism involved, however, by 1997 the results achieved by such dogs as Chad and Rupert had proved sufficiently impressive to have inspired Support Dogs, a British charity based in Sheffield, to train a number of pets to detect seizures in their epileptic owners, and it plans to expand its training scheme further.

Some dogs have been found to be equally sensitive to the onset of diabetic comas in their owners, resulting from a sharp fall of blood sugar (hypoglycaemia). Such dogs tend to be small, lapdog types, who detect their owners' oncoming hypoglycaemia while lying in their arms or in their laps. This has led researchers to suggest that these pets may be reacting to temperature changes experienced by their owners (prior to a hypoglycaemic attack, diabetics frequently become pale, with clammy perspiration breaking out on their hands and face).

## GEORGE, A CANCER-SNIFFING SCHNAUZER

Surely the most amazing example of medical detection practised by a dog is the singular talent of an eight-year-old grey schnauzer called George, as publicly revealed in 1997.

George's remarkable story began several years earlier with Dr Armand Cognetta, a Florida dermatologist who had become fascinated by a number of well-attested medical cases in which a pet dog had revealed the hitherto-unsuspected presence of a cancer in its owner by sniffing compulsively at the location concealing the malignant growth. This had occurred months before its puzzled owner had finally visited the family doctor to seek the reason for his pet's bizarre behaviour, whereupon an examination had uncovered the cancer.

Mindful of the exceptional sensitivity of the canine olfactory system, and anxious to put

*George, the remarkable dog who detects cancer cells.*

these remarkable incidents to the test, Cognetta joined forces with Duane Pickel, a retired police dog handler. Using Pickel's schnauzer, George, as a suitable dog to train in the detection of cancer by smell, he experimented with samples of melanomas stored in test tubes. Once George could recognize and actively seek the scent of the melanoma samples, volunteer patients with known melanomas were brought in, and George would successfully locate each melanoma by delicately placing his paw upon it. The climax to this series of experiments, however, came with a patient called James Garafolo.

Garafolo possessed a number of moles, all of which had been tested and diagnosed as benign, but as soon as George was introduced to him, the dog began obsessively sniffing one particular mole. Unwilling to take chances, Garafolo duly arranged for it to be surgically removed, and afterwards the mole was retested – which revealed that it contained a set of potentially lethal cancer cells. George had saved Garafolo's life.

## THE HEALING FISHES OF KANGAL

There are countless examples of therapeutic thermal waters around the world, but the warm sulphurous spa pools of Kangal, high in the volcanic mountains of central Anatolia, Turkey, have a very special additional ingredient – shoals of tiny fishes that can allegedly alleviate the unsightly and often exceedingly painful skin disorder known as psoriasis.

Since 1917, psoriasis sufferers in Turkey and far beyond its borders have been visiting Kangal. Here, upon the recommendation of the pools' medical attendants, they commence a course of 21 daily baths, each lasting 2 hours, during which time they remain fully immersed and are "treated" by the pools' extraordinary piscean physicians. The tiny fishes, which comprise three distinct types, swim up to the bathers, and while one type swiftly begins nibbling away the white scabs produced by the psoriasis, the second type cleans up any naked red sores, and the third removes any dead skin.

Many patients have subsequently experienced dramatic improvements to their condition. One such case, as documented in media reports during July 1989, was a 32-year-old man named Ali, who had suffered for 15 years from severe psoriasis, and had subjected himself to every available mainstream treatment, but all without success – until Kangal. After being treated by its healing fishes, his skin rapidly improved. Another well-publicized case is that of Belfast psoriasis sufferer Michael Shortt, who despaired of ridding himself of his agonizing condition until, in the mid-1990s, he learnt of Kangal and promptly paid £2,000 for a full course of treatment here. After nine days, the fishes had evidently worked their mysterious (albeit often very painful) magic, because his skin, previously spotted with raised red patches covered in silvery scales, was perfectly clear. Only a few pale pink outlines remained as evidence of his psoriasis's erstwhile presence.

Sadly, not every sufferer visiting Kangal has experienced any benefit, and dermatologists retain an open mind as to the effectiveness of the fishes' treatments. Predictably, however, beneficiaries like Ali and Michael have nothing but praise for their little finned helpers.

As for the fishes themselves: brown and green in colour, and measuring 1–4 inches long, they appear to be of the carp lineage, but their precise species have yet to be formally ascertained. As already noted by me (*Fate*, February 1994), however, they are probably killifishes (cyprinodonts), belonging to the genus *Kosswigichthys*, or, more likely, the genus *Aphanius*. Various *Aphanius* species are known to exhibit similar behaviour in the Dead Sea.

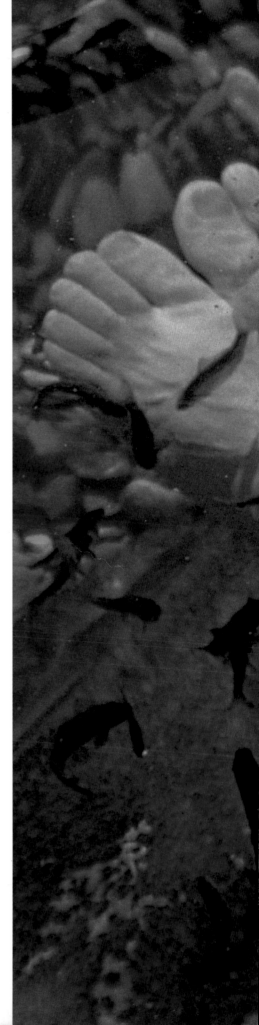

*Kangal's healing fishes at work.*

*The anomalous "Avis Indica" from Adriaan Collaert's book* Avium Vivae Icones.

# MASCARENE MYSTERIES

MANY OF THE UNIQUE SPECIES OF AVIFAUNA NATIVE TO MAURITIUS, LARGEST OF THE MASCARENE ISLANDS IN THE INDIAN OCEAN, WERE WIPED OUT FOLLOWING ITS FIRST MAJOR CONTACT WITH EUROPEAN MARITIME VOYAGERS DURING THE SIXTEENTH CENTURY. SOME OF THESE EXTIRPATED BIRDS WERE FLIGHTLESS, OF WHICH AT LEAST TWO ARE STILL ASSOCIATED WITH MYSTERY AND CONTROVERSY EVEN TODAY, AS EXPOSED HERE.

## THE CONTENTIOUS LEGACY OF LEGAUTIA

For many years, there was much debate within geographical and zoological circles concerning whether the famous Indian Ocean voyage of Huguenot refugee François Legaut

during 1690–98 did actually take place – and, indeed, whether Legaut himself ever existed. Some researchers claimed that Legaut and his travelogue *Voyage et Avantures* [sic] *de François Legaut et de Ses Compagnons en Deux Isles Désertes des Indes Orientales* (1708) were as fraudulent as those of Baron Münchausen and the fictitious Sir John Mandeville, and that his visits to the Mascarene islands of Mauritius and

Rodriguez occurred only in someone's imagination.

In 1926, however, two Paris librarians, J. Vivielle and Henri Dehérain, uncovered much new data substantiating the reality of Legaut and his voyages. Nevertheless, considerable controversy still surrounds this enigmatic explorer, not least of which concerns the identity of a very tall, long-vanished and

Legautia gigantea, *named after a seventeenth-century French explorer, is as enigmatic as its discoverer.*

extremely mysterious Mauritius bird named after him.

Referred to by Legaut as "Le Géant", *Legautia gigantea* was so christened by German zoologist H. Schlegel in 1858, and is usually deemed to have been a giant species of rail. It was reputedly abundant at the time of Legaut's visit to Mauritius, but had entirely vanished shortly afterwards, judging from the fact that no other explorer has reported seeing it.

Two engravings are known (which have inspired a number of much more recent paintings). One is by Legaut himself and appeared in his travelogue, but this seems to have been based upon an earlier engraving of a bird simply dubbed "Avis Indica", featured in an early-seventeenth-century tome of illustrations by Adriaan Collaert, entitled *Avium Vivae Icones*. Both engravings depict a long-necked, squat-bodied, long-limbed bird with enormous toes, a short white-edged tail, small wings and a fairly long, straight, pointed beak. According to Legaut's text, it was 6 feet (1.8 metres) tall, flightless, with wholly white plumage, and inhabited marshes.

Faced with such a highly distinctive bird, yet one that bears no convincing resemblance to any known species, three schools of opinion arose. One claimed that *Legautia* was indeed an unknown species, allied to rails, which had tragically died out long ago. A second proposed that the two engravings were simply ill-drawn, inaccurate representations of some familiar species, of which the two most favoured contenders are a gallinule (i.e. a large relation of the well-known moorhens and coots) or a flamingo. And the third brusquely dismissed *Legautia* (like its human namesake) as wholly fictitious – a dreamed-up, invented species.

Even today, these factions are no nearer reaching an agreement concerning the status and validity (or otherwise) of *Legautia*. It certainly seems strange that none of the many

*The dodo – dead, or just resting?*

explorers visiting Mauritius before or since Legaut has referred to *Legautia*; surely it would be difficult to overlook or fail to mention such a sizeable, eyecatching bird. Yet perhaps at least one explorer did see it – after all, we still have Collaert's enigmatic "Avis Indica" to explain. As for misidentification based upon poor portrayals, flamingos have indeed been reported from Mauritius, but if Collaert's "Avis Indica" is truly meant to be a depiction of a flamingo, then it must surely rate as one of the worst, most outlandishly inaccurate animal illustrations of all time! Equally, it hardly need be pointed out that flamingos are not flightless. Yet if we accept the validity of *Legautia* as a discrete species in its own right, and that its morphology was accurately described and depicted in Legaut's text and the two engravings, why did what Legaut claimed to have been a common species die out so rapidly after his Mauritius visit, and why are there no specimens or preserved remains?

Until answers to such questions as these are forthcoming, *Legautia* seems fated to remain in this ornithological limbo of the lost where it has languished for the past three centuries.

## RETURN OF THE DODO?

Mauritius's most famous deceased denizen of the feathered kind is unquestionably the dodo *Raphus cucullatus*. Indeed, even its name has become synonymous nowadays with obsolescence – as embodied within the oft-reiterated maxim "as dead as the dodo". Consequently, unconfirmed reports that this supposedly demised bird not only persisted long after its official extinction date of 1681, but may even still be doing so today, are particularly intriguing.

It was in 1990, after contacting veteran cryptozoologist Dr Bernard Heuvelmans to inform him that he was planning to visit Mauritius, that Scottish explorer Bill Gibbons (now living in Canada) received with Heuvelmans's letter of reply an accompanying

article that had lately appeared in the colour magazine of London's *The Mail on Sunday* newspaper. The article referred to an Englishman holidaying in Mauritius who, while walking by the sea there one evening, claimed to have spied waddling along the beach a large ungainly looking bird that he felt sure was a dodo. Not surprisingly, his story was not believed. However, a Frenchman had also reported seeing just such a bird in Mauritius two years earlier.

Gibbons himself had heard tell that at a locality now occupied by Mauritius's airport, seemingly fresh dodo remains had been found approximately half a century after the dodo had supposedly died out. Even more tantalizing, however, was some information that he had received when questioning friends and colleagues of his Mauritius-born wife regarding the dodo. They informed him that dodo-like birds have been seen in recent years, at dusk and early dawn, walking along the beach that stretches out to the sea from a large secluded area of rainforest called the Plain Champagne. Even today, this dense expanse is largely unexplored, only occasionally entered by local people seeking monkeys – a popular delicacy.

Could there really be dodos still living in Mauritius? It seems an incredibly remote prospect, and Gibbons freely concedes that even if the supposed sightings on record are genuine, they could merely be misidentifications of some other species – such as the giant petrel *Macronectes giganteus*, a vaguely dodo-like seabird. Nevertheless, remote prospects have been cryptozoologically realized in the past, which is why Gibbons is hoping to launch a serious expedition to Mauritius in search of what may conceivably be the last of the dodos. He also plans to explore some of the tiny, scarcely visited minor Mascarene isles, such as the Cargados Carajos Shoals, whose wildlife is largely uninvestigated.

"As dead as the dodo"? Not if Bill Gibbons has his way!

# BOTANICAL RESURRECTIONS

CRYPTOZOOLOGISTS ARE FAMILIAR WITH THE SENSATIONAL DISCOVERY IN 1938 OF A LIVING SPECIES OF COELACANTH; UNTIL THEN, THIS ANCIENT LINEAGE OF LOBE-FINNED FISHES WAS BELIEVED TO HAVE BECOME EXTINCT OVER 65 MILLION YEARS AGO. FAR LESS FAMILIAR, CONVERSELY, IS THE NO LESS ASTONISHING RESURRECTION IN MODERN TIMES OF VARIOUS OSTENSIBLY LONG-VANISHED SPECIES OF TREE.

## A LONG-OVERDUE MEETING WITH METASEQUOIA

Among the most dramatic resurrections on record is that of the dawn redwood *Metasequoia glyptostroboides*. It was in 1944 when a Chinese forester called Tsang Wang, travelling through Szechuan (Sichuan) Province, came upon a strange-looking tree growing in the valley to the east of the village of Mo-Tao-Chi. Although it superficially resembled a species known as the water pine *Glyptostrobus pensilis*, it was clearly not the same. Fortunately, Wang's curiosity was

*The sturdy trunk of a dawn redwood tree, known only as a fossil until its unexpected rediscovery in the 1940s.*

sufficiently piqued by this botanical enigma to collect some branches from it and take them back to the Division of Forestry in the Ministry of Agriculture, Nanking.

Here, the resemblance of its cones to those of California's *Sequoia* redwoods became the source of great bewilderment among the foresters examining them, and so they were duly passed on to Professor Wan-Chun Cheng at National Central University, an expert on Szechuan trees. He readily perceived that this was not only a new species, but one sufficiently distinct from all others to warrant the creation of a new genus. But that was not all.

One of his colleagues, palaeobotanist Dr Hsen-Hsu Hu from the Fan Memorial Institute of

Biology, recognized that the strange tree's cones were identical with those of a recently named genus of fossil redwood, *Metasequoia*, whose ancient remains, none more recent than 20 million years old, had been found in Manchuria and Japan. Thanks to Tsang Wang's alert eyes, however, *Metasequoia* was a fossil genus no longer. It now had a living, present-day representative, *M. glyptostroboides*, whose scientific name, given to it in 1948 by Hu and Cheng, emphasizes its deceptive outward similarity to the water pine *Glyptostrobus*.

Today, fossil *Metasequoia* are known from North America and many other parts of the world too. Meanwhile, the single living species was introduced into cultivation in 1948, and is now widely grown in temperate regions. It has proved to be quite a hardy tree, and grows up to 140 feet (43 metres) high in the wild, though no more than 6 feet (1.8 metres) in diameter – unlike its much taller, burlier Californian *Sequoia* relatives. It is also set apart from *Sequoia* by its leaves, which are deciduous and arranged in opposite pairs rather than in alternate arrays or spirals.

## THE ONCE AND FUTURE FIR TREE

Another Chinese tree brought back from the dead is the Cathay silver fir *Cathaya argyrophylla*. Professor Zhong Jixin, deputy director of the Guangxi Academy of Sciences, first learnt of what he later revealed to be the Cathay silver fir during the 1950s, when he was informed by an old man from what was then a remote village called Wantian in Guizhou Province that some 30 miles into the mountains was a peak covered with ancient trees. During a subsequent expedition here, one of Zhong's colleagues dug out a seedling of what he considered to be a Fortune's keteleeria tree *Keteleeria fortunei*, but when he examined it Zhong realized that it was something very different, which he did not recognize. More samples, including some of its silver-banded leaves, were obtained by Zhong and his team in May 1955 from the southern slope of Mount Hongya. These were sufficient for botanical taxonomists to declare their species to be new to science and deserving of a new genus.

The biggest surprise came, however, when a Russian botanist called Sugatchey, fortuitously visiting China at this time, saw the Hongya samples and revealed that they shared many similarities with a fossil species whose 10-million-year-old remains had been unearthed in several European localities. Suddenly, the Cathay silver fir had become a "living fossil", reviving a supposedly long-vanished lineage of trees.

## A SUDANESE SURPRISE

More recently, in March 1996, palm tree experts Tobias Spanner and Martin Gibbons announced that after lately driving from Khartoum across the Sudanese desert, they had encountered an old camel herder who had shown them a strange palm tree standing outside a remote abandoned town called Murrat Wells. This tree proved to be a specimen of *Medemia* (= *Hyphaene*) *argun*, traditionally placed in tombs during ancient Egyptian times, but which had hitherto been thought by modern-day botanists to have become extinct long ago. Seeds procured from the precious Murrat Wells tree have now been donated to Kew Gardens and other botanical centres worldwide to perpetuate this remarkable rediscovery.

## ON THE TRAIL OF THE LONESOME PINES

Even more famous was an incredible discovery made during August 1994 by forest ranger David Noble in one of Wollemi National Park's many remote valleys nestling within the Blue Mountains of New South Wales, Australia. The discovery comprised a secluded grove of 23 adult and 16 juvenile trees belonging to a hitherto-undescribed species of evergreen tree. Now christened *Wollemia nobilis*, the Wollemi pine, it is most closely allied to a tree called *Dilwynites*, known only from fossils dating back 150 million years.

Covered in dense, waxy foliage and knobbly chocolate-coloured bark, and up to 130 feet (40 metres) tall, they had escaped previous notice owing to the near-inaccessible nature of their valley hideaway – until intrepid ranger David Noble penetrated it while backpacking, became intrigued by their odd appearance and took a branch back with him for identification. By 1996, moreover, the Wollemi pine had yielded a further, equally significant surprise: its tissues are a source of taxol, a drug used for treating cancer but hitherto derived from yews, as well as four penicillin-producing microbes. A second stand of Wollemis has also been found, in an even more inaccessible valley than the first one. Seedlings have been sent to botanical institutions around the world to ensure the species' continuing survival.

## DENOUEMENT OF THE DINOSAUR VINE

Perhaps the most amazing botanical resurrection of all, however, was just a little too good to be true – and so, indeed, did it prove. In 1989, *Garden News*, a leading British gardening weekly, unveiled a sensational world-exclusive – the revival of a long-extinct prehistoric plant dubbed the dinosaur vine, by germinating seeds extracted from fossilized *Stegosaurus* droppings (coprolites) found with other dinosaur remains in a cave within California's Mojave Desert. In 1988, the droppings had been examined by a scientific team at Utah's University of Eureka, led by Professor Adge Ufult. After the seeds had been successfully germinated, samples were sent to Kew Gardens and also to Alan Durose, technical editor at *Garden News*.

The magazine's coverage included a colour photo of a dinosaur vine, hitherto extinct for over 65 million years, sporting profuse fern-like leaves. It also announced a competition whereby its readers could submit ideas for a suitable official common name for this plant, to replace its temporary "dinosaur vine" appellation. Three weeks later, however, *Garden News* made a second, very different announcement regarding the dinosaur vine – it was a hoax!

Their celebrated plant was nothing more than a slick composite construction, consisting of elderberry stalks, fern leaves and home-made flowers, created by Alan Durose in his own conservatory. In addition, certain clues in the original report's text, written by the production editor of *Garden News*, Trevor Gehlcken, should have alerted readers to the true nature of the dinosaur vine. After all, there is no "University of Eureka" in Utah (or anywhere else?), and the cited professor's name, Adge Ufult, sounds remarkably like "had you fooled". The biggest clue of all, however, should surely have been the date on which the issue of *Garden News* containing the dinosaur vine exclusive appeared – 1 April!

# TECHNICOLOR TIGERS

WHEN WILLIAM BLAKE PENNED HIS FAMOUS LINE "TIGER, TIGER, BURNING BRIGHT", HE LITTLE REALIZED THAT THE FIERY GLOW OF THIS SPECTACULAR CAT'S PELAGE CAN SOMETIMES YIELD A HIGHLY UNEXPECTED, UNCOMMON SPECTRUM OF COLOURS.

## THE BLUE TIGERS OF FUJIAN

The tiger's penchant for colourful controversy is epitomized by the amazing blue tigers sporadically sighted within the dense forests of China's Fujian Province. As yet, science has no specimen of this astounding colour

*Cryptozoological artist William Rebsamen's portrayal of one of the extraordinary blue tigers spied yet never captured in the dense forests of Fujian.*

variety to examine, but one was observed at close range in 1910 by Methodist missionary Harry R. Caldwell. He even attempted to shoot it, if only to verify these creatures' reality to the world, but was prevented from doing so by the presence nearby of two children, who were in danger of being hit by his gunfire. So Caldwell moved his position slightly, to direct his aim away from them, but while doing so he lost sight of the blue tiger and never saw it again. In his book *Blue Tiger*

(1925), he described its fur as deep maltese blue (instead of the usual orange), with black stripes.

His son, John C. Caldwell, who had accompanied him on some of his earlier, unsuccessful searches for blue tigers, recalled seeing on several occasions the beautiful

*Somewhat bigger than the average ginger tom, the golden tabby tiger indicates its mixed parentage in its white underparts.*

maltese hairs of such creatures along the mountain trails. Genetically, Fujian's blue tigers may comprise an example of "blue dilution", an exotic colour form created by the combined expression of two different pairs of mutant alleles (gene forms) – dilute and non-agouti. This combination has occasionally produced blue-furred lynxes and bobcats, and also the maltese blue breed of domestic cat.

## A Whiter Shade of Pale

Less unexpected but no less exotic are India's white Bengal tigers, whose earliest known record dates back to 1561; records are also on file from immediate neighbouring countries as well as China and Japan. Undoubtedly the most famous examples, however, are those recorded from Rewa, especially the strain originating from a superb male specimen called Mohan. Captured on 27 May 1951 and housed within the now-disused summer palace of Rewa's Maharajah, Mohan was mated with many normal-coloured tigresses, ultimately establishing a pure-breeding white lineage yielding moonlight-furred specimens that have been exhibited in zoos worldwide. Characterized by their creamy-white fur patterned with narrow brown stripes, and also by their glacial, ice-blue eyes, for a long time these white tigers' genetics remained a baffling mystery. In 1967, however, Drs Ian W.B. Thornton, K.K. Yeung, and K.S. Sankhala revealed that they are chinchilla albinos.

In other words, instead of possessing a pair of normal (wild-type) alleles for the pelage colouration gene known as full colour, they possess a pair of mutant alleles called chinchilla albino. This allele expresses itself by inhibiting or drastically restricting the production of phaeomelanin, which is the normal yellow pigment in tiger fur.

## Golden and New

Recently, moreover, a dramatic new feline manifestation involving white tigers has

appeared. By mating white Bengal tigers in some zoos and circuses with normal tigers belonging to other tiger subspecies, particularly Siberian tigers, a very striking, hitherto unrecorded variety of tiger has lately emerged. It is popularly referred to as the ginger or golden tabby tiger, owing to its mellow golden-hued pelage, patterned only with faint darker stripes, and complemented by snowy-white underparts. These golden tigers are also extremely large.

## The Tigers That Lost Their Stripes

In the wild state, meanwhile, nature seems to have taken this tigerine transformation even further, by spasmodically yielding tigers that do

## TIGERS OF THE DARK SIDE – PSEUDO-MELANISM IN SIMILIPAL

The Similipal reserve has lately yielded an even more uncommon colour variety of tiger. In July 1993, a young, anomalously patterned tigress was killed at the village of Podagad in the west of Similipal. A few months earlier, moreover, India's National Museum of Natural History had acquired a near-identical skin that had been confiscated from a New Delhi hunter-smuggler. These two skins came to the attention of Dr Lala Singh, who recorded them in a number of Indian publications.

What makes them so remarkable, and entirely different from all previously recorded tiger skins, is their abnormally wide stripes. Indeed, the stripes are so broad that they have coalesced very extensively, reducing the pelage's normal orange background colour to nothing more than a few orange streaks and stripes sandwiched between this expansive mass of fused black striping. The result of such an extraordinary amalgamation of stripes is that, at least on first sight, an observer might well mistakenly assume that the skins possess a black background colour marked with a few thin orange stripes – i.e. the reverse of normal tiger colouration and patterning.

As yet, the genetic mechanism responsible for this aberrant fusion of pelage markings, to the extent that they obscure much of the pelage's normal background colour, remains undetermined. However, its eyecatching result does have a name – pseudo-melanism – and has also been recorded in leopards. As its name suggests, pseudo-melanism is not the same as true melanism, recorded in many species of spotted cat, in which the pelage markings remain unchanged but are concealed by an abnormally dark background colour – exemplified by the leopard's melanistic morph (variant form), the black panther.

not have any stripes at all; instead they are uniformly brown. In 1989, four recent sightings of stripeless tigers were documented by S.R. Sagar (field director of Orissa's Similipal Tiger Reserve) and Dr Lala A.K. Singh (the reserve's research officer), which took place between 1961 and 1988. The most recent of these occurred on 27 July 1988, when the guard at Brundaban (North Similipal) spied a stripeless tiger walking away from a salt lick, leaving behind a footprint noted by the guard. Other reports indicate that these extraordinary animals tend to occur in open sandy tracts – areas where their unstriped pelage would provide good camouflage. Nevertheless, the genetic basis responsible for these feline contradictions is presently unknown.

## CHAPTER TWO

## UP FROM THE DEPTHS, AND DOWN FROM THE SKIES

# ALL THE BIRDS
## OF THE
# AIR

SOME OF THE WORLD'S LEAST-PUBLICIZED MYSTERY CREATURES ARE OF THE ORNITHOLOGICAL VARIETY, INCLUDING THE PHALANX OF AVIAN ESOTERICA PRESENTED HERE.

## A PARADISE CROW FROM GOODENOUGH ISLAND?

**G**oodenough is the largest of the three principal islands constituting the D'Entrecasteaux Archipelago, situated just north of New Guinea's eastern tip. It may also be home to a distinctive species of bird still awaiting formal scientific discovery.

*A possible identity for the mystery bird of Goodenough Island is a species related to the Moluccan paradise crow.*

In 1953, Goodenough was visited by the Fourth Archbold Expedition (named after Richard Archbold, a millionaire explorer from the USA), and while there one of its members spied a curious bird, documented as follows three years later in the expedition's official report:

*In the forest one morning I saw a black bird the size of a small crow which seemed to be a bird of paradise but not* Manucodia comrii *[curl-crested manucode] or* Manucodia keraudrenii *[trumpet*

*manucode], the only members of the family reported from the island. Our native hunter ... described ... a small black bird with a long tail, which dances in the treetops in the mountain forests of Goodenough, a description that suggests an* Astrapia *[long-tailed bird of paradise].*

The next report appertaining to this unidentified species that I have on file appeared in the March 1976 issue of the New Guinea Bird Society's newsletter, and describes a sighting made by

James Menzies, a renowned expert on New Guinea wildlife:

> On Mt. Oiamadawa'a, Goodenough Island 28 December 1975. Altitude about 1600 m [5250 feet], moss forest of Castanopsis, pandanus and tall bamboo. At dawn – a group of medium-sized black birds with long tails moving about in the forest canopy. Observed against the rising sun, without binoculars. Call a short explosive rattle.

Shortly afterwards, these two reports came to the attention of Australian ornithologist Bruce M. Beehler, who resolved to search for this elusive species when visiting Goodenough in 1976, and again in 1980. Unfortunately, he was unable either to observe or to obtain a specimen, so the Goodenough Island mystery bird currently remains just that – a mystery.

Beehler documented his search in his book *A Naturalist In New Guinea* (1991), and, as he noted, there are quite a number of possible identities on offer. For instance, it may not even be a bird of paradise. Instead, it might be a species, known or unknown, of drongo (predominantly black, long-tailed crow-like bird), long-tailed starling, or honeyeater (meliphagid). Yet the Archbold report's author seemed quite convinced that it was a bird of paradise.

For many people, the mere mention of these famous New Guinea denizens readily conjures up images of highly exotic, multi-hued, flamboyantly plumed birds, which is why the extremely showy, ornately arrayed astrapias, despite their long tails, do not yield a very plausible identity for the Goodenough bird. However, not all birds of paradise fit this popular image. Some of the smaller ones, such as the manucodes, are far less colourful, sporting dark metallic plumages instead of dramatic flourishes of vivid, ostentatious plumes. Certain manucodes have fairly long

*Lewin's honeyeater enjoying a piece of papaya; a honeyeater is another candidate for the mystery bird's identity.*

tails too, increasing their resemblance to this cryptic species.

There is also one further candidate – for which we need to look towards the least known, and least spectacular, bird of paradise species. Indeed, so demure is its plumage that its English name has relegated it to a position midway between its more spectacular relatives and the decidedly dowdy species from which the birds of paradise are believed to have evolved.

I am referring to the paradise crow

*Lycocorax pyrrhopterus*, inhabiting the islands of the Moluccan archipelago, lying to the west of New Guinea. Measuring 14–17 inches (35–43 cm) long and crimson-eyed, this bird of paradise is indeed outwardly corvine in appearance, its silky blackish-brown plumage relieved only by a faint greenish gloss on its body and a blue-black sheen on its long tail when viewed at close range, plus a buffish-white tinge on its inner flight feathers. Frequenting the hill forests of its Moluccan homeland, despite being quite a common species the paradise crow is very shy and hence is rarely observed.

Quite apart from its cry, which resembles a terse bark from a somewhat hoarse dog rather than the explosive rattle described by Menzies, its marked zoogeographical separation from Goodenough Island indicates that the paradise crow is not likely to be one and the same as the latter's black-plumed mystery bird. However, an allied, still-undescribed species of paradise crow with similar habitat preference and reclusive nature indigenous to Goodenough would yield a very satisfactory identity for this island's avian anomaly.

## AN AWOL ARGUS PHEASANT

Evidence for the erstwhile reality of the double-banded argus pheasant *Argusianus bipunctatus* is best described as feather-light – in every sense.

Truly a giant among pheasants, an adult male specimen of the great argus pheasant *Argusianus argus* (=*gigantea*) can measure up to 6.5 feet (1 metre) long. It is also instantly recognized by virtue of its extremely long slender tail, and its huge fan-like wings, whose broad feathers are ornately embellished with rows of spectacular ocelli (eye-like markings) with which to capture the attention of female argus pheasants during courtship.

On 8 April 1871, T.W. Wood published a short report in *The Field* documenting a singular partial feather of unknown provenance and very unusual appearance. A portion of a male bird's primary from the right wing, on first sight it resembled those of the great argus. Closer observation, however, revealed that this strange plume bore two bands of speckled, chocolate-brown colouration – one on its broad web and one on its narrow web. In contrast, corresponding plumes from the great argus bear only one such band, on their broad web. Consequently, Wood deemed that the aberrant feather must have originated from a second, hitherto-unknown species of argus, and he duly dubbed this unseen species *Argus* [now

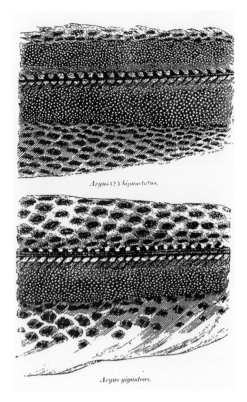

*The unique wing feather of the double-banded argus pheasant (top) is contrasted here with a corresponding feather of the great argus pheasant (bottom).*

*Argusianus*] *bipunctatus*, the double-banded argus pheasant.

The lone feather from Wood's newly created species was presented by Edward Bartlett in 1891 to the British Museum (Natural History)'s ornithological collection at Tring, where it still resides today as the only tangible evidence for the double-banded argus's reality. No sightings of this most mysterious bird have ever been reported either – which can be explained at least in part by the simple fact that no one really knows where to begin looking for it.

Pheasant expert Dr Jean Delacour suspected that Java would prove to be the homeland of this cryptic bird, but his several searches for it here all proved unsuccessful. In 1983, ornithologist G.W.H. Davison nominated Tioman, an offshore island of eastern Malaysia, as a more plausible provenance, though not a very promising one. This is because Tioman has been well-explored scientifically during the twentieth century,

thereby rendering it unlikely that a bird as sizeable as a species of argus pheasant could still exist here undetected.

In other words, if this speculative species was indeed native to Tioman, it must surely now be extinct. Yet if so, this would be exceptionally tragic, because the aerodynamic properties of its unique feather as determined from its precise physical structure are so poor that this seemingly lost species might conceivably have been flightless – and, if so, would have comprised the only species of flightless modern-day pheasant known to science.

## HUMMINGBIRDS IN SUMATRA?

During the late 1950s, as revealed by American cryptozoologist Loren Coleman, a remarkable ornithological sighting was made in Indonesia, which, if the eyewitnesses' description was accurate, assuredly features an extraordinary species of bird still unknown to science.

On two separate occasions while residing in Sumatra in 1957–58, Otto R. Irrgang and his wife, originally from Washington State in the USA, were sitting in their front porch when two tiny birds appeared, and flew to within 12 inches (30 cm) of their faces. According to Irrgang, these birds were yellowish in colour, measured no more than 1.5 inches (4 cm) long, and greatly resembled hummingbirds, with dark brown bellies and small stripes.

However, hummingbirds are found only in the New World; there is not a single Old World species known to science. Here, their ecological niche is occupied by a wholly unrelated but outwardly reminiscent family of birds known as sunbirds. None of these, conversely, is as small as Sumatra's minute mystery birds. A remote option is that the Irrgangs spied two day-flying moths.

## THE KONDLO CONFLICT

Also in need of an identity is Zululand's mysterious kondlo – a large, black, fowl-like bird that incited a considerable conflict of

*An argus pheasant perches in a tree in its native south-east Asia.*

opinion within the pages of the periodical *African Wild Life* during the early 1960s. Its principal champion was Captain G.T. Court of Durban, South Africa, whose letter of December 1962 described the kondlo as a voiceless bird comparable in size and shape to a young female domestic turkey poult, with a feathered head and beak also resembling a hen turkey's. Its irises, beak, legs and feet were red, but its plumage was glossy black, overlain with a greenish-blue sheen – all of which gave it a colouration reminiscent of the chough *Pyrrhocorax pyrrhocorax*, a species of European crow. It did not seem to exhibit sexual dimorphism (morphological differences between the sexes).

During the series of interchanges published in *African Wild Life*, the southern ground hornbill *Bucorvus leadbeateri* and the bald ibis *Geronticus calvus* were offered as putative identities, but both were vehemently rejected by Captain Court. His views were based upon personal experience of the kondlo:

from many years of hunting, not only was he fully acquainted with every species of game bird in this region of South Africa, but in

addition he had actually shot and eaten several specimens of kondlo. Consequently, he was readily able to differentiate between the ground hornbill, bald ibis and kondlo.

Furthermore, quoting from a scholarly Zulu-English dictionary compiled by priest Father Alfred Bryant during many years of work here, Court pointed out that these three birds even had their own wholly separate local names. The ground hornbill was known as the tsingizi, the bald ibis was the xwagele, and the kondlo was only ever termed the kondlo.

According to Court, this mystifying bird occurred in groups of four to eight on the grass-covered ridges of Mtonjaneni and Mahlabatini, and when it took to the air it flew low, in a manner resembling the flight of a guineafowl. Ominously, Court also noted that although once abundant, the kondlo seemed lately to be disappearing from its former haunts; his most recent sighting was in about 1956. Surely this species could be systematically sought and conclusively identified by ornithologists – always assuming that it hasn't already died out?

*As the fowl-like kondlo of Zululand may already have become extinct, will its identity remain for ever unresolved?*

# UNTANGLING
## THE THREADS IN
## A WEB OF CONFUSION

ANGEL HAIR IS THE POPULAR NAME GIVEN TO MYSTIFYING FILAMENTOUS PRECIPITATION SPASMODICALLY DESCENDING TO EARTH FROM ABOVE. DOCUMENTED CASES DATE BACK AT LEAST AS FAR AS 679 AD AND HAVE BEEN REPORTED FROM MANY PARTS OF THE WORLD, BUT PARTICULARLY NORTH AMERICA AND EUROPE.

The occurrence of angel hair shows a marked seasonal fluctuation, with most cases taking place during autumn, especially October. They also seem more frequent during warm dry weather, as opposed to colder damp conditions.

One of the most dramatic cases occurred in October 1881 at Milwaukee and Green Bay, Wisconsin, in which the sky was filled with sheets of angel hair, as later reported by the journal *Scientific American* in a report entitled "A Rain of Spider Webs":

*White magic: sheets of gossamer lie draped across the grassy tussocks on Overton Down in Wiltshire.*

*In the latter part of October the good people of Milwaukee (Wis.) and the neighboring towns were astonished by a general fall of spider webs. The webs seemed to come from a great height. The strands were from two feet to several rods in length. At Green Bay the fall was the same, coming from the direction of the bay, only the webs varied from sixty feet in length to mere specks, and were seen as far up in the air as the power of the eye could reach. At Vesburg and Fort Howard, Sheboygan, and Ozaukee, the fall was similarly observed, in some places being so thick as to annoy the eye. In all*

*instances the webs were strong in texture and very white. Curiously there is no mention, in any of the reports we have seen, of the presence of spiders in this general shower of webs.*

No less amazing was the angel hair of 20 September 1892 that fell extensively at Gainesville, Florida, and at many other locations too in the south-eastern USA. Letters from a number of eyewitnesses were assimilated within a report by George Marx published later that same year in the Entomological Society of Washington's Proceedings:

*It was first discovered late this afternoon floating in the air or falling from the clouds. I have seen people, who live at least ten miles [16 km] apart, who tell the same story – that it sometimes falls in long strands like spider webs, two and three thousand yards [up to 3000 metres] long, then doubled up into strands and wads ... great white sheets were seen floating with the daily showers, resembling large, pure white spider-webs, some of them fifty yards or more in length. The trees in many cases are covered. Near the small stream, about 100 yards from the house, some of it extended as an immense web; in other places it rolled up into a ball.*

Judging from the above descriptions, not to mention the fact that the angel hair was openly referred to as spiders' webs, one might assume that there is no mystery – that this filamentous phenomenon is nothing more than masses of loose spider silk floating in the air. And, indeed, in many cases this is precisely what angel hair appears to be.

It is not widely realized that although spiders are wingless, some species, such as the tiny *Linyphia* money spiders, are capable of migrating through the air, via an ingenious technique known as ballooning. A money spider simply orients itself facing the wind, which draws out a fine thread of silk from the spinnerets at the posterior end of the spider's body. Then, as soon as the thread is lifted up into the air by the wind, the spider grips tightly to it and is carried aloft on a silken hang-glider, which can carry it great distances through the sky.

Money spiders exist in vast concentrations, sometimes over a million individuals per acre. This means that after they have ballooned en masse (which usually occurs on warm days in autumn, i.e. the weather and seasonality reported for angel hair), the threads left behind once these tiny aeronauts have returned to earth can yield very sizeable sheets of silk.

These silvery silken sheets are in turn broken up by rising air currents, which lift them up into the sky, whereupon they are correctly termed gossamer. And it is this gossamer, normally lacking attached spiders, that seemingly constitutes much of the material referred to in reports of angel hair – which is indeed usually said to lack any associated spiders.

Certainly, as revealed by angel hair researcher Dr Robert W. Morrell in a paper presented at a MUFORA conference on 6 June 1981, the fundamental properties of *Linyphia*

*Spiders' webs found in India show how a concentration of these threads create sheets of "angel hair".*

spiders' gossamer correspond very closely with those reported for angel hair. Thus, just like angel hair, the gossamer yielded by these spiders' amalgamated ballooning threads is very fragile, swiftly dissolving when handled; it is not affected by boiling water; it leaves behind neither ash nor smell when burnt in a naked flame; and in some cases is non-adhesive.

Another likely zoological origin for angel hair is the cobweb-like mass produced by the larvae of certain moths. As exemplified by a report of ermine moth larvae that I have on file from Strathardle in Perthshire, Scotland (*Scots Magazine*, October 1981), congregations of these larvae can rapidly cover great expanses of tree foliage with their webs.

However, some samples of angel hair have been shown when analysed not to have a biological origin. In such cases, it is conceivable that these filaments may comprise long strings of dust particles linked together electrostatically – a process that can occur only on warm days. Worth noting here is that some angel hair witnesses have claimed that when they attempted to touch this gauzy substance, they discovered that it was electrically charged.

It is also plausible that certain cases of angel hair owe their origin to plasma phenomena, which have recently been implicated in the formation of ball lightning. There are some intriguing reports on file in which angel hair has been seen spilling down to earth from apparent UFOs – explaining why this substance is frequently documented in ufological publications. The most famous instance took place at midday on 17 October 1952, when a white cylindrical object and at least 30 domed saucer-like entities were seen in the sky above Oloron-Sainte-Marie and various villages nearby in south-western France.

As they flew by, the saucers discharged trails of a long thread-like substance that drifted downwards, ultimately draping itself in profuse quantities over trees, roofs, walls and other exposed surfaces, but when touched it rapidly vanished. Ball lightning, which (despite its name) can occur in several different shapes, has been found to emit filamentous strands when observed at close range. Accordingly, some investigators have opined that the Oloron-Sainte-Marie UFOs were examples of filament-extruding ball lightning.

Like many other apparent mysteries, it may well be that angel hair is not one but several wholly separate yet outwardly similar phenomena that have been erroneously lumped together by investigators. If so, then only by identifying and disentangling these heterogeneous strands will the web of confusion encompassing the subject of angel hair be dispersed.

# FISHY TALES
## OF THE ONES
## THAT GOT AWAY

EVERY ANGLER HAS A TALE OF "THE ONE THAT GOT AWAY", BUT THOSE DOCUMENTED HERE CONCERN
TRULY EXCEPTIONAL FISHES THAT HAVE "GOT AWAY" FROM FORMAL SCIENTIFIC DETECTION AND
RECOGNITION TOO.

### MYSTERY MANTAS OF THE STRIPED VARIETY

Also dubbed the great devil-fish, the Atlantic giant manta ray *Manta birostris* is the world's largest species of ray, courtesy of its huge wing-like pectoral fins, which are black above, white below, and known to span up to 22 feet (6.7 metres) – features that make this huge fish readily noticed and identifiable. Conversely, whereas the mysterious manta ray once spied briefly by eminent American naturalist William Beebe off Tower Island in the Galapagos Archipelago was certainly noticed, it could not – and still cannot – be identified.

As noted in his book *Galapagos: World's End* (1924), Beebe had been aboard his vessel *Noma* on 27 April 1923 when a large manta measuring at least 10 feet (3 metres) across its

---

*The striped manta ray spied by William Beebe has never been conclusively identified.*

pectoral fins suddenly collided with *Noma*. After catching sight of the specimen responsible, however, he was even more startled, because it did not resemble any species known to science:

> [It was] of somewhat the usual manta or devil-fish shape, except that the wings were not noticeably concave behind, and the lateral angles were not acute. The cephalic horn-like structures [formed from the pectoral fins and arising at each end of the mouth] were conspicuous and more straight than incurved. In general the back was dark brown, faintly mottled, while the most conspicuous character was a pair of broad, pure white bands, extending halfway down the back from each side of the head. The wing tips also shaded abruptly into pure white.

Over 70 years later, Beebe's white-banded manta remains uncaptured and undescribed – but it is no longer unique. As recently revealed by German researcher Gunter G. Sehm in the journal *Cryptozoology*, a photograph published in 1976 of a strange-looking manta spied in the sea around New Caledonia clearly shows that it has the same symmetrical white dorsal bands. Moreover, on 28 December 1989, when a documentary programme, *Sharks: Hunters of the Seas*, was screened on German television, Sehm paid great attention to a 30-second or so clip of a large manta sporting brilliant white, symmetrical v-shaped bands on its dorsal surface. The manta had been filmed by Sigurd Tesche, the programme's producer, at close range in the waters off Cabo San Lucas, at the southern tip of Baja California, Mexico.

Also worth noting here is the small blue-black manta bearing two very large pale chevrons dorsally that was harpooned during 1924 off the shore reef of Fanning Island, in the tropical Central Pacific. In 1934, it was formally documented as a new species, *Manta fowleri*, but no additional specimens, or sightings, appear to have been recorded since.

Although highly distinctive, these odd mantas may simply comprise an aberrant pattern mutation of a known manta species, analogous to rare specimens of striated crows and other banded anomalies. However, recalling Beebe's statement that his striped manta's cephalic horns also differed from those of the known giant manta, it is by no means impossible that an unknown species is present. Even so, only a procured specimen subjected to a full scientific investigation can expose the true taxonomic nature of these eyecatching enigmas.

## A BLENNY FOR YOUR THOUGHTS

In his book *Dangerous To Man* (1975), Roger Caras included a tantalizingly brief mention of a small black, but potentially lethal, mystery fish said to inhabit the Shatt al Arab River in Iran, and to possess a swift-acting venomous bite that had allegedly claimed the lives of 28 human victims. As I revealed in a detailed investigation of this deadly species (*Fortean Times*, December 1996), a number of possible identities can be put forward as contenders.

As with so many reports of strange-sounding animals, it might owe its "existence" solely to the misidentification of a species already known to science. One possible contender is *Heteropneustes fossilis*, a small species of black catfish that was quite recently introduced into the Shatt al Arab River from India and Thailand as a food fish. It does not have a venomous bite, but its pectoral fins do contain poisonous spines that can inflict painful wounds. Also worthy of consideration is whether young specimens of the long-tailed moray eel *Thyrsoidea macrura*, swimming up the river from the sea, could be the answer. Although their bite is not thought to be venomous in the technical sense, rotting particles of flesh attached to their teeth can cause septic wounds (just like the bites of lions and tigers).

Alternatively, there is the prospect that the Shatt al Arab's tiny terror is indeed an unknown species, but one that may conceivably be related to a certain species of small freshwater blenny. Blue-grey and yellow in colour, the blenny in question frequents the Red Sea as well as the Gulf of Suez and Aqaba, and is known

*Could this innocuous-looking blenny have a more sinister relative that inhabits the Shatt al Arab River?*

scientifically as *Meiacanthus nigrolineatus*. Unlike the various candidates already discussed here, this species does possess a genuinely venomous bite, thanks to a series of large sharp teeth in its lower jaw that have grooved sides and venom-producing basal tissue. True, no human fatalities have so far been recorded with this particular blenny – but if a darker version capable of producing a more potent venom exists in the Shatt al Arab River, and a specimen of it is captured here one day, science will assuredly have unmasked this river's cryptic mini-killer at last.

## THE WHALE-FISH OF LAKE MYLLESJÖN

I am greatly indebted to Swedish cryptozoological artist Richard Svensson for kindly informing me of a water monster not previously brought to the attention of cryptozoologists.

Lake Myllesjön is situated in Richard's home province of Blekinge, in southernmost Sweden, and since at least the middle of the nineteenth century reports have been circulating of a piscean monster inhabiting its cool waters, which is popularly referred to as the whale-fish. A flurry of sightings occurred during the 1920s and 1930s. One eyewitness, while riding by the lake on his bike, saw what he initially thought to be a massive log – until the water surrounding it began to churn, and the "log" abruptly dived out of sight. Another observer claimed to have seen a huge fin-crested back rise above the surface, and considered it to be an immense pike, but no one else supported this identity. Pike or not, local fisherman Sven Johan discovered two of his fishing nets ripped apart after hauling them out of the lake, and yet another man stated that he had seen a whale-like beast frolicking at the water's edge.

These and other sightings encouraged local talk about attempting to capture the monster, and after three girls fled from the lake, screaming in terror, after supposedly spying an animal resembling a whale basking in shallow

water near the shore, an official plan of action was drawn up and set in motion. As Richard revealed in his account that he sent to me:

*The local blacksmith made a hook the size of a ping-pong bat, a piece of board was made as a float, and a steel wire chosen as line and tied around a slim oak tree. A butcher donated a dead piglet for bait, and the entire contraption was hurled out into the lake. The next day the oak tree was found uprooted, bobbing about in the middle of the lake, where it stayed for a whole week until it sank. Nothing more happened and the monster was believed to be dead.*

Until August 1962, that is, when sightings of "logs" splashing in the lake gained attention all over again. This time, the local response was to unleash a veritable hunting party in the monster's wake, consisting of 425 fishermen, each one competing against all of the others not only for the honour of procuring (and thence himself becoming) a living legend, but

victim of modern-day urbanization. In 1996, he visited its watery domain and discovered to his horror that a two-lane motorway had been constructed right next to the lake and that the few houses still nearby are themselves newly built, with their owners having little or no knowledge of the monster. Richard has learnt of one other lake that was once said to harbour something similar to the Myllesjön whale-fish, but he now considers it likely (as do I) that both of these unidentified water beasts were specimens of *Siluris glanis*, commonly known as the wels or European giant catfish. According to Richard, the largest confirmed specimen ever caught in Sweden, in 1871, measured 3.6 metres (11.8 feet) long; but the largest recorded specimen of all, as listed by the *Guinness Book of Records*, was a true monster of a fish, measuring 4.5. metres (15 feet), which was caught in Russia's Dneiper River during the 1850s.

## GIANT BLUE EELS OF THE GANGES?

And finally: Ctesias, Solinus, Aelian and several other famous scholars of ancient times soberly attested that giant worm-like eels (or eel-like worms?) with vivid blue bodies dwelt amid the dank riverbed ooze of the Ganges. According to Solinus, these astonishing creatures were 30 feet (9 metres) long, but their dimensions grew ever more prodigious with repeated tellings by later writers – until they ultimately acquired sufficient stature to emerge from their muddy seclusion beneath the dark mantle of night and prey upon camels and oxen!

It will come as no surprise to learn, however, that this spectacular species of eel has never been brought to scientific attention – a classic case, no doubt, of "the one that got away"!

also for the financial recompense of 1000 Swedish kroner. Perhaps, however, it was a case of too many anglers spoiling the lake, because the biggest fish caught was a 2.9-lb (1.3-kg) perch.

Returning to Richard's account of Myllesjön's monstrous history:

*In November 1962, several large hooks were manufactured and baited with dead chickens and calves' heads. Most newspaper stories say that the efforts went resultless,* *but others claim that at least one of the calves' heads disappeared. During 1963, the diving log was seen again, and in September another fishing competition was held: now with the prize of 10,000 Swedish kroner. Again, it proved to be an uneventful event.*

Nevertheless, Richard knows of reports concerning Lake Myllesjön's mystifying whale-fish from as late as the 1970s. However, he fears that it may have since become an unsuspected

# HANDLING SOME WEIRD
# WATER MUSIC

MYSTERIES MAY BE MANY THINGS, BUT MELODIOUS IS NOT ALWAYS ONE OF THEM – WHICH IS WHY THE ACOUSTIC ENIGMA ASSOCIATED WITH SHOSHONE LAKE AND YELLOWSTONE LAKE IN WYOMING IS SUCH A NOTABLE EXCEPTION. NUMEROUS VISITORS HAVE BEEN ASTOUNDED TO HEAR WEIRD YET ETHEREAL MUSICAL SOUNDS ECHOING OR WHISPERING IN THE AIR ABOVE THESE TRANQUIL BODIES OF WATER, YET LACKING ANY EVIDENT SOURCE OR DISCERNIBLE EXPLANATION.

One of this audible phenomenon's most notable "earwitnesses" was Professor S.A. Forbes, a scientist working for the US Fish Commission, who experienced it during the early 1890s while researching Shoshone Lake's aquatic invertebrate fauna, and duly reported it in 1893:

*Here we first heard, while out on the lake in the bright still morning, the mysterious aerial sound for which this region is noted. It put me in mind of the vibrating clang of a harp lightly and rapidly touched high up above the tree tops, or the sound of many telegraph wires swinging regularly and rapidly in*

*the wind, or, more rarely, of faintly heard voices answering each other overhead. It begins softly in the remote distance, draws rapidly near with louder and louder throbs of sound, and dies away in the opposite distance; or it may seem to wander irregularly about, the whole passage lasting from a few seconds to half a minute or more. We heard it repeatedly and very distinctly here and at Yellowstone Lake, most frequently at the latter place. It is usually noticed on still bright mornings not long after sunrise, and it is louder at this time of day; but I heard it clearly, though faintly, once at noon when a stiff breeze was blowing.*

Another US Fish Commission scientist who heard these mystifying refrains was Edwin Linton, when working at Yellowstone Lake in 1890. He likened them to slightly metallic echoes or reverberations, sounding forth in the air above Shoshone Lake before moving south-west. Yet there was no sign of any wind, either on the lake or in surrounding trees.

One of the most interesting encounters with this whimsical water music occurred at about 8 am on 30 July 1919, when pisciculture experts A.H. Dinsmore and Hugh M. Smith set off across the waters of Shoshone Lake in a canoe:

*The fog-shrouded waters of Lake Shoshone, source of unaccountable musical sounds.*

*The canoe had barely gotten under way and was not more than twenty meters from the shore when there suddenly arose a musical sound of rare sweetness, rich timbre, and full volume, whose effect was increased by the noiseless surroundings. The sound appeared to come from directly overhead, and both of us at the same moment instinctively glanced upward; each afterward asserted that so great was his astonishment that he was almost prepared to see a pipe organ suspended in midair. The sound, by the most perfect gradation, increased in volume and pitch, reaching its climax a few seconds after the paddling of the canoe was involuntarily suspended; and then, rapidly growing fainter and diminishing in pitch, it seemed to pass away toward the south. The sound lasted ten to fifteen seconds, and was subsequently adjudged to range in pitch approximately from a little below center C to a little above tenor C of the piano-forte, the tones blending in the most perfect chromatic scale.*

But more was to come. Once the men began paddling swiftly again, the strange music resumed, and died whenever they stopped paddling. Experimenting, they found that its onset always coincided with the canoe's attainment of a certain minimum speed, and ceased when the canoe's speed fell below that critical threshold. Intrigued, they looked for further clues:

*A search for the cause of the sound disclosed the following situation ... the waxed silk line [of a jointed bamboo salmon rod touching the side of the canoe] was reeled in, but about a meter of line with the lure at the end was wrapped several times around the terminal joint; a lead sinker weighing one hundred grams ... was dangling from the end of the rod about five centimeters [2 inches] below the surface of the water. As the canoe moved through the water, the short length of free line, held taut by the sinker, rapidly vibrated in conformity with the speed of the boat; the vibrations were transmitted through the bamboo rod to the canoe, whose thin, curved, rigid sides and bottom acted as a sounding board and gave out an augmented volume of sound that seemed to be concentrated or focused overhead. The combination of essential factors present in this case seems to have been a smooth water surface, a vibrating cord, a resonant body to which the vibrations were transferred, and still air, with perhaps other favorable atmospheric conditions.*

*The scene for a symphony: early morning light over Yellowstone Lake.*

Nevertheless, as Smith openly conceded, even if it were indeed responsible on that occasion, such a set-up cannot be offered as an all-encompassing explanation for the lakes' phantom music, because canoes were seldom used here, yet the music had frequently been reported.

Today, the mystery of these strange sounds remains unresolved. A popular theory is that the wind blowing across the peaks surrounding the lakes in some way engenders this mellifluous effect, possibly yielding standing sound waves. However, this does not account for cases in which the music has been heard on placid, windless days. Another suggestion is that the sounds are seismic in origin, emitted by the surrounding mountains when stressed by the upwelling hot magma underlying this particular region.

Less famous than the ghostly music of Shoshone and Yellowstone Lakes but equally mystifying is the wailing waterhole at Wilga, which is part of the Barcoo waterway near Ruthven Station, leading to Isisford in central-western Queensland, Australia. Reports by European settlers of this aural anomaly date back at least as far as the 1870s. One encounter on record featured two sheep shearers who camped by this uncanny waterhole one fine summer evening in the 1890s. Suddenly, as subsequently documented by Bill Beatty in a collection of Australian traditions and lore, an eerie noise pierced the stillness:

*... there came a soft, distant wailing that grew rapidly nearer and louder. To the astonished men the cries appeared to be in different keys – devilish, unearthly shrieking, such as no human voices ever uttered. One thing was certain – the screaming, now ringing in their ears at deafening pitch, was coming from the waterhole. The shearers thought their ear-drums would burst, but they were too terrified to move. Then, to their fervent relief, the shrieking diminished in volume until it was merely a weird wailing. Moments later, it ceased utterly, and once more the bush was deathly silent. Throughout it all, not a ripple or movement marked the surface of the lagoon from whence the noises had emanated. Without waiting for the dawn the shearers caught their horses and rode off.*

Many theories have been proposed by researchers seeking to solve this mystery. Perhaps the most publicized is the possibility that the eerie wail is caused by the rushing of water through some subterranean channel linking the Wilga water-hole to others. Extensive investigations, however, have consistently failed to substantiate this notion.

# THE PARROT
## IN THE PAINTING

I AM GREATLY INDEBTED TO ACCLAIMED ORNITHOLOGICAL AUTHOR AND PAINTER ERROL FULLER FOR KINDLY BRINGING THE FOLLOWING CASE TO MY ATTENTION, WHICH HAS NEVER PREVIOUSLY BEEN DOCUMENTED.

The modern-day history of George Edwards's red mystery parrot from Jamaica began in June 1996, when Errol Fuller attended the annual Olympia Antiques Fair in London. While walking round, he noticed on the stall of one dealer a picture that he knew at once to be the work of English bird painter George Edwards (1694–1773), author and illustrator of *A Natural History of Uncommon Birds* (1743–51) and *Gleanings of Natural History* (1758–64). Yet although he was very familiar with all of the paintings in both of these books, Errol did not recognize this particular example on the dealer's stall, and suspected that it was an unpublished, unknown work of Edwards. Greatly intrigued, Errol purchased this painting, and after researching it thoroughly he was able to confirm that it was indeed unknown.

Errol has very generously granted me permission to publish the painting here, the first time that it has ever appeared in print. As can be seen, it depicts a predominantly red, vaguely amazon-like parrot – which only serves to deepen further the mystery encompassing this picture. For there is no known species of parrot anywhere in the world that corresponds with this specimen. So what could it be and where did it come from?

The painting bears an inscription at the bottom: "A very uncommon parrot from Jamaica. Drawn from Nature of the size of life [i.e. life size] by G. Edwards. July 1764". A more detailed note, clearly penned by Edwards himself, is written on the painting's reverse:

*George Edwards's painting of the red parrot owned by Dr Alexander Russell; the bird's identity remains a mystery.*

Left: *Neptune's fireworks: oceanic wheels of light defy explanation.*

Over a hundred different cases of oceanic light wheels have been reported. Apart from their often immense size (sometimes spanning a mile or more in diameter), however, these incredible entities are so varied in form, and so versatile in their ability to transform, that it is difficult to state with certainty what constitutes a typical example. Consequently, the following report documents what can best be described as a fairly simple variation on an exceedingly enigmatic theme. It was filed by the S.S. *Delta*'s second officer, S.C. Patterson, who witnessed this giant light wheel in the Malacca Strait, and was duly published in 1907:

*I noticed shafts of pale yellow light moving rapidly over the surface of the water. During the major part of the time, the shafts seemed to move round a centre – like the spokes of a wheel – and appeared to be about 300 yards long, the appearance being very similar to that of the reflection of a powerful electric quick-flashing light (of the type of Ushant) thrown on the clouds on a clear dark night.*

Not all light wheels appear singly. On 19 December 1927, the S.S. *Arracan* witnessed a series of wheels while sailing through the Andaman Sea. The phosphorescent phenomenon began as shapeless clusters of light, but these soon resolved themselves into bars that began to revolve. Each revolution took approximately 30 seconds, but these remarkable fiery wheels were not content to revolve unidirectionally. Every five minutes, they changed their direction of rotation, from anticlockwise to clockwise, then back to anticlockwise again.

Even more astonishing was the scene witnessed on 24 April 1953 by crew aboard the merchant vessel *Rafaela* in the Gulf of Thailand. After encountering a patch of sea exhibiting flashing luminescence, they saw three rotating wheels of light abruptly appear. Unlike most light wheels on file, however, the spokes of these examples were curved, not straight, with the concave side of each spoke facing the direction of rotation. Moreover, the three wheels were not discrete but overlapped one another, two rotating anticlockwise, the third clockwise, each rotation taking just 20 seconds. The wheels were visible for 20 minutes.

Two of the most amazing incidents of all, however, occurred during the 1970s. On 14 February 1977, eyewitnesses on board the S.S. *Cardigan Bay* in the Strait of Malacca initially

This strange luminous swirl near the sea's surface is caused by a swarm of plankton.

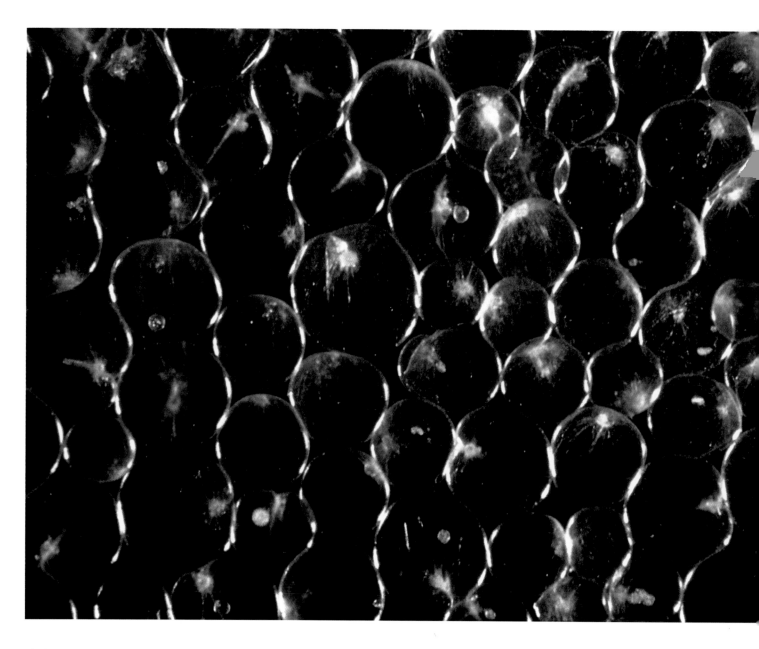

*The bioluminescent marine organism* Noctiluca.

observed a single clockwise-spinning wheel with curved spokes and a dark centre, whose spokes, each with a width of 3 metres (10 feet), were spaced at 7.5–9-metre (25–30-foot) intervals. Each rotation of the wheel lasted 20 seconds. Soon, however, this horizontal, phosphorescent Ferris wheel of the sea metamorphosed before their unbelieving eyes into a series of parallel, inverted chevrons (v-shapes) that moved under their vessel without effect, before swiftly transforming into an anticlockwise wheel, and thence into a clockwise wheel.

Suddenly, a second light wheel manifested itself, rotating anticlockwise about its own hub, but as it did so, the first light wheel changed back into a series of chevrons, and thence into an anticlockwise wheel. The entire *Cardigan Bay* sighting, including the rapid succession of transformations, lasted no more than 10 minutes, by the end of which the light wheels had gradually faded away.

Yet even this scintillating spectacle was as nothing compared with the sighting made by the merchant vessel *Border Shepherd* in the South China Sea on 28 March 1970. It began with the appearance of a series of parallel white

bands of light – positioned a few feet *above* the surface of the water!

As the crew watched in amazement, these luminous bands transformed into a clockwise-revolving wheel, which retained this form for several minutes – still airborne above the water surface – before changing back into parallel bands. Moreover, a second set of bands also appeared, moving perpendicularly to the first. Both sets then moved rapidly towards the ship, at times being visible over the deck as well as over the water. After about 20 minutes, however, these astounding aerial light wheels dimmed, becoming a general,

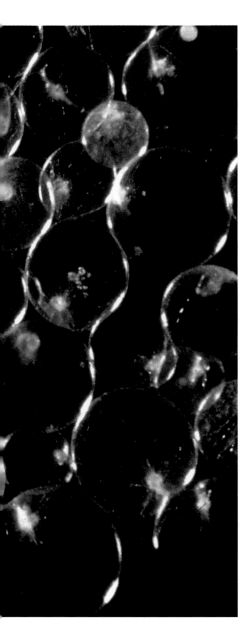

amorphous haze of pulsating green-hued luminescence that flashed once every half-second for a short time before disappearing completely. The entire display had been exclusively airborne; no light whatsoever had been observed in the water.

So many sightings of oceanic light wheels have been reported, frequently by highly experienced maritime observers and travellers, that scientists readily accept the authenticity of this phenomenon. Explaining it, conversely, has proven to be another matter entirely.

Among mainstream researchers, the theory that has attracted most support is that of Kurt Kalle. In his study of light wheels, published in 1960, Kalle proposed that these marvellous manifestations are created by seaquake activity beneath the sea's surface yielding an interference pattern in the water shaped like a spoked wheel with a central hub. The force of this interference pattern in turn stimulates the glowing of tiny bioluminescent marine organisms (such as *Noctiluca*, a dinoflagellate protozoan) in a selective manner that recreates this distinctive wheel shape in vivid luminescent form.

However, in what is assuredly the most detailed, significant analysis of the oceanic light wheel phenomenon published in recent times (*Fortean Studies*, 1995), Michael T. Shoemaker skilfully revealed that Kalle's theory is severely flawed on several separate counts.

To begin with: if Kalle's shockwave-based theory were indeed correct, some of the most characteristic features of light wheels would be unlikely to occur – such as the preponderance of straight (as opposed to curved) spokes, the occurrence of stationary wheels and deepwater wheels, the high proportion of sightings featuring multiple wheels, the failure of ships to disrupt light wheel formation, and the apparent lack of perceived shockwaves.

Even more damning, however, are the following light-wheel characteristics, which Shoemaker claims would be impossible if Kalle's theory were correct. These include aerial light wheels, light wheels of short and/or long duration, wheels with glowing hubs or moving hubs, and non-interaction between waves.

Similarly, the theory of physicist Wallace L. Minto, who also favoured the creation of an interference pattern as the precursor of light wheels, but nominated sound waves emitted by dolphins and other cetaceans rather than seismic vibrations as the source of the interference pattern, fails to explain many of the above-listed features of light wheels.

In Shoemaker's opinion, the theory which is compatible with more light-wheel features than any other so far propounded is that of Captain A. Carpenter, a British sea captain. He first proposed it at a meeting of the Royal Meteorological Society, whose journal published it in 1902. Carpenter suggested that light wheels and other phosphorescent maritime phenomena were due directly to the spontaneous (not shockwave-induced), synchronized glowing activity of tiny bioluminescent marine organisms. Even so, this theory yet again fails entirely to address or resolve sightings of light wheels that appear to hover above the water's surface.

A meteorological origin for these latter examples, conversely, might not experience such difficulties, especially if it functioned in conjunction with the glowing talents of the oceans' bioluminescent fauna. But what might the nature of that meteorological origin be? As suggested by veteran anomaly chronicler William R. Corliss, perhaps electromagnetic stimulation could be responsible, as with the mountain-top glows seen along the Andes in South America.

One thing is certain. Unlike many unexplained phenomena, the mystery of the oceanic light wheels is one that could well be solved within the near future, if only science would make a determined effort to investigate it thoroughly. After all, as Shoemaker pertinently notes:

> ... *lightwheels occur with enough regularity to make scientific observations possible. A ship stationed at a cluster site in a peak month would have a reasonable chance of seeing one within a few years. Note that only a few months of actual expedition time would be necessary, and this might be combined with other researches.*

So if there are any marine biologists or thalassologists reading this who feel in need of a stimulating new challenge, you need look no further!

# LESSER NESSIES

EVERYONE HAS HEARD OF NESSIE, THE REPUTED MONSTER OF LOCH NESS, BUT FEWER PEOPLE REALIZE THAT SIMILAR MYSTERY BEASTS HAVE ALSO BEEN REPORTED FROM SEVERAL OTHER SCOTTISH LOCHS.

## MORAG, MONSTER OF LOCH MORAR

The most famous lesser Nessie is Morag, the supposed monster of Loch Morar, whose history, like Nessie's, dates back many centuries, as testified by a very old Scottish song:

> *Morag, Harbinger of Death,*
> *Giant swimmer in deep-green Morar,*
> *The loch that has no bottom ...*
> *There it is that Morag the monster lives.*

Loch Morar is 11 miles (18 km) long, approximately 1.5 miles (2.5 km) wide, and with a maximum depth exceeding 1000 feet (300 metres) it is Britain's deepest freshwater lake. Unlike the waters of Loch Ness, however, which are extremely peaty, Morar's are very clear, enabling objects situated at quite a distance beneath the surface to be perceived with remarkable clarity – as exemplified by visitor Robert Duff's extraordinary sighting on 8 July 1969. A joiner from Edinburgh, Duff was

fishing from a boat in Meoble Bay on the loch's southern shore, where the water is no more than 16 feet deep and very lucid, when he spotted what he described as a "monster lizard", lying motionless on the loch's white, leaf-strewn bottom, looking up at him.

---

*Above: Loch Shiel, whose deep waters are claimed to be home to Seileag, a monster of considerable size.*
*Right: In the remote fastness of Caledonia's highlands a Scottish loch monster ensnares its hapless victim. The reality may be less fearsome, but no less intriguing.*

Duff estimated the creature to be 20 feet (6 metres) long, with a snake-like earless head, slit eyes and a wide mouth. Its body was grey-brown with rough skin, and it had four limbs, with three toes visible on each front foot, plus a tail. He was so startled that he revved up the boat and made off at once. Later, however, he returned to the same spot, but the animal had gone.

Even more dramatic was the 5-minute confrontation experienced on 16 August 1969 by Duncan McDonell and William Simpson. At about 9.00–9.30 pm, but while still daylight, their motor boat was travelling along the loch at a speed of 6–7 knots when McDonell, at the wheel, saw a creature in the water about 20 yards (20 metres) behind but moving directly towards them. A few seconds later it caught up, and collided with the side of their boat, seemingly unintentionally but nonetheless with sufficient force to hurl a kettle of water off the boat's gas stove and on to the floor. McDonell attempted to fend the beast away with an oar, frightened that it may capsize the boat, but because the oar was old it snapped in half.

When Simpson saw this, he picked up his rifle, ran out of the cabin and aimed a shot at the creature, which slowly sank away from the boat. They did not see it again, but they did not see any blood either, or any other sign to indicate that Simpson's bullet had hit it.

According to Simpson and McDonell, the portion of the creature that they had observed was 25–30 feet (7.5–9 metres) long, with rough, dirty-brown skin, and three humps or undulations standing about 18 inches (45 cm) above the water surface at the highest point. The head was brown and snake-like, measuring approximately 1 foot (30 cm) across the top, and raised 18 inches (45 cm) out of the water.

On 1 August 1996 came the electrifying news that Cameron Turner, a diver from Darlington, had discovered some bones from a large unidentified animal at a depth of 60 feet (18 metres) in Loch Morar. Could these be the

mortal remains of a Morag? Sadly, no – the following day a biologist formally identified them as the bones of a deer.

## SEILEAG, WEE OICHIE, LIZZIE AND OTHERS

Morar is a remote lake, much of which can be reached only by boat. This is also true of Loch Shiel – Scotland's fifth largest loch, with a length of 17 miles (27 km), a width ranging from 100 yards to a mile (0.1–1.6 km), and a maximum depth of 420 feet (128 metres) – whose own resident monster is known as Seileag. Its most diligent investigator was Father Cyril Dieckhoff, from the Benedictine Abbey at Fort Augustus, who collected many reports but died in 1970 before completing a book that he had been preparing. One of his reports, dating from 1905, featured Ewan MacIntosh, two young boys, and an old man called Ian Crookback, all of whom observed three humps above the water surface with the aid of a telescope while travelling across the loch opposite Gasgan aboard the little mail steamer *Clan Ranald*. And a massive creature with a broad head, wide mouth, long thick neck and seven "sails" (humps) on its back was viewed through a telescope by Ronald MacLeod as it emerged from the water at Sandy Point one afternoon in 1926, and was claimed by MacLeod to be bigger than the *Clan Ranald*!

Other mainland Scottish lochs where monsters have been reported include Arkaig, Beiste, Lochy, Lomond, Oich, Quoich and Treig. In a diary entry for 3 October 1857, English politician Lord Malmesbury recorded that his game stalker, John Stuart, had twice seen the horse-like head and hindquarters of a "lake-horse" basking at the surface of Loch Arkaig.

Intriguingly, "Wee Oichie" of Loch Oich, directly below Loch Ness, traditionally sports a flattened head rather than the familiar equine form noted for other Scottish loch monsters. Having said that, the head of the very big, black, serpentine beast that rose to the surface one summer's day in 1936 was vaguely dog-like,

according to A.J. Robertson, who spied it while boating at the loch's south-western end. Others have likened Oichie to a huge otter.

At Easter 1980, a Mr and Mrs Maltman and their daughter were camping near the edge of Loch Lomond at Luss when a head and slender neck rose up to a height of about 5 feet (1.5 metres) above the water surface, no more than 200 yards (200 metres) away, with a long curved back visible behind. This amazing spectacle lasted for 30 seconds or so, then the head and neck swiftly submerged and were not seen again. The Maltmans were so frightened that they fled, later returning only to pack their belongings before journeying back home.

The lesser Nessie that has attracted most media attention lately, however, is Lizzie, the

monster of 10-mile- (16-km) long Loch Lochy – Scotland's third deepest loch, sited immediately below Loch Oich. With no publicized sightings for 36 years, Lizzie reclaimed the headlines in September 1996, when a 12-foot- (3.6-metre) long, dark-coloured mystery beast with a curved head and three humps reared up out of the water and began moving round in circles in full view of several staff and guests at the Corriegour Lodge Hotel, overlooking the loch. According to Aberdeen University psychology student Catriona Allen, who studied this amazing sight through binoculars, "It certainly wasn't a seal, otter, porpoise or dolphin".

In late July 1997, a six-man expedition featuring previous Loch Morar diver Cameron Turner and led by Gary Campbell, president of the Official Loch Ness Monster Fan Club, arrived to conduct a sonar sweep of Loch Lochy. Encouragingly, they achieved success on their very first day, when their equipment detected a large unidentified object swimming in the middle of the loch and estimated at 15–20 feet (4.5–6 metres) long – far bigger than anything known to be there. Turner came back to Lochy in September 1997, but no new evidence was obtained.

As with the Nessie saga, many sober sightings have been reported at these Scottish lochs that do appear to feature something more than misidentified otters, seals, sturgeons, eels, birds, boats, algal mats, and suchlike – but what? All of the familiar Nessie contenders can be offered – a surviving plesiosaur, an undescribed species of long-necked seal, an elusive evolved version of the officially long-extinct elongate zeuglodont whales – but with no physical evidence to examine, no firm taxonomic identification can be offered. If such reports as those documented here are indeed genuine, however, it seems likely that the species responsible is one that can actively migrate overland, or via connecting rivers, from one loch to another – thus explaining sightings in bodies of water that are too small or insufficiently stocked with fish and other potential prey to sustain a permanent, viable population.

*Ben Nevis towers over a deceptively tranquil Loch Lochy.*

# ARE
# PHOSPHORESCENT
## OWLS A HOOT?

As noted in Chapter 1, it is well known that certain invertebrates and fishes emit light by producing light-releasing compounds – a process known as bioluminescence. Far more extraordinary, however, are recorded encounters with very ordinary, non-bioluminescent birds (and even certain mammals) that for some undetermined reason were also glowing – radiating a spectral, unearthly phosphorescence (i.e. luminescence that yields an after-glow).

For example, the following passage appeared in an article by John Welman (*Blackwood's Magazine*, September 1948) concerning a visit to Anatolia, Turkey, in 1918:

*A luminous blob ... swung round a clump of trees about 200 yards [200 metres] away, and came winging, swiftly and silently, towards us. It was a bird ... and when it came nearer, I saw that every feather of its plumage glittered with tiny points of light, a kind of frosted fire which, without the power to dazzle, was bright enough to illuminate the branches of a tree through which it passed. Its wide, luminous wings seemed to beat the air*

*without disturbing it, for they made no sound whatever. I found myself ... cowering down as it approached looming bigger and brighter every instant, until, seeming about to fly right in among us, it swerved aside and shot up in an arc to pass above our heads.*

Phosphorescent owls and other glowing birds have a very extensive documented history, dating back at least as far as Pliny the Elder (c.23–79 AD), who mentioned them in his *Historia Mundi* (Vol. X). His account was regurgitated two centuries later by Solin, in his *Polyhistoria*, and in 1555 Conrad Gesner published an entire tome devoted to luminous animals. In 1647, a mighty three-

volume treatise on this subject appeared, penned by Thomas Bartholin and entitled *De Luce Animalium*, of which one volume was devoted wholly to glowing birds. This appeared at an opportune time: only a few years earlier, in 1641, some luminous fowl had attracted so much attention at a market in Montpellier, France, that even Henri de Bourbon, Prince de Conde, paid a special visit there to see them.

The most frequently reported glowing birds are owls. As lately documented by David W. Clarke

*The light plumage of the barn owl makes it look striking at dusk; even more so are those specimens that appear to glow.*

(*Fortean Studies*, 1994), one such bird seen in 1897 near King's Lynn in Norfolk, England, was shot by a gamekeeper, Fred Rolfe, who identified it as a barn owl *Tyto alba*. R.J.W. Purdy and his son spied a glowing owl at Twyford, Norfolk, on 3 February 1907, and Purdy Snr saw it several more times in December, as did various other eyewitnesses. Its phosphorescence was so powerful that even the branches upon which it sat were illuminated, and its radiance compared with that of a bicycle lamp seen 300–400 yards (300–400 metres) away. However, this eerie glow was apparently confined to its breast, because its brightness was much less powerful when it flew directly *away* from Purdy (i.e. when only its back, tail and wings were visible to him). Throughout the months spanning these sightings, the owl's phosphorescence showed no sign of diminishing. Moreover, it transpired that such uncanny birds were far from unknown to the locals, who referred to them as lampmen and were afraid of them.

Several notes concerning glowing birds appeared in the *Revue Français d'Ornithologie* during that same period, and in 1917 *Scientific American* published an account by Patrick Brennan regarding phosphorescent skunks. Charles Fort documented some avian examples, and by the mid-1940s Dr W.L. McAtee of the US Fish and Wildlife Service had accumulated numerous eyewitness reports of glowing birds worldwide, from night-herons to barn owls, and even Australian finches. Clearly the phenomenon is genuine, but how can it be explained? Several theories have been proposed, but none provides a conclusive solution.

Contact by a bird with phosphorescent wood in tree-holes would cause some of the bacteria or fungi creating the phosphorescence (very commonly the honey fungus *Armillaria mellea*) to adhere to the bird's feathers, thereby making them glow. However, whereas the regions of a bird's body most likely to make contact with wood when entering or exiting a tree-hole would be its wings and head (brushing against the hole's edges), in some specimens that have been formally

*A possible explanation for phosphorescent feathers is contact with honey fungus, often found growing on trees.*

examined the body region actually glowing has been the breast, with the wings and head giving out little or no light. Also, glowing examples of some extremely large birds have been recorded, such as North America's 4-foot- (1.2-metre) tall great blue heron *Ardea herodias* – not the most likely species to be frequenting tree-holes!

The phosphorescence of glowing birds is external, sometimes disappearing after moulting. Hence it is evidently a phenomenon intrinsic to the bird's plumage, rather than to any internal process. Nevertheless, one can speculate that phosphorescent microbes ingested by the bird

could pass out of its body within its faeces and might then become in some way smeared upon its feathers. This is not very plausible, however, as a complete solution.

A third theory is that phosphorescent bacteria or fungi may actually grow upon a bird's breast feathers if the latter have become damp or dirty, especially as the breast feathers are very dense, thereby encouraging microbial proliferation. Also, the breast is not always a region readily reached by birds when preening. Within an article on luminous birds (in *Knowledge*, 1913), Count Louis de Sibour noted that the glow is particularly powerful during flight, and he sought to explain this occurrence as an effect of super-oxygenation, pointing out that if a medium containing phosphorescent particles is agitated, the particles' glow increases. Even so, coupling the comparative rarity of glowing birds with the likelihood that a great many birds must surely possess damp or dirty feathers at some time or another, this theory still falls short of providing a wholly satisfactory answer.

In short, and despite published protestations to the contrary, the anomaly of glowing birds is not as easy to explain as contemporary mainstream science would like to believe.

*Occasional sightings have been recorded of luminescent great blue herons.*

# UFO-LOGICAL ENCOUNTERS OF THE
# INSECT KIND?

DURING THE 1960S, AMATEUR SCIENTIST NORTON NOVITT FROM DENVER, COLORADO, BECAME INTERESTED IN THE POSSIBILITY THAT CERTAIN UFO SIGHTINGS FEATURED INSECT SWARMS THAT HAD SOMEHOW BEEN RENDERED LUMINOUS. THIS IDEA STEMMED FROM A SIGHTING THAT HE HAD MADE ONE DAY OF TWO GLOWING ANTS IN FLIGHT, THEIR APPARENT LUMINOSITY ACTUALLY COMPRISING REFLECTED SUNLIGHT.

Some species of ant engage in mass nuptial flights at certain times of the year, and as these mating swarms can contain several million insects, they often attain a very considerable size – large enough to resemble glowing orbs in the sky if there is sufficient sunlight to bounce back to earth from the swarms. Even so, luminous UFO sightings made at night could not be explained by this theory – or could they?

As described by Robert Chapman in his book *Unidentified Flying Objects* (1968), Novitt wondered whether it was conceivable that flying ants could generate their own luminosity (i.e. as distinct from merely reflecting rays of sunlight). To pursue this thought-provoking line of speculation, he attached some winged ants to a ping-pong ball, which in turn was connected by

*Could some sightings of UFOs be insect swarms rendered luminous in the evening sky?*

a thin wire to a static generator placed in a darkened room – and sure enough, when the generator was set in motion, the ants' bodies began to glow brightly. Although certainly interesting, such an experiment may appear rather futile at first, because in the natural world (as Chapman drily commented in his own coverage of Novitt's researches) ants are not normally attached to generators! However, it just so happens that nuptial flights of ants often take to the air shortly after thunderstorms – weather conditions that give rise to very strong atmospheric electrical fields. Under such conditions, it is quite likely that the swarms would indeed glow, and with a light

strong enough to be easily observable at night. So perhaps some UFO reports on record were inspired by swarms of flying ants after all.

A few may have involved swarms of moths too. In a paper published by the journal *Applied Optics* in 1978, insect behaviouralists Drs Philip Callahan and R.W. Mankin from the USA provided independent support for Novitt's findings by revealing that light can be generated by placing specimens of Canada's spruce budworm moth *Choristoneura fumiferana* in electrical fields. This discovery confirmed that during those weather conditions when the air is heavily charged with electricity, insects are capable of emitting light.

*In the right atmospheric conditions, swarms of flying ants are capable of emitting light.*

Of course, the amount emitted by each insect would be minute, but as migrating swarms of spruce budworm moths can measure up to 60 miles (96 km) long and 15 miles (24 km) wide, the total amount of light emitted per swarm would be of very appreciable magnitude – more than enough, surely, to mimic a glowing UFO. And as Callahan and Mankin pointed out, it is noticeable that a number of UFO sightings of this latter type that they have analysed occurred at times when mass migrations of this moth species would be expected.

# STELLER'S SECRET FAUNA

Dr Georg Wilhelm Steller·was a German physician and naturalist participating during the early 1740s in the last of Danish explorer Vitus Bering's Russian expeditions to the Arctic waters (now called the Bering Sea) separating Siberia's Kamchatka Peninsula from Alaska. During this expedition, Steller documented many new species of animal, including three very contentious forms that continue to arouse cryptozoological curiosity even today.

## SURVIVING SEA-COWS?

Distantly related to elephants, the manatees and dugongs are herbivorous aquatic mammals known as sirenians, with fish-like tails, no hind limbs and flippers for forelimbs. Nowadays, the largest living sirenian is the Caribbean manatee *Trichechus manatus*, which is up to 15 feet (4.5 metres) long, but there was once a much bigger species, called Steller's sea-cow *Hydrodamalis gigas* (=*Rhytina stelleri*). Measuring up to 35 feet (10.6 metres)

long and weighing several tons, this gigantic sea mammal was discovered in 1741 in the shallow waters around Copper Island and nearby Bering Island – named after Vitus Bering, whose expedition was virtually wrecked here that year. While marooned on this island, Steller studied the sea-cows (the only scientist ever to do so), which existed in great numbers, but the other sailors slaughtered them for food.

When he returned to Kamchatka with news of this enormous but inoffensive species,

it became such a greatly desired source of meat for future sea travellers that by 1768 – just 27 years after Steller had first discovered it – every single sea-cow appeared to have been killed. Not one could be found alive, and since then science has classified this species as extinct. Every so often, however, sailors and other maritime voyagers journeying through the icy

---

*First recorded more than 250 years ago, Steller's sea-cow may still exist in the icy Arctic waters.*

waters formerly frequented by Steller's sea-cow have spied extremely large, unidentified creatures closely resembling this officially vanished, giant sirenian.

In 1879, while exploring the polar waters traversed more than a century earlier by Steller, Swedish naturalist Baron Erik Nordenskjöld visited Bering Island in his vessel, *Vega*. He was startled to learn from one islander, Pitr Vasilijef Burdukovskij, that for the first 2–3 years after his father had settled here from mainland Russia in 1777, sea-cows were still being seen – and were still being killed, their tough hides used for making baydars (native boats).

Even more intriguing was the testimony of two other islanders, Feodor Mertchenin and Nicanor Stepnoff, who claimed that as recently as 1854, they had encountered on the eastern side of Bering Island a very large sea mammal wholly unfamiliar to them: it had brown skin, no dorsal fin, small forefeet and a very thick forebody that tapered further back. It blew out air, but through its large mouth instead of through blow-holes like a whale, and about 15 feet (4.5 metres) of its body's length rose above the water surface as it moved.

Nordenskjöld was sure that they had seen a Steller's sea-cow, because their description contained details of sea-cow morphology given in Steller's documented account, which they had never seen. However, when American researcher Leonhard Stejneger later interviewed Stepnoff, he concluded that the creature encountered by them had actually been a female narwhal *Monodon monoceros* (a species of whale whose males characteristically possess a single long spiralled tusk, once believed to be the unicorn's horn). Stejneger also felt that Nordenskjöld had misunderstood Burdukovskij's statement regarding when his father had settled on Bering Island, and considered that the correct date was 1774, not 1777.

Sometime between 1911 and 1913, a fisherman claimed to have seen a dead Steller's sea-cow, brought in by the sea current towards the Cape of Chaplin on Siberia's easternmost tip, close to the Bering Strait. Frustratingly, this potentially sensational discovery was never investigated.

Perhaps the most compelling sighting occurred in July 1962 near Cape Navarin, south of the Gulf of Anadyr, lying north-east of Kamchatka's coast. Six strange animals were spied in shallow water by the crew of the whaling ship *Buran* about 300 feet (100 metres) away. They were said to be 20–26 feet (6–8 metres) long, with dark skin, an upper lip split into two sections, a relatively small head clearly delineated from its body, and a sharply fringed tail. Scientists postulated that these animals must have been female narwhals. However, the description provided by the *Buran* whalers fits Steller's sea-cow more closely than a female narwhal, and it seems unlikely that experienced whalers would fail to recognize such a familiar creature.

In summer 1976, some salmon factory workers at Anapkinskaya Bay, just south of Cape Navarin, reported seeing, and actually touching, the carcase of a stranded sea-cow. One of them, Ivan Nikiforovich Chechulin, was interviewed by Vladimir Malukovich from the Kamchatka Museum of Local Lore, and stated that the mysterious animal had very dark skin, flippers and a forked tail. Reaching out to touch this creature, they had noticed that it also had a prominent snout. When Malukovich showed Chechulin various pictures of sea creatures to assist him in identifying what he and his colleagues had seen, the creature whose picture he selected as corresponding with their mystery beast was Steller's sea-cow.

In the late 1970s, British explorer Derek Hutchinson launched an expedition to search for sea-cows off the Aleutian Islands, as did Soviet physicist Dr Anatoly Shkunkov in the early 1980s off Kamchatka. Neither met with success. Even so, as speculated by cryptozoologists such as Professor Roy P. Mackal in his book *Searching For Hidden Animals* (1980), and Michel Raynal (*INFO Journal*, February 1987), some sea-cows may have avoided annihilation by moving away from their former haunts, into more remote regions – of which the freezing waters and bleak coastlines around Kamchatka, the

*A skeleton of Steller's sea-cow is preserved in the Swedish Museum of Natural History in Stockholm.*

## STELLER'S SEA-RAVEN – UNMASKED BUT UNRECOGNIZED?

Whereas Steller's sea-cow, even if indeed extinct today, has been extensively documented and is physically represented in museums by skeletal material, we still have next to nothing on file (let alone in the flesh) concerning Steller's most cryptic avian discovery.

While shipwrecked on Bering Island during 1741–42, Steller briefly referred in his journal to a mystifying species that he called a "white sea-raven" – a rare bird "... not seen in the Siberian coast ... [and which is] impossible to reach because it only alights singly on the cliffs facing the sea". However, this species has never been formally identified; nor does it appear to have been reported again by anyone else. So what could it be?

Seeking an answer to this baffling riddle, I communicated in June 1998 with Chris Orrick, who has made a special study of Steller's own writings as well as other Steller-related works. Orrick speculated that Steller's white sea-raven may actually be some species that is known to science today, but was unknown at least to Europeans back in the early 1740s – possibly a species native to the Aleutians but rarely if ever seen around Kamchatka. One candidate offered by Orrick was the surfbird *Aphriza virgata*, a white-plumaged wader from Alaska and America's western Pacific that may not have been familiar to Steller.

Danish cryptozoologist Lars Thomas from Copenhagen Museum was also intrigued by the mystery of the white sea-raven's identity, and he offered me his own opinion about it. Steller was German, and Thomas pointed out that cormorants are referred to in German as sea-ravens. Indeed, a hitherto unknown species of cormorant, the now-extinct spectacled cormorant *Phalacrocorax perspicillatus*, discovered by Steller during this same expedition, was referred to by him as a sea-raven. Consequently, Thomas argued that Steller's mention of a white sea-raven may in reality refer to a white cormorant (either an albino or a young specimen, as some juveniles are much paler than the dark-plumed adults). Alternatively, it may be a bird that superficially resembles a white cormorant, such as the pigeon guillemot *Cepphus columba* in winter plumage, or possibly even a vagrant gannet or booby.

During our communications, Orrick revealed that in a letter to the Russian Academy, dated 16 November 1742, Steller announced that he had prepared and sent two scientific papers – one dealing with North American birds and fishes, the other with Bering Island's birds and fishes. In view of Steller's meticulous manner of documentation, it is likely that the latter paper would have contained a detailed description of the white sea-raven. Unfortunately, however, neither of these manuscripts is known today, but they may still exist, albeit possibly unrecognized, amid the Academy's vast archives in St Petersburg.

Unless these or other additional eighteenth-century documents on this incognito seabird are uncovered, however, its identity will probably never be exposed. Ironically, as Orrick noted, we may already know what Steller's sea-raven is, but without realizing that we know!

## MANDARIN-WHISKERED SEA-MONKEYS

None of the many creatures documented by Steller, however, is as curious, or controversial, as the bizarre animal observed by him for over two hours during the afternoon of 10 August 1741, at approximately 52.5°N latitude, 155°W longitude. He described it as follows:

> It was about two Russian ells [about 5 feet or 1.5 metres] in length; the head was like a dog's, with pointed erect ears. From the upper and lower lips on both sides whiskers hung down which made it look almost like a Chinaman. The eyes were large; the body was longish round and thick, tapering gradually towards the tail. The skin seemed thickly covered with hair, of a gray color on the back, but reddish white on the belly; in the water, however, the whole animal appeared entirely reddish and cow-colored. The tail was divided into two fins, of which the upper, as in the case of sharks, was twice as large as the lower. Nothing struck me more surprising than the fact that neither forefeet as in the marine amphibians nor, in their stead, fins were to be seen ... For over two hours it swam around our ship, looking, as with admiration, first at the one and then at the other of us. At times it came so near to the ship that it could have been touched with a pole, but as soon as anybody stirred it moved away a little further. It could raise itself one-third of its length out of the water exactly like a man, and sometimes it remained in this position for several minutes. After it had observed us for about half an hour, it shot like an arrow under our vessel and came up again on the other side; shortly after, it dived again and reappeared in the old place; and in this way it dived perhaps thirty times.

After watching this extraordinary creature frolicking comically in the water with a long strand of seaweed for a time, Steller, greatly desiring to procure their strange sea visitor in order to prepare a detailed description, loaded his gun and fired two shots at it. Happily, the animal was not harmed, and swam away, though they saw it (or another of its kind) on several subsequent occasions in different stretches of the sea.

No known species corresponds with Steller's description of this peculiar beast, which became known as Steller's sea-monkey or sea-ape. Moreover, until fairly recently, no further sighting of such a creature had ever been reported either, leading scientists to speculate that whatever it had been, its species must surely now be extinct. On a clear afternoon in June 1965, however, eminent British yachtsman-adventurer Brigadier Miles Smeeton was sailing by the central Aleutian Islands aboard his 46-foot (14-metre) ketch *Tzu Hang*, with his wife, daughter and a friend aboard, when he and the others sighted a remarkable sea-beast.

As since documented by explorer-journalist Miles Clark (*BBC Wildlife*, January 1987), lying in the water close off the port bow was what seemed to be a 5-foot- (1.5-metre) long animal with 4–5-inch- (10–13 cm) long reddish-yellow hair, and a head more dog-like than seal-like, whose dark intelligent eyes were placed close

together, rather than set laterally on the head like a seal's. Indeed, Henry Combe, the Smeetons' friend aboard their ketch, stated that it had a face rather like a Tibetan shih-tzu terrier "... with drooping Chinese whiskers". As the vessel drew nearer, this maritime mandarin "... made a slow undulating dive and disappeared beneath the ship". No one spied any limbs or fins. Their observation of it had lasted 10–15 seconds, and they have remained convinced that it was not a seal. Although sea otters occur in these waters, this creature did not resemble any sea otter previously spied by them either.

Conversely, it closely corresponds with Steller's description over two centuries earlier of

his mystifying sea-monkey, thereby giving cryptozoologists hope that its species still exists. As for its identity, however, there is still no satisfactory explanation. Its inquisitive, playful, intelligent, supremely agile behaviour are all characteristics of seals and otters, yet Smeeton and his fellow observers are convinced that their creature was neither of these. It certainly does not bear any immediate resemblance to such animals, set apart by its apparent absence of forelimbs, its asymmetrical vertical tail and its mandarin-style whiskers. Equally, it seems highly improbable that any wildlife observer as experienced and as meticulously accurate in chronicling his observations afterwards as Steller would fail to recognize it as a type of seal or otter if this is truly all that it was. In fact, Steller was so perplexed by the creature that he made no attempt whatsoever to classify it.

Via independent lines of research, Steller scholar Chris Orrick and Jay Ellis Ransom, formerly executive director of the Aleutian-Bering Sea Expeditions Research Library in Oregon, have both formulated theories that Steller's sea-monkey may have been a vagrant specimen of the Hawaiian monk seal *Monachus schauinslandi* – one that had wandered north far from its normal Hawaiian archipelago domain. Orrick also suggests that it may have been undergoing its annual moult at the time, explaining its fur's appearance as documented by Steller. Nevertheless, it still requires an appreciable stretch of the imagination to convert the sea-monkeys described here into any form of seal, Hawaiian monk or otherwise.

Perhaps one day a zoologist voyaging in the Bering Sea will espy Steller's most enigmatic discovery, which seems still to survive in these frigid waters, and in so doing may finally resolve a fascinating zoological mystery that has persisted for more than 250 years.

*The strange animal known as Steller's sea-monkey has yet to be conclusively identified.*

# IN PURSUIT OF PWDRE SER,

## THE ROT OF THE STARS

ALSO TERMED STAR JELLY, ROT OF THE STARS, AND A GELATINOUS METEOR, PWDRE SER IS AN
EXCEEDINGLY STRANGE JELLY-LIKE SUBSTANCE, WHICH REPUTEDLY FALLS DOWN TO EARTH FROM THE
SKIES DURING METEOR SHOWERS, BUT NO ONE KNOWS WHETHER IT REALLY DOES, OR WHAT IT IS.

Nevertheless, pwdre ser has been widely reported, and documented, for many centuries – so much so, in fact, that it has even been alluded to by poets such as John Dryden and Sir John Suckling, as well as in popular novels. These latter include Sir Walter Scott's *The Talisman* (1825), which contains the line:

*Are meteor showers the source of star rot, or is there a terrestrial origin for this strange jelly?*

"Seek a fallen star and thou shalt only light on some foul jelly".

Today, conversely, this subject has become one of the many derided uncertainties of science – once readily accepted as fact, now discounted as fallacy or outright fiction. Such an attitude makes all the more ironic the fact that possibly the most comprehensive report of pwdre ser on file features the examination of a sample by a well-respected scientist. The event

occurred in Amherst, Massachusetts, and was recorded by the *American Journal of Science* in 1819:

*On the 13th August, 1819, between eight and nine o'clock in the evening, a fireball, of the size of a large blown bladder, and of a brilliant white light, was seen in the atmosphere. It fell near a house, and was examined by Rufus Graves, esq. former*

lecturer of chemistry at Dartmouth College. It was of a circular form, resembling a sauce or salad dish bottom upwards, about eight inches [20 cm] in diameter and one [2.5 cm] in thickness, of a bright buff color, with a fine nap upon it similar to that of milled cloth ... On removing the villous coat, a buff-colored pulpy substance of the consistence of good soft soap, of an offensive suffocating smell appeared; and on a near approach to it, or when immediately over it, the smell became almost insupportable, producing nausea and dizziness. A few minutes exposure to the atmosphere changed the buff into a livid color resembling venous blood. It was observed to attract moisture very rapidly from the air. A half-pint tumbler was nearly half filled with the substance. It soon began to liquefy and form a mucilaginous

*A meteor track, or "falling star", photographed in a sky full of star trails over Tucson Mountain Park, Arizona.*

substance of the consistence, color, and feeling of starch when prepared for domestic use.

A few days later, all that remained of this substance in the tumbler was a dark-coloured

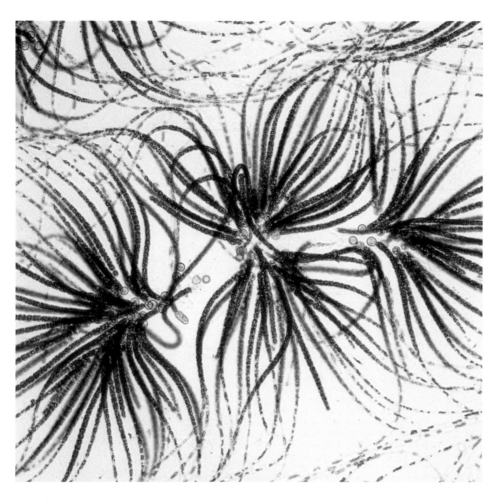

*Types of blue-green algae have been suggested as one possible identity for pwdre ser.*

complex life cycle of these strange species includes a maturation stage in which numerous individuals aggregate to produce an amorphous gelatinous colony called a pseudoplasmodium. This acquires some surprisingly animal-like capabilities, as its component individuals function collectively to yield what is to all intents and purposes a single composite "super organism".

It is even quite plausible that some of the more modern cases of pwdre ser owe their origin to an equally modern man-made device – the aeroplane, or, more specifically, to the waste disposal systems of aeroplanes.

Nevertheless, there are still a number of reports on file that cannot be so readily explained. Take, for instance, the weird wonder that abruptly fell into the backyard of Miami police officer Faustin Gallegos on 28 February 1958. Described by Gallegos as resembling a large medicine ball, it was 20 inches long, 8 inches high, and shaped like an American football. When inspected by Gallegos and his wife, Dorothy, however, they discovered that this enigmatic object was lined with "... thousands of minute cells resembling those of a honeycomb, it ... was clear like glass [and] ... was pulsating over its entire body". This singular event had attracted interest from one of Gallegos's neighbours as well as his mother, who watched with bated breath as he gingerly touched this grotesque ovoid. Nothing happened, so he carefully gathered it up, placed it into a large jar, and drove off to his station to show it to his police colleagues – but before he arrived, the mysterious object had evaporated.

As with angel hair, documented earlier in this chapter, it seems evident that several wholly discrete gelatinous substances and sources have been erroneously lumped together in the past by chroniclers and investigators, yielding the impossibly heterogeneous, composite mystery

residue that became a fine odourless ash when rubbed between the fingers.

The house near which this supposed meteor (falling star) had landed was owned by Erastus Dewey, who discovered the jelly about 20 feet (6 metres) from his front door on the following morning. Moreover, two women eyewitnesses testified to seeing its light reflected upon one of the walls of Dewey's house just before it hit the ground.

This is significant, because, as sceptics readily point out, few reports of pwdre ser are complete, i.e. containing both a sighting of a falling star and the finding of pwdre ser at the spot where the falling star landed. And even in those few cases that do, it is very rare that someone actually sees the falling star land. Usually, it is only supposition that the site where some pwdre ser is found is indeed the site where a recently spied falling star has landed.

Most accounts of supposed "star jelly" merely feature the discovery of strange gelatinous deposits on the ground, often in a field or on a lawn, and quite frequently following a rainstorm. Analyses of such samples have yielded a variety of results. In some cases, they have been found to be the disgorged, partially digested remains of a bird's meal, containing slimy portions of earthworms, frogs, fishes, etc. Occasionally, the bird in question, which has included herons, gulls and a bittern, has actually been observed in the act of disgorging a gelatinous sample. Other biological identities for pwdre ser include the blue-green alga *Nostoc*, and a type of fungus known as *Tremella* or devil's butter.

In a few decidedly dramatic cases, involving blob-like specimens of alleged star rot that have physically crawled across a lawn or up a telegraph pole, they have been found to be an extraordinary type of fungus known as a myxomycete or slime mould. The highly known to us today as pwdre ser, rot of the stars, star jelly, and suchlike. Moreover, as revealed here, most of its component forms are unquestionably of terrestrial origin.

Even so, is it conceivable that certain cases do actually feature a genuine mystery, i.e. the "real" pwdre ser – transported to earth on meteors? The overriding problem with this notion is that such a fragile organic substance would surely be incinerated when the meteor entered our planet's atmosphere from space. However, there is one theory on file that offers a startling solution to this problem. What if these apparent meteors did not derive from Outer Space, but originated from within our planet's own atmosphere, and that their organic content, pwdre ser, was due to the fact that these supposed meteors were actually living entities – veritable sky beasts and cloud creatures?

Whereas living organisms populate every conceivable ecological niche on land and in the water on our planet, there does not appear to be any life form adapted for an exclusively aerial, airborne existence in our skies' rarified realms – a mysterious omission in the otherwise comprehensive scheme of evolution. Consequently, as documented by me in detail within my book *The Unexplained* (1996), down through the years a number of researchers have speculated that perhaps some such entities do exist. Quite possibly they would be of immense size but of exceedingly fragile, lightweight consistency, living their entire lives in the upper reaches of our planet's atmosphere, and generally hidden from human view – except when one is occasionally spied and duly documented afterwards as a UFO.

Perhaps the most famous proponent of this "living UFO" scenario is Trevor James Constable, a US radio officer, who promulgated his fascinating theories in his book *Sky Creatures* (1978). In this he claimed that any such sky-dwellers would probably consist principally of pure energy, encased within only the lightest, flimsiest outer shell or skin.

Whether or not such highly specialized life-forms as these do (or even could) really exist is beyond the scope of this present account's consideration – except, that is, for one very pertinent aspect. If there are indeed such things as sky-beasts, in the form predicted by Constable and others, what would happen to one of these creatures when it died?

Although this is all entirely speculative, one might assume that its notably insubstantial, probably gelatinous corpse would simply plunge down from the skies to earth, breaking up as it fell, thereby releasing the contents of its energy-rich interior – an event that would resemble the descent of a bright falling star to eyewitnesses observing it from the ground. And if they should happen to see where it fell, and hurried over to look for its remains, what would they discover? Not the rocky debris that would mark the landing of a genuine meteorite. Instead, all that would be found would be a mass of jelly – popularly referred to as pwdre ser or star rot, but in reality the gelatinous outer skin of a dead sky beast.

## FOAM OF THE MOON

Even more mysterious than the rot of the stars is an enigmatic substance variously known as the foam of the moon, moon-drop, aphroselenos (by the ancient Greeks) and virus lunare (by the Romans) – a diversity of names mirrored by the considerable variety of descriptions, interpretations and properties attributed to it.

In Classical Graeco-Roman times, for instance, it was claimed to be a venomous vaporous foam shed on to certain herbs by the moon when conjured downwards during witchcraft ceremonies, after which these herbs were collected for magical purposes. Accordingly, this arcane substance was even mentioned briefly in *Macbeth* (III, v) by Shakespeare:

*Upon the corner of the moon*
*There hangs a vaporous drop profound;*
*I'll catch it ere it come to ground.*

Moreover, in the Roman epic poet Lucan's *Pharsalia* (vi, 699), the character Erichtho is introduced using it: "Et virus large lunare ministrat".

According to an ancient Egyptian papyrus dealing with magic and dating from the third century AD, conversely, moon foam was a white glass-like stone (moonstone?) that could be rubbed into tiny fragments.

In modern times, however, moon foam in all its conflicting forms had been largely forgotten, until it recently became the subject of an extensive, fascinating review by historical anomalies researcher Steve Moore (*Fortean Studies*, 1995). After surveying a host of ancient texts and references to moon foam, Moore concluded:

> *… we have a catalogue of different possible meanings: a secretion of the Moon; a magical ingredient; a poison; opium; sexual and menstrual fluids; a prophylactic against snakes; moonstone and selenite; and finally, a name for quicksilver. Aphroselenos is not a single substance, variously described; rather it is a single word, variously applied at various times – to substances mineral, medical, magical and entirely mythical. It meant different things to different people at different times; but we must also bear in mind that it may well have carried more than one meaning at any one time as well, with shadings, nuances and connections that defy easy interpretation. It is, indeed, as nebulous as foam, and as changeable as the Moon herself.*

In short, this ambiguous substance has been defined and documented in so many ways in the past, spanning such fields of study as witchcraft, eclipse lore, medicine and alchemy, that there is no guarantee that it ever actually existed as a single entity – if, indeed, at all?

# GLOBSTERS AHOY!

IN 1998, A 20-FOOT, 4-TON CARCASE-LIKE OBJECT DRIFTED ASHORE ON TASMANIA'S FOUR MILE BEACH.

Extremely decomposed, and with a white fibrous hair-like covering, it also sported several sturdy but elongate projections resembling tentacles. However, it lacked any recognizable head, sensory organs, or internal skeleton, and it baffled the many local people who came to observe this maritime mystery. Even experienced fishermen claimed that it did not resemble any decayed shark, whale, squid, turtle or seal carcase previously seen by them.

Hairy, grotesque-looking carcases cast up on to beaches in the past have proven to be the rotting remains of basking sharks, whose exposed connecting tissue had yielded their deceptive

"hair", but this blob-shaped mass bore scant resemblance to such corpses. By 13 January, marine biologist Barry Bruce from the Marine Research Division of the CSIRO (Commonwealth Scientific and Industrial Research Organisation), and officers from the Tasmanian Parks and Wildlife Service had examined the carcase for themselves.

They came away sharing the opinion that it was merely a lump of decomposing whale blubber, whose "hairy" surface resulted from dried-out exposed sinews. Nevertheless, tissue samples were taken for DNA analyses in order to ensure that a conclusive identification was obtained this time.

Because this was not the first time that an anomalous blob-like entity had been washed ashore in Tasmania, or elsewhere, for that matter.

Indeed, back in the 1960s American cryptozoologist Ivan T. Sanderson was so intrigued by these huge, amorphous and mystifying carcases that he coined a specific term for them – globsters, of which the massive shapeless lump of hirsute flesh constituting the Tasmanian Four Mile Beach specimen from January 1998 is a typical example. Regrettably, another typical feature in the history of globsters has been the consistent failure by scientists to provide an unequivocal identity for them, as exemplified by the infamously confused saga of an earlier Tasmanian example.

It was in August 1960 when this particular globster made its debut, discovered at Sandy Cape, near Temma and Smithton in western Tasmania. Hard and rubbery, with a hump standing roughly 4 feet (1.2 metres) high at one end but tapering gradually to no more than 6 inches (15 cm) at the other, the Temma globster was approximately circular in shape, measuring about 20 feet (6 metres) long, 18 feet (5.5 metres) wide, and probably weighed 5–10 tons. As with the later Four Mile Beach specimen, it was covered in pale hair-like strands, which felt greasy to the touch. It also bore a series of long vertical gill-like slits around its fluted perimeter, but did not possess any head, limbs, bones or visible organs.

Even so, more than 18 months passed before news of this bizarre entity finally attracted zoological attention, in the shape of CSIRO scientist Dr Bruce Mollison. In early March 1962, he led a small team of CSIRO members and local naturalists to observe the globster, then came home bemused by what he had seen. Shortly afterwards, he returned, hacking off with great difficulty a sizeable segment of flesh from the globster for study by experts at the Royal Prince Albert Hospital, who were unable to identify it as deriving from any known animal species.

Media reports containing diverse views and suggestions as to the globster's identity soon appeared, leading by late March to yet another expedition, this time by a government research team, who collected tissue samples for analysis. When their official report appeared, it announced that the globster was nothing more than a huge mass of whale blubber. However, as a number of independent observers of the globster pointed out, the report seemed to describe a globster very different morphologically from, and much smaller than, the one that had attracted all the attention. This gave rise to speculation that the government team may not have examined the correct carcase, especially as they did not take along any of the original carcase's discoverers to show them the way. Thus the Temma globster case ended unsatisfactorily.

Several other notable globsters have turned up since then. These include a 30-foot- (9-metre) long specimen at New Zealand's Muriwai Beach in March 1965; a grey 8-foot (2.5-metre) example discovered in May 1988 on a Bermudan beach; and another New Zealand specimen, resembling a pale lump of rotting carpet, washed up in autumn 1997 on a beach about 100 miles (160 km) from Wellington; as well as Tasmania's Four Mile Beach globster.

In 1992 a similar carcase to the Temma globster was spied by tourist Louise Whipps (not Whitts, as media accounts erroneously claimed) on the shore of Benbecula, a small island in Scotland's Outer Hebrides. Like the Temma specimen, the Benbecula globster had long vertical slits, but these seemed more numerous and elaborate, approaching the tentacular projections of the Four Mile Beach globster. Whipps took a photo of herself beside the beast (see page 6), thus providing a useful size scale with which to check her estimate that it was about 12 feet (3.5 metres) long. She later took the photo to the Hancock Museum in Newcastle, but its staff could not identify the creature. On 21 August 1996, Dr Alec Coles, the museum's curator and keeper of natural sciences, conceded in a *Newcastle Journal* interview: "We haven't got a clue ... We have taken it around to all the experts and they don't know what it is either. We haven't seen anything like it before."

Although Whipps's photograph was publicly exhibited in August 1996 by the Hancock Museum, the globster has still not been positively identified. However, in 1996 I sent a newspaper report containing Whipps's photo to Copenhagen Museum zoologist Lars Thomas, who is also a keen cryptozoologist. On 21 October, he replied as follows:

*Regarding the mysterious animal from Benbecula. I might have a suggestion for you. In the summer of 1989 a completely similar creature stranded itself on the beach some miles south of Godthaab, or Nuuk, as the capital of Greenland is called nowadays. We received a sample of the creature, and some videofootage of it at the museum in Copenhagen, where it was later analysed. It looked almost exactly like the one in the newspaper clipping you sent me. The Greenland creature turned out to be a long gone, and very decomposed shark. Just about the only thing left of it was fatty and connective tissue. Anyway, the biochemical results showed it to be from a shark, although the species couldn't be determined. Judging from the size though, it could either have been a basking shark or a greenland shark (Somniosus microcephalus), which is rather common in the area. My suggestion for the Benbecula creature would be a shark, probably a basking shark.*

In 1995 a fish identity was also put forward as the solution to the Bermuda globster mystery, following microscopical and chemical analyses of its tissue by a zoological team from Maryland University. However, this team also claimed that their analyses of tissue samples from another amorphous sea-discarded anomaly – the controversial carcase washed ashore on a Florida beach in 1896, and claimed by its original observers as well as various previous biochemical analyses to have been a gigantic octopus – revealed its probable identity to be mammalian. Similarly, the New Zealand globster of 1997 was deemed by Dr Steve O'Shea to be a partly decomposed sperm whale.

Presumably, then, there is some ill-defined process of decomposition that can transform mammalian and piscean carcases into similar globsters – but if so, why are there not more globsters turning up on beaches worldwide? Alternatively, could it be that the methods of tissue analyses applied to globster tissue so far are not sufficiently discriminating? If the latter is true, might it be that globsters are in reality the mortal remains of some radically different animal group still undiscovered by science?

# MYSTERIES OF THE
# SUPERNATURAL
# WORLD

*Every great scientific truth goes through three stages. First, people say it conflicts with the Bible. Next they say it had been discovered before. Lastly they say they always believed it.*

Professor Louis Agassiz, pioneering nineteenth-century palaeontologist

EVERY SO OFTEN, A SCIENTIFIC DISCOVERY IS MADE THAT DOES NOT MERELY PROVIDE AN EXTENSION OF KNOWLEDGE WITHIN A CURRENTLY EXISTING FIELD, BUT REVEALS A DRAMATIC, ENTIRELY NOVEL, HITHERTO-UNSUSPECTED SCENARIO, AS IF THE KEY TO A PREVIOUSLY UNEXPLORED, LOCKED ROOM HAD SUDDENLY BEEN UNCOVERED. IN 1896, FRENCH PHYSICIST HENRI BECQUEREL MADE ONE SUCH DISCOVERY, WHEN HE ACCIDENTALLY FOUND THAT URANIUM SALTS WERE EMITTING ATOMIC RADIATION. LATER RESEARCH BY BECQUEREL REVEALED THAT RADIOACTIVITY CAUSES THE TRANSFORMATION OF ONE ELEMENT INTO ANOTHER — A CONCEPT HITHERTO CONFINED TO THE MEDIEVAL CLAIMS OF ALCHEMISTS, BUT NOW CONFIRMED BY SCIENTIFIC EXPERIMENTATION, AND GIVING RISE TO THE FIELD OF NUCLEAR PHYSICS. SIMILARLY, SCOTTISH BACTERIOLOGIST SIR ALEXANDER FLEMING'S DISCOVERY OF PENICILLIN IN 1928 ULTIMATELY LED TO THE DEVELOPMENT OF ANTIBIOTICS, A REVOLUTIONARY NEW TOOL IN THE ADVANCEMENT OF MEDICINE.

PERHAPS THERE IS ALSO A BECQUEREL OR FLEMING WAITING IN THE WINGS OF THE FUTURE WHO WILL FIND THE KEY TO THAT SEALED, VEILED ROOM OF SCIENTIFIC REVELATIONS LABELLED "THE SUPERNATURAL".

## CHAPTER THREE

## WELCOME TO THE TWILIGHT ZONE
# CLOSE ENCOUNTERS OF THE
# CREEPY KIND

GHOSTS, PHANTOMS, SPECTRES AND OTHER INCORPOREAL ENTITIES HAVE BEEN REPORTED WORLDWIDE FROM THE EARLIEST TIMES TO THE MOST RECENT TIMES, AND ARE AS DIVERSE AS THEY ARE DAUNTING. YET FEW ARE WEIRDER THAN THE LITTLE-PUBLICIZED, EERILY CAPTIVATING, ANIMALIAN APPARITIONS THAT COMPRISE THE FOLLOWING SPINE-CHILLING MISCELLANY OF THE MACABRE.

As will be seen, the forms assumed by these "creatures" are far too outlandish to be explicable by even the most generous, broad-minded cryptozoological hypotheses, yet were only too real to their terrified eyewitnesses. Hence they are best described as zooform phenomena – entities that outwardly resemble animals (real or, more often, mythical) or sometimes even grotesque animal-human

*An artist's impression of the sinister horse-man encountered on a country road in Ireland.*

composites, but which seem to be paraphysical rather than zoological in nature.

## APOCALYPTIC HORSE-MEN

The following case was brought to my attention in February 1996 by a telephone caller when I appeared on GMTV's "This Morning" breakfast television show, hosted by Richard Madeley and Judy Finnigan, and was subsequently written up in the magazine *Animals and Men*.

It was a very late evening in 1994 when the husband of Nicky Knott, while driving home

through King's Lynn, Norfolk, took a back road that led him to a living nightmare:

*It was very dark and quite rural in that area – lots of fields and trees around. As I drove down the road I noticed a shape in the fields at the right hand side. I thought it was probably a horse or a deer, as it seemed to be the right size and shape. But, as I got closer it moved nearer towards the road and I got the shock of my life – it had the body and legs of a horse but a man's face!*

*It was very scary and unpleasant. I didn't hang around, but put my foot down hard on the accelerator and "got the hell" out of there! I had the sensation that it was following me down the road. I didn't look back – I was terrified.*

*When I got home I told my wife and friends about it, but most people just laughed ... but I am convinced about what I saw. I know it seems impossible, but I did see it and it wasn't just a horse or a deer.*

A remarkable account – but even more so is the fact that it has a notable precedent. As recalled in John J. Dunne's *Haunted Ireland* (1977), one evening in spring 1966, 21-year-old Margaret Johnson (spelt "Johnston" in some accounts) and her boyfriend John Farrell were driving past the estate of Lord Dillon in County Louth, Ireland, when a huge creature suddenly loomed up on the road ahead, and Farrell braked. It seemed to be an extremely large horse, but then it turned to look at them, and to their absolute horror they could see that it had a grotesque, leering human face! Its eyes bulged malevolently as it stared down at them, blocking their way for almost two minutes. Then, wholly without warning, it vanished, leaving two very frightened eyewitnesses to drive on home – so shocked that they could hardly believe the evidence of their own eyes, and so scared that Johnson was ill for several days afterwards. One of the most feared supernatural entities of Irish mythology is the pooka, which often assumes the guise of a demonic pony or horse. Is this what the two travellers saw that night? But pookas are only imaginary – aren't they?

And just to show that the British Isles do not hold the monopoly on equine enigmas: on 18 May 1963, Centerville in Illinois was apparently visited by a veritable centaur, which pranced and gambolled its way into local history by inciting more than 50 calls to the police over the next few nights. One of its very startled eyewitnesses was James McKinney, who observed this escapee from a Classical Greek legend cavorting directly in front of his house. "It looked like a half-man, half-horse" was McKinney's succinct description.

## DOG-MEN AND GOAT-MEN

Another popular being from the realms of myth and legend is the dog-headed man, ranging from the Shetland Isles' wulver to the Nicobar Islands' cynocephali. However, something that sounds disturbingly like a real-life version has been reported for more than a century from the northern woods of Michigan. Dubbed the Michigan dog-man, and said to combine a canine head with a human body, it supposedly stands in excess of 7 ft 4 in (2.24 metres), walks upright like a man, and, curiously, is very often sighted in the seventh year of each decade, i.e. 1967, 1977, 1987, and so on. It has been held responsible for many mysterious mutilations of livestock and pets, and has been spied from Big Rapids northwards to Mackinaw City.

Yet another legend come to life is Goatman, the name given to a frightening satyr-like entity long reported from northern Prince George's County, Maryland. Indeed, Maryland University's folklore archives contain a sizeable dossier of Goatman stories, which tell of a fearsome woodland-frequenting humanoid entity with the legs and hoofed feet of a goat, coarse black hair covering its lower body, the upper torso of a man, and a pair of short white horns projecting from its brow. Although largely dismissed as an urban legend, possibly inspired in part by sightings of hermits and even an occasional bigfoot report, Goatman is still reported spasmodically, and has been blamed for the savage deaths of many dogs, as well as the vandalizing of cars and trucks. Its most diligent investigator is Mark Opsasnick, whose article "On the Trail of the Goatman" (*Strange Magazine*, fall 1994) is the most detailed enquiry into the Goatman phenomenon's origin. Intriguingly, a similar horned entity, also nicknamed Goatman, has allegedly been reported from Wisconsin too.

## HOWARD LELAND AND THE DEMON CAT OF WORLD WAR II

And speaking of horns: one evening in October 1943, during the terrifying bombing blitz inflicted by German aircraft upon London in World War II, English air-raid volunteer Howard Leland was seeking shelter from yet another explosion when he spied a deserted house and ran inside. Its interior was inky-black and silent, but while sitting at the bottom of a flight of stairs Leland became convinced that he was not alone – that something else was close by, watching him. Switching on his torch, he illuminated his immediate surroundings, and there, to his horror, crouching at the top of the stairs, was an enormous cat, with black and brown tabby stripes, blazing eyes and, most monstrous of all, a pair of sharp pointed horns sprouting from its skull!

Frozen with fear, Leland could only gaze in terror at this evil apparition. Then, without warning, it sprang down into the shadowy room below, in which Leland was standing. Before it had reached the ground, however, it had already vanished, but a spine-chilling yowling cry filled the air. Enquiries revealed that Leland was only one of many people who had encountered this feline monster here during the past several years, and on every occasion it had been squatting at the top of the stairs.

Still unnerved by his experience, Leland subsequently consulted John Pendragon, a renowned clairvoyant, and recalled his encounter to him. After listening, Pendragon perused a large map of London and placed his finger on the precise spot marking the site of the cat-haunted house. Immediately, his mind was filled with a whirling vista of cats, a vortex of screeching feline fury and hate, located at the top of the house's stairs, and at whose epicentre he could clearly visualize a despairing man, about to hang himself.

After revealing his vision to Leland, Pendragon asked him to gather whatever information he could find concerning the

*Wolfie, the weird entity often spied in Abbey House in the early years of the twentieth century.*

house's previous occupants, and a week later Leland returned to the clairvoyant with some remarkable news. He informed Pendragon that one of the house's former inhabitants had been a student of the black arts, who had slaughtered many cats during one particularly grisly, vile ceremony of sacrifice. Eventually, his mind had become unhinged, and he had committed suicide by hanging himself from the top of the stairs.

After learning this, Pendragon suggested that the monstrous horned cat witnessed by Leland and others was probably an elemental spirit – one that had been created or "moulded" into a hate-imbued feline guise by the restless ghosts of the numerous cats slain here during the wizard's foul rituals, and which may well linger in this accursed dwelling indefinitely.

## WOLFIE – A WEIRD WONDER OF ABBEY HOUSE

Abbey House in Cambridgeshire is no stranger to supernatural visitations, with several sightings of a mysterious ghostly Grey Lady on record. Even more mystifying, however, are reports of an extraordinary "animal" sighted by the Lawson family who lived here from

1904 to 1910. According to a description given in Enid Porter's *Cambridgeshire Customs and Folklore* (1969), which served as the basis for Richard Svensson's excellent illustration reproduced here, Abbey House's zooform apparition walked on its hind legs, was covered in brown fur, sported flipper-like front paws and a long beak.

Another account, included in Graham McEwan's *Mystery Animals of Britain and Ireland* (1986), cites Mrs Lawson's description of it as "a nondescript kind of animal resembling a large-sized hare, but with close-cropped ears. It was always seen and heard running about on its hind legs, the patter of its footsteps being very distinct and characteristic. It was never seen standing still or moving slowly."

Frequenting the ground floor of the house, it was usually seen at twilight, but was also observed quite clearly in the drawing room when illuminated with artificial light. This uncanny entity became so familiar a sight to the Lawsons' children that they nicknamed it "Wolfie", and despite its impossible form it seemed to be solid, rather than insubstantial, at least in Mr Lawson's opinion – after he had encountered it at close range in a corridor.

In 1910, the Lawsons moved out, but Wolfie evidently remained, because a mysterious "animal" was sighted in the house on more than one occasion by Charmian, the young daughter of the Sharps, who had moved into Abbey House in 1920. What may be the final appearance of Wolfie occurred in 1947, when an elusive "tiny doggie" was spied in the kitchen by the young son of Celia Schofield, a friend of the then tenant. It is interesting to note that most (though not all) sightings of Wolfie were made by children, suggesting that they were somehow more receptive than adults to this strange entity.

Other reports of what may have been Wolfie (or perhaps another of its kind) come from Merton Hall (also in Cambridge but situated quite a distance away from Abbey House) during the early 1920s, when it was occupied by Roman Catholics. In 1924, however, several priests stayed here during the Pax Romana Conference held in Cambridge, and said Mass each day – after which the anomalous animal was not seen in Merton Hall again.

## THE VAMPIRE CATERPILLAR OF EDINBURGH

Some zooform phenomena, like Wolfie, seem so bizarre that they defy belief, let alone categorization, yet their eyewitnesses vehemently affirm that they were real. Another notable example is the entity that Godfrey H. Anderson claimed to have spied on 23 November 1904 while walking along a street in Edinburgh, Scotland. Suddenly, he saw a grotesque "something" rise out of the gutter and spring up at the throat of a horse. According to Anderson's description, cited in *Creatures of the Outer Edge* (1978) by Jerome Clark and Loren Coleman, the horse's weird attacker was a "vague black shape about four feet long and two and a half feet high ... [it was shaped] like an hourglass and moved like a huge caterpillar." The horse reared up in terror, and as it did so its assailant vanished.

## THE MAN-MONKEY OF STAFFORDSHIRE

No less sinister, and certainly no less hostile to horses, than Edinburgh's vampire caterpillar was the Staffordshire man-monkey, which allegedly haunted a stretch of the Birmingham and Liverpool Junction Canal (now part of the Shropshire Union Canal). Several reports are on file, but the most famous was the terrifying encounter that occurred at 10 pm on the evening of 21 January 1879, as a man was about to cross a bridge on the canal while driving his cart home from Woodcote in Shropshire to Ranton in Staffordshire. Only a few weeks after this event, Charlotte S. Burne spoke to the man's employer and received full details of his shocking experience, which she duly recorded in her book *Shropshire Folk-Lore* (1883):

*Just before he [the eyewitness] reached the canal bridge, a strange black creature with great white eyes sprang out of the plantation by the road-side and alighted on his horse's back. He tried to push it off with his whip, but to his horror the whip went through the Thing, and he dropped it to the ground in his fright. The poor tired horse broke into a canter, and rushed onwards at full speed with the ghost still clinging to its back. How the creature at length vanished the man hardly knew. He told his tale in the village of Woodseaves, a mile further on, and so effectually frightened the hearers that one man actually stayed with his friends there all night, rather than cross the terrible bridge which lay between him and his home. The ghost-seer reached home at length, still in a state of excessive terror (but, as his master assured me, perfectly sober), and it was some days before he was able to leave his bed, so much was he prostrated by his fright. The whip was searched for next day, and found just at the place where he said he had dropped it.*

But the story does not end there. Several days later, the man was visited by a policeman, wishing to take details under the assumption that he had been robbed. When the man told him that he had not been robbed and informed him of his bizarre encounter, however, the policeman was far from surprised:

*"Oh, was that all, sir?" said the disappointed policeman. "Oh, I know what that was. That was the Man-Monkey, sir, as does come again at that bridge ever since the man was drowned in the Cut!"*

So now you know. Nothing more mysterious than a phantom man-monkey after all!

But what exactly are zooform phenomena? Some, such as the horned demon cat, may indeed be elemental entities, created by intense emotions, or externalized psychic projections, and hence akin to tulpas and other mentally moulded thought-forms. Others, such as Goatman, probably owe more to colourful local humour than to any hardcore history of genuine encounters. The concept of interdimensional visitors briefly entering our world through "window areas" (see the monastery imp item, Chapter 5) is another popular explanation offered, and not only for zooforms but also for humanoid entities such as the Little People, devas and even Grey aliens. Hallucinations, possibly originating from temporal lobe aberrations (see Chapter 4), offer a further identity for certain, but not all, zooforms: the sightings of Wolfie at different times by different people of different ages, for instance, would seem to rule out hallucinations as a satisfactory explanation. As with more typical ghosts and phantoms, the true nature – or natures – of zooform phenomena continues to defy elucidation.

*The terrifying man-monkey once reputed to haunt a canal-side tract in Staffordshire.*

# DON'T FEAR
# THE REAPER

THE SETTING FOR HER INCREDIBLE ENCOUNTER WAS A PATIENT'S ROOM AT THE DIAGNOSTIC HOSPITAL IN HOUSTON, TEXAS, ON A HOT DAY IN THE MID-1960S. A PRIVATE DUTY NURSE WAS HURRYING PAST, ON HER WAY TO ONE OF HER OWN PATIENTS, BUT WHAT SHE SAW AS SHE GLANCED INTO THIS ROOM IS SOMETHING THAT SHE HAS NEVER FORGOTTEN, EVEN THOUGH SHE IS TODAY ALMOST 80 YEARS OLD:

*O*n the bed was a little grey-haired lady dressed in lace, propped up with pillows. Beside the bed stood this tall figure dressed in a monk's robes with its head covered. It looked up at me when I appeared in the door. His face was a skull with tiny red fires for eyes. His hands, skeletal, were patiently folded over each other inside the dark sleeves. My impression was that he was very patient, waiting.

*I remember the terrible smell of death – something rotting in the sun – when I looked into the eyes... When he looked at me I became almost frozen in the couple of seconds I looked at him. I stepped back, turned, went down the hall to my patient's room. When the*

*male nurse I shared my patient with saw me, he grabbed a blanket off the bed and wrapped it around me. I was freezing. He wrapped me in four blankets and put some hot chocolate in me and it took nearly two hours before I could even talk to him and I told him what I saw. He said, "Yes, the lady had been fighting death for over seven days."*

The old lady died shortly afterwards, the eerie darkness that had filled her room vanished, and her macabre visitor was gone.

Although not publicly released, the identity of this nurse is known to eminent Maryland-based Fortean researcher Mark Chorvinsky, who holds full details of her case on file – together with many others. For this was not an isolated incident. During his lengthy investigations, Mark has learnt that numerous people have encountered a spine-

chilling entity, most commonly witnessed in death-bed situations, that corresponds precisely with the traditional image of the Grim Reaper. Yet until Mark's thanatalogical researches, this astonishing phenomenon was largely unsuspected.

Predictably, given the circumstances behind this entity's appearances, a considerable number of eyewitnesses have been nurses or other carers. Of particular interest is that, as with ghosts and other paranormal entities, not everyone can see the Reaper. Mark obtained the following testimony from another experienced nurse:

*I have worked as a registered nurse for almost 20 years, but I can't really say when I first noticed the Reaper. I've worked in hospitals and nursing homes and have noted the figure regularly. Usually, I just see a dark figure, robed, standing near the nurse's station...*

---

*Classic Grim Reaper: Gustave Doré's engraving of the Vision of Death from the Book of Revelation.*

*Very rarely, the figure will be white. I've never heard it speak, but someone always dies within a few days of its appearance.*

*Of all these many encounters, one stands out clearly in my mind. Since 1993, I have worked at a local long-term care facility in Erie, Pennsylvania. As usual, I've often seen the figure before the death of a resident. One night, a resident lay dying, with no friend or family to be with him. He was the only person in the room; the other bed was empty.*

*The LPN (Licensed Practical Nurse) and I stood in the hall outside his room, talking softly. Suddenly we both stopped speaking, stared and gasped, "Did you see that?"*

*"That" was a black robed figure, with hood, standing at the foot of the resident's bed. He seemed to be waiting, and was "facing" the resident – "looking" at him. He made no move toward the resident, but seemed content to stand, waiting. In fact the resident did not die that night, but the next.*

*Needless to say, the LPN and I were stunned. Another nurse standing with us saw nothing. If the resident saw anything, he gave no indication.*

Sometimes, however, the Grim Reaper's appearance does not precede someone's death, but has actually prevented it. A man publicly identified by Mark only as "A.L." told him how, while living in an apartment in Yonkers, New York, during 1974, he had been sitting on the sofa in his living room one evening at about 10.15 pm when he felt that he was being watched – and when he glanced to his right, he was horrified to see the classic form of the Grim Reaper standing beside him, even holding a long scythe in its hand! Petrified, A.L. watched as this eerie figure glided backwards, its white skull gleaming but never turning away from him, until it passed right through A.L.'s front door and vanished.

Stricken with fear in case it had come not for him but for some other family member, he called out to his wife, asleep in bed, but received no reply.

Racing to her side, he found her lying unconscious, with an empty bottle of pills at her side. Unable to wake her, A.L. telephoned his sister, who lived nearby. She came at once with her husband, and they succeeded in reviving her before taking her to hospital, where she was saved. Since that incredible episode, A.L. is convinced that the Grim Reaper is able to save lives by bringing warning, as well as waiting to take the dying elsewhere.

Indeed, Mark has several cases on file in which the Grim Reaper has refused to take someone because it was not their time. He also has some fascinating histories in which this

entity appears to have abandoned its classical gothic guise in favour of a more contemporary image. One of the most compelling of these accounts came from nurse Charlene Williams:

*My mother was dying of a brain tumour in the hospital; she had cancer throughout her body. She also was a sensitive [psychic] as was my grandmother. She stated that a nice man dressed in black with his hat in his hand visited at her bedside for three nights in a row. The Man in Black visited my grandmother three nights also. He introduced himself as the angel of death. He held her hand and took the pain away. He*

*brought peace and love to mother; he also told her about heaven and that she would come with him on the fourth night, and that she did. He was the same spirit that came to a lady that lived with us, old Nanny Lou, all under the same circumstances. "Don't fear him honey," she told me, and I don't.*

It would be tempting to dismiss such accounts as hallucinations of the dying brain, were it not for the earlier cases cited here, in which the witnesses were the carers, not the dying patients. Apparently, therefore, the ability to see the Reaper depends upon whether or not someone is sensitive or psychic. But why does this entity appear in different guises – sometimes as a stereotyped Reaper, other times in modern-day guise?

Perhaps – to borrow a theory previously applied to the diversity of reported extra-terrestrials and Little People – the Grim Reaper deliberately adopts whichever image it considers to be the most influential for a given situation. The frightening, scythe-carrying, skull-headed, robed figure was necessary in order to compel A.L. to check whether his wife was well; whereas the reassuring, kindly image adopted when visiting Charlene Williams's relatives helped them not to be afraid at the end of their lives. Alternatively, perhaps the eyewitnesses are imposing their own visual expectations upon the Reaper, translating its visual form into whatever they anticipate or hope such an entity will look like.

Few mysterious phenomena of modern times are as thought-provoking as the concept of a bona fide Grim Reaper – or Reapers, as it is scarcely conceivable that a single entity can simultaneously attend the dying all over the world. Moreover, despite centuries of bad press, the Grim Reaper's eventual arrival may not be an event to be feared. And that, as much as any other facet emerging from Mark Chorvinsky's casebook, is a very precious insight indeed.

---

*Another dramatic image of death, in Arnold Bicklin's painting "The Plague".*

# THE ECTOPLASMIC MENAGERIE OF
# FRANEK KLUSKI

DOWN THROUGH THE AGES, MANY MEDIUMS HAVE CLAIMED THAT WHEN THEY ENTER A TRANCE DURING A SEANCE THEY CAN MATERIALIZE SPIRIT FORMS COMPOSED OF ECTOPLASM – A MYSTERIOUS GELATINOUS, MILKY-COLOURED SUBSTANCE OFTEN SEEN TO EXUDE FROM THE MEDIUM'S MOUTH. IN MOST CASES, HOWEVER, SUCH MATERIALIZATIONS HAVE ULTIMATELY BEEN EXPOSED AS FRAUDULENT, BUT THERE IS AT LEAST ONE VERY NOTABLE EXCEPTION – A POLISH MEDIUM KNOWN PROFESSIONALLY AS FRANEK KLUSKI.

An engineer and writer by trade, during the first half of the twentieth century Kluski became famous for materializing all kinds of extraordinary manifestations. Some of the most spectacular took the form of animals, which could be seen, heard, touched, smelled, even photographed, before vanishing again.

---

*This photograph of a Warsaw seance on 25 December 1919 shows Kluski (second from right) and behind him the Pithecanthropus.*

For instance, he could materialize a large feathered bird, which was photographed on 30 August 1919 perching upon his shoulder with its wings outstretched, peering around at its bemused audience at a seance in Warsaw. This entity has often been described as a hawk-like or owl-like bird. In fact, it is identifiable as a nightjar – an insectivorous, highly elusive bird of nocturnal life-style also termed a goatsucker or caprimulgid, of which there are many species worldwide. Sometimes, Kluski's winged

manifestation would launch itself into the air, flying rapidly around the room and beating its wings very audibly against the ceilings and walls of the room, then abruptly vanish.

A second Kluski "creation" of equally dramatic, mercurial temperament was an animal likened by some sitters at Kluski's seances to a lioness or maneless lion. According to a report published in April 1926 by *Psychic Science*, it was tawny in colour and as large as a very big dog, with glowing feline eyes, a mouth

*Kluski's ectoplasmic bird perches on his shoulder.*

brimming with sizeable teeth, and a slender neck. Even more of an extrovert than the ectoplasmic nightjar, this curious entity enjoyed licking its human observers, with a moist prickly tongue, and also exuded a potent, palpably feline odour. Perhaps the most astonishing aspect of its materializations, however, was that even *after* the seances featuring it were over, the sitters remained "impregnated with this acrid scent as if they had made a long stay in a menagerie among wild beasts".

A third mystery animal of the materialized kind was smaller but no less remarkable. It resembled a weasel in appearance and ran freely over the table, sniffing the hands and faces of the sitters with a small cold nose.

Perhaps the most celebrated member of Kluski's menagerie, however, was the shambling humanoid figure that became known as the Pithecanthropus – in dubious deference to an ancestral species of human formerly called *Pithecanthropus* [now *Homo*] *erectus*. Colonel Norbert Ocholowicz, who attended a Kluski seance at which this being materialized, likened it in form to an ape, with low (but benevolent) intelligence and astounding strength. When documenting his observations, Ocholowicz stated: "It could easily move a heavy bookcase

filled with books through the room, carry a sofa over the heads of the sitters, or lift the heaviest persons in their chairs into the air to the height of a tall person."

Regrettably, however, reputed photos of the Pithecanthropus are somewhat less impressive, depicting a tall lumpy figure resembling a stout man wrapped in a sack with a second sack over his head. Yet according to another, very eminent eyewitness, Dr Gustav Geley – director of the Institut Metapsychique International, based in Paris – one of his fellow sitters at a seance held on 20 November 1920 felt the Pithecanthropus's large head press hard against his right shoulder and cheek, revealing that its head was covered in coarse, shaggy hair. When another sitter offered his hand, the Pithecanthropus took hold of it and licked it slowly three times with a large soft tongue. In addition, not only could this eerie entity be seen and felt, but just like the manifested lioness it could even be smelled – suffusing the room with an odour likened by the sitters to that of a deer or wet dog.

As with all of Kluski's animal materializations, however, none of his audience, which often included seriously sceptical scientific investigators, was able to detect any means by which the Pithecanthropus could have been surreptitiously introduced into the room, hidden there or removed without being detected.

Kluski was also celebrated in psychical circles for his success in providing permanent physical evidence of spirit manifestations via a highly novel technique. Upon request, he would materialize the hand or even the face of a spirit entity directly into a bowl containing molten wax, and then plunge it via psychic control into cold water – while remaining in a trance, and holding the hands of his attending sitters, throughout the procedure. The wax rapidly solidified, creating a detailed three-dimensional "glove" impression of the spirit's hand, or a macabre mask of its face. This could then be filled with plaster of Paris, yielding a

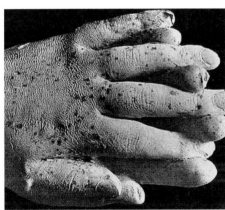

*A wax impression of spirit hands apparently created by Kluski entirely by psychic means.*

lasting mould. During these amazing activities, the sitters could clearly hear splashing sounds as Kluski psychically transferred the spirit hand or face from the wax to the water. Equally, the wrist holes of the hand moulds were so narrow that anyone attempting to create them by normal means would inevitably destroy them when trying to withdraw their own hands.

Franek Kluski died in 1949, but photos as well as hand and face moulds from various of his manifested spirit forms still survive. So far, they have continued to defy all attempts by science to expose them as hoaxes, or explain them by natural means, thus perpetuating for Kluski the title bestowed by Dr Geley upon him in the 1920s – "The King of the Mediums".

# THE SHAPELESS ONES –
# MALIGN MISTS AND FOGGY PHANTOMS

PERHAPS THE MOST MYSTERIOUS (AND TERRIFYING) CATEGORY OF ALLEGEDLY SUPERNATURAL APPARITION CAN BEST BE DESCRIBED AS A MALIGN MIST – AS DEMONSTRATED BY THE FOLLOWING SELECTION OF WEIRD, TRUE-LIFE ENCOUNTERS WITH EERIE MIST-LIKE MANIFESTATIONS THAT SEEM TO EXUDE A PALPABLE SENSATION OF EVIL, AND ARE ON RECORD FROM MANY DIFFERENT PARTS OF THE WORLD.

## EERIE IN ENGLAND

B ritish folklore contains several tales of amorphous, insubstantial entities, such as the Shetland "It" and "Boneless" from Oxfordshire. The latter is said to resemble

"... a shapeless Summat as slides behind and alongside in the dark night. Many's have died of fright through his following on. They can't never tell about him except he's a big shadow and shapeless". Judging from the next couple of

testimonies, however, there are also a number of noticeably similar reports that appear to have a firm foundation in fact.

*Mist hovers amidst the mountains of China.*

The sister-in-law of one terrified eyewitness, a Somerset policeman, gave English folklorist Ruth Tongue a concise account of his frightening encounter with one of these "boneless" entities – whose details were confirmed by Colonel Luttrell and a Mr H. Kille. One evening sometime after World War I, the policeman had been cycling on his beat along the Minehead-Bridgwater road, in the vicinity of Putsham Rise:

*... the tide was in far below – he could hear it plain down two hill fields, and then his lamp lit up a white Summat across the road. It weren't fog. It were alive – kind of woolly like a cloud or a wet sheep – and it slid up and all over him on his bike, and was gone rolling and bowling and stretching out and in up the Perry Farm Road. It was so sudden he didn't fall off – but he says it was like a wet heavy blanket and so terrible cold and smelled stale.*

The policeman was so unnerved by this hair-raising incident that he insisted upon being transferred forthwith to another district, some distance away. Intriguingly, in Shetland folktales the formless "It" is sometimes said to resemble a bag of white wool.

One September night during the 1950s, railwayman John Davies was riding his motorbike back home along a bright moonlit road leading to his cottage in Derbyshire's Longdendale Valley, a region noted for strange sightings and mystifying occurrences, when he suddenly experienced a profound desire to stop. There seemed no reason for him to do so, yet so strong was the compulsion that he braked at once. It proved a wise decision, for as he pulled up his motorbike to one side, he observed a spine-chilling sight ahead in the road. As Davies later recalled to Fortean writer David Clarke (*Fortean Times*, February 1998), it was:

*... like a big black slug sliding across t'road and up t'moor making a funny gritty noise like feet on wet gravel...as it came slowly across the road in front of me I could see it was completely black and really peculiar, like a huge whale. It had a head like a whale and white eye, with a black pupil going round and round. It disappeared and I went to have a look, but it had gone. I've been over there thousands of times but never seen anything like that before.*

Others, conversely, have indeed seen this entity. One, a friend of Davies, was afforded a view of it one night after striking a series of matches – whose glow revealed its inky form sliding across the valley below Ogden Clough, before its observer fled, panic-stricken. Another of Davies's friends encountered it in the same locality, also at night, and was certain that it was trying to follow him as he raced away. Both felt sure that it was definitely evil.

## SMOKY AND SPECTRAL, BONELESS AND BLUE

A sentry on guard in the much-haunted Tower of London one evening during 1954 observed a strange cloud of smoke that seemed to be moving quite independently of any prevailing breeze or other propulsive agents. For several minutes, he watched his nebulous visitor change shape and drift in what looked very like a purposeful, deliberate manner. But when he approached this smoky spectre, in the hope of examining it, it promptly vanished.

No one has been buried at Bachelor's Grove Cemetery in Chicago, Illinois, since 1965, but over a hundred claims of paranormal activity have been reported here, including such memorable materializations as a two-headed male ghost, a phantom farmhouse, a White Lady and a glowing blue "Boneless". According to Tony Vaci, who spied (and photographed) the latter one evening in 1974, this apparition resembled a dense and animate yet shapeless mass of glowing misty blue light. Happily, it made no attempt to envelop or pursue him.

## SAVED BY A STREET LAMP

The entity of unconstrained form met by Phyllis Duncan Brown in Australia, conversely, was unremittingly sinister. As recalled in *Fate*

*The glowing blue mist seen in Bachelor's Grove Cemetery, Chicago – captured on film.*

(February 1953), Phyllis, who was 19 at the time, was walking one evening with a Sydney University engineering student down a narrow track winding along the waterfront of Sydney Harbour's North Shore, by the water's edge. Nearing her home, they turned off this track and on to the main road, close to a street lamp.

Without warning, Brown suddenly sensed that something menacing was behind them, and at that same moment her companion asked her, in a raised, nervous voice, whether she felt anything. Before she had chance to answer, however, they were both enveloped by what she described as "a faint darkening of the air", visible against the brightness of the street lamp. Yet despite its insubstantial appearance, it weighed down upon the two of them so heavily that their knees were bent, and both felt certain that if they fell to the ground under this oppressive presence "it" would kill them. Worst of all, however, was the overpowering sense of evil that emanated from their amorphous assailant:

*Whatever it was, we were distinctly aware that it had a malign intelligence that was directed against ourselves. And there was a physical pain in the region of my heart as though I had been struck. But the very worst of all, was the encompassing sense of boundless and unclean evil. You and I have often read books with passages that describe an impression of evil. None that I have read has even touched on the quantity of this.*

Somehow, in the midst of their terror and physical labours to free themselves from this malign mist's vile embrace, they managed to push their way forward a few yards until they reached the street lamp's emanating light, and as they entered its golden glow their caliginous (smoky) foe released them. To their horror, however, they could still perceive it in the shadows outside the limits of the lamp's illumination – waiting. Fortunately, the short distance remaining to Brown's house was well-lit, enabling them to reach it safely, but as they entered inside they could see "the thing" outside, lurking in the darkness.

Brown's student colleague was petrified at the thought of confronting it again, as he would have to do in order to depart to his own home, so her family allowed him to stay overnight in their spare room. But their chilling experience was still not over. Spasmodically, all through the night, their front door resounded to the din of heavy pummelling, as if some gigantic fist were pounding upon it over and over again. And even worse was to come.

When they dared venture outside in the bright sunlight the next day, they were horrified to find dozens of dead birds on the road, which seemed to have fallen from the trees lining it – the road along which Brown and her colleague had been pursued by "the thing", shielded from its malevolent grasp only by the street lamp's light.

Although Brown never saw "the thing" again, the fear that it had generated remained with her for years. And despite media interest and documentation, no one ever did discover why all those birds had died.

*Known as "pea-soupers", clouds of dense fog were once a common sight in London, creating a sense of lurking mystery and foreboding in the city's alleys and byways.*

This is not a unique case. Many notable scientific discoveries have stemmed directly from amazing examples of creative dreaming, as illustrated by this selection of examples.

## ELEMENTARY, MY DEAR MENDELEEV

The periodic table of chemical elements utilizes these substances' atomic masses as the basis for classifying them into periods and groups. This universally accepted system of element tabulation was the brainchild – or should that be dreamchild? – of Russian chemist Dmitri Mendeleev in 1867. After many unsuccessful attempts to create an accurate means of categorizing the elements, one night Mendeleev had a vivid dream in which the periodic table that we still use today was laid out in front of him, fully constructed. When he awoke, Mendeleev could clearly recall the table's format and wrote it down straight away. In the years that followed, only one value in the table needed correcting. Initially, there were gaps in it, because no elements were known at that time which precisely exhibited some of Mendeleev's predicted properties, but all of those missing elements were indeed discovered in due course – including gallium, scandium and germanium within his own lifetime.

## A FISHY KIND OF DREAM

A similar instance of creative dreaming was experienced by Swiss-born American palaeontologist Professor Louis Agassiz. His major work *Researches On Fossil Fish* (1833–44) described and classified more than 1700 species, but during his exhaustive studies while preparing this book he experienced profound difficulties in ascertaining the structure of one particular species. One night, however, he visualized its structure in a dream – but he could not recall it when he awoke. The same frustrating scenario

Left: *Dreaming of dragons – an ourobouros makes a continuous ring.*

*Professor Louis Agassiz, whose research into fossil fish was aided by an extraordinary dream.*

took place the following night too. And so at the onset of the third night, Agassiz placed a pen and paper next to his bed, just in case he experienced this uncanny dream yet again. Happily, he did, and as soon as he woke up he jotted down the fish's structure as detailed in the dream. Although it seemed bizarre to look at, his continuing studies confirmed that the dreamed structure was wholly accurate.

## A DREAM IN TIME SAVES NINE

Now renowned as the inventor of the world's first double-thread sewing machine, back in 1844 Elias Howe had experienced a year's worth of disappointments in his attempts to design one. Then one night, he dreamed a very odd dream, in which he was fiercely confronted by a host of belligerent warriors armed with peculiar spears bearing holes shaped like eyes. The image of these spears stayed with him when he awoke, and inspired him to create the curved, eyed needle that became an integral part of his eventual stitching machine.

## A COUPLE OF SHOCKING DREAMS

A major figure in establishing the science of acoustics, German physicist Dr Ernst Chladni (1756–1827) invented several types of musical instrument, but perhaps his most

*William Blake owed his successful engraving method to a subconscious revelation.*

## ENGRAVED WITHIN A DREAM

Poet, illustrator and visionary William Blake owed much of his financial support to a vision-like dream that came to him at a time when he was experiencing severe monetary woes. He desperately needed to devise a means of inexpensive engraving, but even his extraordinary genius seemed unable to provide an answer – until he dreamed one night that his deceased brother, Robert, had visited him and had revealed to him the technique for a revolutionary new method of engraving, using copper. The next day, Blake dispatched his long-suffering wife to purchase (using most of what little money remained to them) the materials required for testing this innovative process. And, just as Robert had predicted in the dream, it proved to be a great success.

## THE DREAM THAT CHANGED THE COURSE OF WORLD WAR II?

Events in World War II may have followed a very different path had it not been for a truly memorable dream experienced in 1940 by D.B. Parkinson, an engineer at Bell Labs. At that time, he was engaged in designing a carded potentiometer, for civilian telephones. One night, however, he dreamed a strange dream in which he saw his potentiometer being put to a rather different use. After watching an Allied crew utilizing an artillery piece to shoot down German aeroplanes with unerring accuracy, Parkinson was permitted to examine the gun, and found to his surprise that mounted on to the exposed end of its left trunnion was his own potentiometer. Parkinson mentioned this dream to his fellow

celebrated example was a euphonium composed of metal and glass rods, which would vibrate when rubbed with a wet finger. The design for this ingenious instrument came to Chladni in a dream, causing him to wake at once in a state of tingling, electrified euphoria.

Even more electrifying, quite literally, was the dream experienced by eminent German physiologist Dr Otto Loewi (1873–1961). In 1936, he was a joint winner of the Nobel Prize for Physiology/Medicine, honouring his discovery that the stimulation of one neuron (nerve cell) by another is caused by a chemical substance (now known to be acetylcholine), rather than entirely by electrical means, as previously thought. Loewi attributed his discovery to a remarkable dream, in which he was presented with the design of an experiment, utilizing a frog's heart, to test this theory of chemical neurostimulation. When he awoke, he performed the experiment exactly as he had witnessed it in his dream, and duly confirmed his theory.

*A crew manning an anti-aircraft gun during World War II: remarkably, these machines owed their accuracy to an idea revealed in a dream.*

engineers at Bell Labs, who accordingly came up with a means of converting his dream into reality in the field of anti-aircraft gun control. The result was the M9 gun director, and as revealed in a *New Scientist* article (31 May 1997) documenting this extraordinary episode, in a single week in August 1944 Bell Labs' remarkable invention was deemed responsible for destroying all but two of 91 V-1 buzz bombs launched towards England from an enemy site based near Antwerp.

## NOVELS OF THE NIGHT

Nor should we overlook the many famous examples of literature inspired by dreams. Mary Shelley's classic horror story *Frankenstein* owes its origin to a peculiarly vivid nightmare that she experienced one summer evening. Robert Louis Stevenson's story *The Strange Case of Dr Jekyll and Mr Hyde* has a similar provenance: indeed, so in tune was Stevenson with his dreams as sources of inspiration that he claimed the ability to continue with dreaming one novel at the section where his previous dream had ended. Equally, Charles Dickens and H. Rider Haggard stated that many of their novels' memorable characters and plots arose Athena-style, fully formed, in daydreams and snatched bouts of dozing between writing sessions.

Perhaps the most glorious dream-derived piece of literature, however, was denied in its entirety to the world by that curse of modern-day life – the door-to-door canvasser. One evening in 1797, after sedating himself with opium while recovering from an illness, the great English poet Samuel Taylor Coleridge penned an epic poem of scintillating brilliance while asleep, drawing in his dream upon the magnificent Mongol Empire when ruled by Kubla Khan. Awakening in a state of great excitement the next morning with the many-versed poem, of some 200–300 lines in total length, still illuminated brightly in his mind, Coleridge began at once to transcribe it in written form, before the words began to fade from his memory. To the great detriment of world literature, however, he had committed only 54 lines to paper before an unwelcome caller from Porlock arrived at his house, and earnestly engaged him in trivial but protracted conversation.

An hour later, Coleridge finally succeeded in bidding him good-day, and returned to his study to continue recording his dream epic – but it was too late. No longer were the words etched in fire upon his mind; while he was detained by the Porlock procrastinator, they had dimmed and vanished, like ghosts from a bygone evening. Only the words that he had already written down survived, yielding the incomplete masterpiece known today as *Kubla Khan*, and opening with the majestic lines "In Xanadu did Kubla Khan a stately pleasure dome decree".

Many theories have been offered to explain creative dreaming, including telepathy,

*The inspiration for Coleridge's poem was the Mongol Empire of Kubla Khan.*

*Samuel Taylor Coleridge's famous poem "Kubla Khan" was composed while he slept, but remains incomplete as he was interrupted when transcribing it.*

prescience, divine influence, and contact with the spirit world. However, it is noticeable that discoveries or insights gained by a person during a bout of creative dreaming generally seem to be confined to an area of experience or knowledge in which that person is already well-versed. That is, a dream-inspired revelation experienced by a palaeontologist is concerned with palaeontology (rather than, for instance, acoustics, or engraving, or the classification of chemical elements). Hence it would appear most likely that during sleep, a person's unconscious mind is merely continuing the investigation of problems previously tackled by that person's conscious mind when he was awake. Mostly, the outcome is a jumbled, seemingly senseless muddle, but occasionally an exceptionally lucid result is achieved. Offered to the dreamer either directly or in symbolic but discernible form (as with Kekulé's ourobouros), if recalled upon waking it yields the long-sought-after solution.

# SUPERSTARS
## AND THE SUPERNATURAL

THE SUPERNATURAL WORLD IS NO STRANGER TO THE WORLD OF SHOWBUSINESS, AS REVEALED BY THIS
TRIO OF EXCEPTIONALLY STRANGE EVENTS EXPERIENCED BY FAMOUS SCREEN CELEBRITIES.

### UNEASY RIDER – BIKER ERIK AND A PRESCIENT DREAM

One of the most entertaining TV shows of the cops'n'robbers genre during the late 1970s and 1980s was "CHiPs", featuring the high-speed, not-too-serious, crime-combating antics of two motorbike cops, Frank "Ponch" Poncherello and Jon Baker, in the Californian Highway Patrol (hence "CHiPs"). This was due in no small way to the considerable popularity of Erik Estrada, who played biker Ponch throughout the show's six-year life – despite an incident that nearly brought the likeable star's own life to a tragic end.

Erik did his own biking scenes in "CHiPs", and while shooting one scene he had a very severe smash – so severe that he almost died. However, according to psychical researcher Jenny Randles in *Beyond Explanation?* (1985), while unconscious in hospital Erik underwent

*The actor Erik Estrada, who had an out-of-the-body experience after a serious accident.*

an OBE (out-of-the-body experience), in which he viewed his body, and his relatives sitting all around it, as if he were an external observer.

After deciding that he was too young to die, Erik re-entered his body and duly recovered, but this was not the only paranormal aspect of his accident. Three days before it had occurred, Erik had been telephoned unexpectedly by his mother, in a state of unease, warning him to take especial care while riding his motorbike when shooting his next scenes, because she claimed that he had visited her in a dream and she had sensed great danger for him.

### WRITTEN IN THE CLOUDS

Supernatural messages have allegedly been transmitted via many types of media, from ouija boards and planchettes to telephones and word processors. But few are any stranger than the mechanism by which Vincent Price prematurely learnt of fellow actor Tyrone Power's death.

It was November 1958 and Price was flying

from Hollywood to New York. During the flight, he idly looked out of the aeroplane window at the vista of nearby clouds, and was astonished to see what looked just like an enormous newspaper headline superimposed upon their pale fleecy forms. It consisted of bright shining letters that spelt out the message "Tyrone Power is Dead". As one might expect, Price was thoroughly bemused by this sight – and even more so once it became apparent that no one else on the aeroplane had seen it. When his plane landed, he was met by some friends; but before he was able to speak to them about his weird experience, they gave him some news of their own: sadly, his fellow actor Tyrone Power had unexpectedly died just a few hours earlier.

### RUDOLPH VALENTINO – LORD OF THE CURSED RING?

Amid jewellery of much greater value and splendour, the plain silver ring decorated only with a single semi-precious stone was decidedly

*In a scenario stranger even than those of his many films, Vincent Price witnessed an unearthly message about his fellow actor Tyrone Power.*

commonplace. Nevertheless, on that day in 1920 when no less famous a film star than the great Rudolph Valentino happened to gaze into the humble San Francisco jewellery shop's window where it was displayed alongside all of its much showier companions, it was this ring that captured his attention – so much so, in fact, that he entered the shop and informed the shopkeeper that he wished to buy it at once.

Surprisingly, however, the shopkeeper seemed reluctant to sell it, even to so illustrious a customer as Valentino. When Valentino asked why, the man informed him that the ring was cursed, having brought death or disaster to all of its previous owners. In Valentino's eyes, however, this made the ring an object of dark romance and made him even more eager to purchase it. This he did, wearing it afterwards with great zest. He also wore it while filming *The Young Rajah*, which became his first failure. He wore it again when making *The Son of the Sheik*,

which in 1926 proved to be his last film – because shortly afterwards, with this sinister ring still on his finger, he died unexpectedly of acute peritonitis.

Following Valentino's death, the ring was given to one of his Hollywood friends, actress Pola Negri. Not long after first wearing it, she too fell ill, stalling her previously successful career. After a year, her health recovered, unlike her career, which never revived again.

As for the ring, she gave it to Russ Colombo, a young singer who reminded her of Valentino. Delighted to own a ring that had once belonged to so famous a film star, Colombo wore it proudly, but briefly: he died soon afterwards in a shooting accident. The next owner of this jinxed jewellery was a friend of Colombo's called Joe Casino. Mindful of its baleful history, he placed it in a glass case, but one day he succumbed to temptation and decided to wear it, which he did, until he was killed just a week later in a traffic accident.

Only one owner of this ring seemed somehow immune to its inimical effects – Joe Casino's brother, Del, who delighted in wearing it and scoffing when reminded of its evil history. Eventually, however, he placed it inside a safe in his house, where it remained until the house was robbed by a burglar, James Willis. After inadvertently activating the house's burglar alarm, Willis tried to escape, but he was shot dead by a policeman alerted by the alarm. When they examined Willis's body, they found Valentino's ring in his pocket.

The ring was consigned once again to Casino's safe, where it remained until he

received a request from film producer Edward Small to borrow it in order for it to be worn by a young unknown called Jack Dunn, whom Small wished to screen-test for the starring role in a planned film of Valentino's life. Casino loaned Small the ring, Dunn wore it, and duly passed the screen-test, only to die less than a fortnight later of a rare, unsuspected blood disease.

This doom-laden finger band was returned once more to Casino, who decided this time to seal it away from the world inside a safe deposit box in a Los Angeles bank. As noted by Margaret Ronan, whose absorbing book *Strange Unsolved Mysteries* (1974) first publicized the macabre chain of death linked to this lethal bauble, it has remained there ever since – despite several robberies, strikes and a fire suffered by the bank since the ring's arrival!

*Rudolph Valentino's cursed ring seems to have claimed several victims.*

# WEIRD ENCOUNTERS

## ON THE WING

WINGED HUMANS SPIED IN FLIGHT, A BLATANTLY BIZARRE ENTITY APTLY DUBBED "BATSQUATCH", A
CHILEAN "BIRD" COVERED WITH SCALES AND SPORTING THE HEAD OF A LOCUST-LIKE INSECT,
PHANTASMAL BAT-LIKE HORRORS FREQUENTING THE SUMMIT OF MOUNT EVEREST – THESE ARE JUST
SOME OF THE OSTENSIBLY IMPOSSIBLE "THINGS WITH WINGS" WHOSE SHOCKED EYEWITNESSES
VEHEMENTLY AVER ARE FRIGHTENINGLY REAL, YET WHICH REMAIN RESOLUTELY UNEXPLAINED BY SCIENCE.

## A BEING CALLED BATSQUATCH

One of the most bizarre apparitions ever reported made its debut at 9.30 am on 19 April 1994. Brian Canfield, an 18-year-old high-school student, was driving a truck from Buckley to his home at Camp One in the foothills of Mount Rainier, above Lake Kapowsin in Washington State. Abruptly, for no good reason,

his truck came to a halt. Then, about 30 feet (10 metres) ahead, descending on to the road with a sizeable thud, appeared a creature of nightmare!

Standing perfectly still on its hind legs, at least 9 feet (3 metres) tall, and covered in bluish fur, it had a wolf-like face, yellow eyes with half-moon pupils, tufted ears, a large mouth well supplied with sharp white teeth

(but no fangs), bird-like feet, powerful arms and fingered hands. It also had a pair of huge wings, which lay folded behind its broad shoulders as this monstrous being gazed at the

*A visual interpretation of Brian Canfield's description of his spine-chilling encounter with a "batsquatch".*

*An image of a deva or nature spirit, found in Eastern religions – but less common in the English Lake District!*

unbelieving trucker for several minutes in a terrifying face-off.

Canfield's macabre confrontation finally ended when his astonishing visitor began twitching its fingers, then unfolded its wings, which were so enormous that they spanned the entire width of the road, and slowly took off into the air – stirring up such extensive turbulence before soaring away towards Mount Rainier that Canfield's truck rocked and swayed. Once the creature had departed, his truck inexplicably came alive again, enabling him to drive home.

Later that day, still greatly frightened but this time accompanied by his mother and a neighbour, Canfield returned to the location of his incredible encounter. He hoped to find something that could provide physical proof of his story's veracity, but was unable to do so. Notwithstanding this, his reputation for honesty and abstemious life-style were such that no one acquainted with him had any doubt that he was telling the truth. Even newspaper columnist C.R. Roberts, who interviewed him in the

*Tacoma News Tribune* (1 May), was convinced of his sincerity. As for the amazing creature seen by him, its surrealistic similarity to a bigfoot (sasquatch) incongruously sprouting a pair of bat-like wings was sufficient for the media to dub it "batsquatch" – a memorable name for a truly unforgettable entity.

## A DEVA IN THE LAKE DISTRICT

Although no further reports of batsquatch appear to have emerged, when first reading Canfield's description of it I thought of another remarkable encounter on file, which Geoffrey Hodson claimed to have experienced while visiting England's Lake District in June 1922. He later documented it in his book *Fairies at Work and at Play* (1925):

> My first impression was of a huge, brilliant crimson, bat-like thing, which fixed a pair of burning eyes upon me. The form was not concentrated into the true human shape, but was somehow spread out like a bat with a human face and eyes, and with wings outstretched over the mountainside. As soon as it felt itself to be observed it flashed into its proper shape, as if to confront us, fixed its piercing eyes upon us, and then sank into the hillside and disappeared. When first seen its aura must have covered several hundred feet of space, but in a later appearance, in which it again showed itself, the actual form was probably ten to twelve feet high.

Hodson was a Theosophist, and believed that the above entity was a deva – an elemental nature spirit. Devas advising and assisting the human workers at Findhorn in Scotland and Perelandra in the USA were deemed to be responsible for the astonishingly successful cultivation of extra-large vegetables and flowers in the gardens of these experimental spiritual communities, despite the poor quality of the soil and the adverse climate.

Could batsquatch have been a deva? In spite

of its daunting appearance, it made no attempt to harm or even threaten Canfield, merely observing him for a time before disappearing, just like the being observed by Hodson in the Lake District.

## A MONSTROUS MIXTURE FROM CHILE

In addition to publishing the more traditional genre of natural history sightings and reports, *The Zoologist*, a popular English journal of the 1800s, was not afraid to devote space to the more controversial, mystifying facets of nature too – but few were more mystifying than the following account, which it published in July 1868. Its author witnessed the entity in question three months earlier, while at a mine in Copiapó, Chile:

> Yesterday, at about five o'clock in the afternoon, when the daily labours in this mine were over, and all the workmen were together awaiting their supper, we saw

*The mystifying creature that soared over the heads of Copiapó's bemused miners.*

*Mount Everest, believed by many Tibetans to be guarded by spirits.*

*coming through the air, from the side of the ternera, a gigantic bird, which at first we took for one of the clouds then partially darkening the atmosphere, supposing it to have been separated from the rest by the wind. Its course was from north-west to south-east; its flight rapid and in a straight line. As it was passing a short distance above our heads we could mark the strange formation of its body. Its immense wings were clothed with a grayish plumage, its monstrous head was like that of a locust, its eyes were wide open and shone like burning coals; it seemed to be covered with something resembling the thick and stout bristles of a boar, while on the body, elongated like that of a serpent, we could only see brilliant scales, which clashed together with a metallic sound as the strange animal turned its body in its flight.*

Bearing in mind that this winged monstrosity was observed by all the mine workers, not just a single eyewitness, it hardly seems likely that a hoax was involved, or that a misidentification of some familiar species of bird was responsible. Mass hallucination is often offered as a solution to bizarre sightings when all else fails. Yet one would have thought that some shadowy tunnel-dwelling entity might have been a more plausible nightmare to be conjured forth by the minds of possibly over-worked, over-stressed miners; the stimulus for such men to espy a locust-headed, scaly-bodied, serpentine bird can scarcely be conceived.

## THE PHANTOMS OF EVEREST

The Tibetans refer to Mount Everest, the world's tallest mountain, as the Throne of the Gods. Few, moreover, choose to ascend to its summit, because they believe that spirit entities fiercely guard the sanctity of this rarefied zone at the rooftop of the world.

Perhaps they do. Certainly, mountaineer Frank Smythe is someone with an Everest-related experience that gave him cause to reflect upon these traditional local beliefs. In 1933, as later recounted by him in *Kingdom of Adventure, Everest*, Smythe was engaged upon his first of three Everest expeditions. On the day in question, he had been climbing alone, as his partner had fallen ill and turned back. Later that day, having ascended to within 1000 feet (300 metres) of the summit, Smythe too began to make his way back, climbing down towards Camp Six. At such an altitude the air was very thin, and he struggled manfully, gasping for breath in this oxygen-impoverished zone, unobserved and alone – or was he?

Suddenly, half-hidden in the swirling mist, Smythe perceived two eldritch apparitions, hovering silently and motionless in the sky above the north-east shoulder of Everest. Dark in colour and shaped like kites, both of them were enormous, and at least one seemed to have a pair of wings, like a giant phantom bat. They also appeared to have beaks. Most unnerving of all, however, was that their bloated bodies were pulsating, as if they were breathing.

Sitting in the snow and scrutinizing these weird entities in spite of his disbelief at what he was seeing, Smythe attempted to rationalize them as optical illusions engendered by a potent combination of mental stress and anoxia (oxygen starvation). Yet although he tested his own reactions via a number of standard methods in the hope of exposing these twin terrors as mere hallucinations, they refused to be dispelled. Only when the mist eventually swept over them and concealed them thereafter from his view did Smythe finally lose sight of their eerie presence. He never saw them again and remained unconvinced that they were the result of hallucinations.

Encounters with purportedly paraphysical beings at lofty altitudes have been reported by climbers from a number of other mountains around the world too. One of the most famous is Ben MacDhui in the Scottish Cairngorms, which, according to numerous reports, is alleged to be frequented by a malevolent paranormal presence known as Am Fear Liath Mor – the Big Grey Man. And one might expect seasoned, professional mountaineers to be readily adept at recognizing the difference between the hallucinatory effects of anoxia and the presence of a bona fide entity.

## ALOFT WITH A DRAGON

Perhaps the most bizarre high-altitude encounter on record is one that appeared in an article published by the *Occult Review* (December 1917). Written by someone referring to himself only as "A Philosophical Aviator", the article presented the recollections of an unnamed correspondent described as an experienced World War I pilot. According to the philosophical aviator, while flying his aeroplane at a considerable height this pilot had supposedly spied on several occasions a quite literally unearthly apparition that he described as "a curious coloured dragon-like animal apparently floating in the air", and which approached him at a rapid speed. Not surprisingly, the pilot made haste in descending back to earth.

This extraordinary incident was discussed in a fascinating article on aerospatial anomalies (*Fortean Times*, winter 1982) by Fortean investigator Nigel Watson, who suggested that the pilot was probably suffering from oxygen deficiency. However, there are two other possible factors to be considered here. First, as neither the pilot himself nor the author of the article presenting his recollections was identified, the prospect of a hoax cannot be ruled out.

Secondly, this episode bears a strong resemblance to the basic plot of a memorable short story by Sir Arthur Conan Doyle called "The Horror of the Heights", first published only six years earlier by the *Strand Magazine* (November 1913). In this fictional account, a pilot ascending to a great altitude in his plane is astonished to discover that the sky's upper reaches are inhabited by a diverse host of gigantic, exclusively airborne life-forms, including gargantuan sky medusae and huge varieties of vaporous aerial serpents not dissimilar in appearance from some depictions of the fabled Chinese dragon.

## THE BIRD-MEN OF BROOKLYN

*New York Times* readers were given a brief respite from mundane reality and offered a tantalizing glimpse of veritable surreality on 12 September 1880, when their daily newspaper carried the following report:

*One day last week, a marvellous apparition was seen near Coney Island [part of Brooklyn]. At the height of at least 1000 feet [300 metres] in the air a strange object was in the act of flying toward the New Jersey coast. It was apparently a man with bat's wings and improved frog's legs. The face of the man could be distinctly seen and it wore a cruel and determined expression. The movements made by the object closely resembled those of a frog in the act of swimming with his hind legs and flying with his front legs ... When we add that this monster waved his wings in answer to the whistle of a locomotive and was of a deep black color, the alarming nature of the apparition can be imagined. The object was seen by many reputable persons and they all agree that it was a man engaged in flying toward New Jersey.*

*Ben MacDhui in the Cairngorms is another mountain with ghostly associations.*

*Flying dragons are a familiar feature in the legends and folklore of China.*

It would have been good to know the names of those "many respectable persons" who reputedly spied this frog-legged bat-man during his aerial activity, and also to ascertain the means by which they observed it – given that a distance of 1000 feet does not typically enable an eyewitness to discern a person's features even on the ground, let alone those of someone soaring overhead in the sky. Having said that, it should be noted that a Mr W. Smith wrote a letter to the *New York Sun* in which he detailed his sighting of what he termed a winged human form flying over Brooklyn on 18 September 1877. Several other reports are on file from North America of flying humanoids, but these were generally rendered airborne by various mysterious contraptions strapped to them, rather than with the assistance of wings.

In *The Complete Guide To Mysterious Beings* (1994), veteran anomalies researcher John Keel refers to winged men rather delightfully as *Homo avis* – "bird man" – and suggests that they may be responsible for many stories of angels during the past two millennia. Whether or not winged men do indeed have a heavenly link may be debatable, but one thing is certain – they clearly do not fall into any orthodox zoological category native to planet Earth.

## GONZWELL VS. MR GONZWELL

This final report, which has not previously appeared in print, is presented with no comment – other than to say that it was passed on to me by a reliable correspondent who spotted it on an online "mysteries" message board in 1997, and contains the familiar elements common to many paranormal "bedroom invader" scenarios, i.e. hypnotic gaze and disturbing ability to render its observers mute and immobile without involving any physical contact. Neither my correspondent nor I have been able to uncover any details regarding its author or veracity:

*During the early 1950s to 1964 [while living in the Bronx, New York City] before our family moved into The Butler Houses Complex, among the many visitations we had was a creature that me and my younger brother Ralph called a Gonzwell [which] would come and stand on the roof outside our bedroom window and stare in at us. Sometimes it entered the room. It was dark grey and seemed to have very smooth feathers or fur and was like a cross between an ostrich, a bat, a huge bird, and a man. What was ostrich about it was it seemed to be able to stretch its neck when it wanted to get close to your face and look into your eyes. I don't know if this was a physical thing it could do, or an illusion it projected. For sometimes it seemed it would not leave the roof but somehow put only its head into the room right up in your face but you had to look into its eyes first, it seemed, before it could do that. It had huge reflective fish eyes that seemed to at times [shimmer like?] mother of pearl from red to yellow, or green. I can't say if the light was reflected or projected but it was hypnotic. It seemed to only come during the warmer months and when the moon was out. If it came at any other times we did not see it for, because of the bed factory roof outside our window, very little light reached our room from the street. Once you looked into those eyes you no longer could move or even scream. We called this thing Mr. Gonzwell when it took on the more human form and a Gonzwell when it manifested in its more birdbat like form. It never ever looked totally human though, only humanoid. Of course when we spoke to our parents of it we were told it was a nightmare, and rightly so. If you wake up the next morning in bed, it had to be a dream, right? It was not until the seventies that I first heard of a creature that somewhat fit the Gonzwell's description. It was in a book called* The Mothman Prophecies *by John Keel I think the author's name*

was [this book concerns a series of eerie visitations by a bizarre red-eyed winged entity dubbed Mothman to Point Pleasant, West Virginia, during the 1960s]. So I am left asking was it a dream or not, this creature that would come to stand outside our bedroom window and gaze in at us?

Dream or reality? Fiction or fact? Make of it what you will!

In his guide to mysterious beings, Keel offers a thought-provoking opinion that may be relevant not only to the apparitions featured in this item's winged encounters of the weird kind but also to many others that I have documented in this present section:

*There is something out there that we can't see except under special conditions. We probably never see It in its real form. We see only what It wants us to see, filtered through our conscious and unconscious minds, manipulated into forms that are acceptable to our particular belief systems. If we are young and living in a*

*Seen flying over New Jersey in 1880, this weird entity was described as part man, part bat and part frog – an aerial amalgamation of spare parts!*

---

*Catholic community, It becomes a BVM [Blessed Virgin Mary vision]. If we are atheistic and immersed in science and technology, It appears in a mechanical-looking contrivance in the guise of a being from some distant galaxy.*

Or perhaps a batsquatch, a winged man, even an insect-headed scaly bird – who can say?

# EDEN

## WHERE WAS THE GARDEN OF GOD?

HOME TO ADAM AND EVE BEFORE THEIR EXPULSION BY GOD AS PUNISHMENT FOR BEING TEMPTED BY THE SERPENT TO EAT THE FRUIT FROM THE TREE OF KNOWLEDGE OF GOOD AND EVIL, THE IDYLLIC GARDEN OF EDEN IS DESCRIBED IN THE BIBLE (GENESIS 2:8–15) AS FOLLOWS:

*And the Lord God planted a garden eastward in Eden; and there he put the man whom he had formed.*

*And out of the ground made the Lord God to grow every tree that is pleasant to the sight, and good for food; the tree of life also in the midst of the garden, and the tree of knowledge of good and evil.*

*And a river went out of Eden to water the garden; and from thence it was parted, and became into four heads.*

*The name of the first is Pison: that is it which compasseth the whole land of Havilah, where there is gold;*

*And the gold of that land is good: there is bdellium and the onyx stone.*

*And the name of the second river is Gihon: the same is it that compasseth the whole land of Ethiopia [=Cush; not to be confused with modern-day Ethiopia, a totally separate region].*

*And the name of the third river is Hiddekel: that is it which goeth toward the east of Assyria. And the fourth river is Euphrates.*

*And the Lord God took the man, and put him into the garden of Eden to dress it and to keep it.*

The river Hiddekel is known today as the Tigris, but what of the rivers Pison (also spelt "Pishon") and Gihon? Do they exist too? Through the centuries, theologians, geographers and archaeologists have united in their efforts to identify these missing rivers and, in so doing, relocate the Garden of Eden itself. Many theories have been aired in the process.

The most popular, and plausible, location is in southern Iraq, specifically at Sumer (lower Mesopotamia, between Babylon and the

Above: *"Paradise" by Lucas Cranach the Elder (1530); the painting depicts Adam and Eve in the Garden of Eden.*

*The idyll of Eden – Roeland Savery's seventeenth-century painting entitled "Paradise".*

Persian Gulf), where the Tigris and Euphrates unite. As for the other two, missing rivers, these may simply have been tributaries that have since dried up. The land of Cush is deemed by some scholars to have been situated somewhere in present-day Iran, in the vicinity of a dried-out gully called Wadi Karun, which unites with the Tigris and Euphrates at the Persian Gulf's head. Could this once have been the Gihon?

Further support for this notion was obtained in 1993 when satellite photography revealed that a dry Iraqi riverbed called Wadi Batin, which runs directly into the head of the Persian

Gulf where the Tigris, Euphrates and the Iranian gully Wadi Karun unite, has a long dried-out underground river hidden beneath it, which extends to the mountains of Hijaz. Researchers believe that this dead river may be the vanished Pison. Some claim that a second Iraqi gully here, Wadi Rimah, may also be a vestige of the Pison.

Based upon this information, Dr Juris Zarins of Southwest Missouri State University has concluded that today the Garden of Eden may in reality be submerged beneath the Persian Gulf. His theory is supported by palaeontological and archaeological evidence showing that many millennia ago this was a lush, fertile region of land.

Iraqi scholars, however, favour a terrestrial

site near Al Quma, again at the confluence of the Tigris and Euphrates, in marshland about 45 miles (72 km) north of Basra. Here, the petrified remains of a large tree claimed in local legends to be from the Garden of Eden can be seen. These legends also state that the readily visible wavy line where those two rivers unite, yielding the Shatt al Arab, was made by the serpent when it departed from the Garden.

As for the land of Havilah, this has traditionally been identified with the Arabian Peninsula. Moreover, there is a specific Arabian site known as Mahd edh-Dhahab ("Cradle of Gold") that is situated near the Hijaz mountains and is famed for its high-quality deposits of gold – as claimed for the land encircled by the Pison in the Genesis account.

Conversely, there is also a quite different school of opinion that, although in agreement with the placement of Havilah within the Arabian Peninsula, believes the Garden of Eden to have been situated in what is today the land of Israel. Pursuing this premise, the river that flowed into it must have been the river Jordan, and the Gihon was actually the river Nile.

Additional Middle Eastern localities proposed for the Garden of Eden include Egypt and Turkey, but there are still others that have been suggested which lie far beyond Asia Minor. Take, for instance, the Seychelles archipelago – a site favoured by no less famous a figure in history than General Charles George Gordon. He arrived at this intriguing conclusion after visiting the island of Praslin during a survey for the British government in 1881, where he was amazed by the idyllic scenery and tranquillity of the Vallée de Mai. Furthermore, this island is also noted for the extraordinary coco-de-mer *Lodoicea maldivica* (=*seychellarum*).

A rare species of palm tree, it is famed for its enormous seeds, resembling double coconuts, which are the world's largest seeds – growing up to 15 inches (38 cm) long, and weighing up to 33 lb (15 kg). Found elsewhere only on Curiense, another island in the Seychelles group, this exotic tree was deemed by Gordon to be none other than Eden's celebrated Tree of Knowledge:

> *As we generally believe that there was a tree*
> *of Knowledge of Good and Evil, and a tree of*
> *life, actual trees set aside for a time to be*
> *imbued with mystic powers, there is no*
> *reason why these trees should not exist now*
> *… relegated back to ordinary trees.*

Even further from the Middle East than the Seychelles is Sinkiang in China. Nevertheless, noting that the river Tarim has four tributaries flowing eastward, in his book *The Creation, the Real Situation of Eden, and the Origin of the Chinese* (1914) scholar Tse Tsan Tai nominated Chinese

Turkestan in the plateau of eastern Asia as Eden's true original site.

Similarly, pointing out that the Apalachicola River is today the world's only four-headed river system, and that high-quality deposits of gold, onyx and bdellium are indeed to be found nearby, American Baptist minister Elvy E. Calloway has claimed that the Garden of Eden was situated on the banks of the Apalachicola, a mile east of Bristol, in Florida!

Other locations proposed in the past include Java, India, East Africa, Galesville in Wisconsin, the lost continent of Lemuria – and Mars! The most recent investigation, however, has focused once more upon the Middle East.

After conducting three expeditions in search of the likely site of the Garden of Eden, in his book *Legend: The Genesis of Civilisation* (1998) English scholar David Rohl has postulated that Eden itself was a sizeable mountainous region around two extremely large lakes, Urmia and Van (Turkey's biggest lake), on the borders of Iran, Iraq and Turkey – hence within the traditional land of the Kurdish people. And its divine Garden, planted by God, is, according to Rohl, a 200-mile- (320-km) long valley east of Lake Urmia, watered by the river Adji-Chay, and surrounded by tall snow-capped mountains.

Within this valley are verdant vineyards and orchards. Truly an idyllic spot – or at least it would be, but halfway along this same valley is the Iranian city of Tabriz, encompassed by industry and its associated atmospheric pollution. However, Rohl notes that this is only to be expected, for as revealed in the Bible, the Garden of Eden was lost to humanity after Adam and Eve were banished. What we are seeing, therefore, is the post-Adamite Garden of Eden, not as it was when still inhabited by Adam and Eve. There's a moral in there somewhere.

*The end of an idyll – "Expulsion from Paradise", a woodcut by Julius Schnorr von Carolsfeld.*

# THE HAND OF
# FIRE

SELDOM (IF EVER?) MENTIONED IN POPULAR-FORMAT BOOKS DEALING WITH THE UNEXPLAINED, BUT KNOWN TO SPECIALIST RESEARCHERS OF MYSTERIOUS RELIGIOUS PHENOMENA, IS THE EXISTENCE OF SACRED BOOKS AND OTHER ITEMS THAT BEAR SCORCHED FIERY HANDPRINTS, TRADITIONALLY CLAIMED TO HAVE BEEN MADE BY SPIRITS OF THE DEAD WHILE SUFFERING IN PURGATORY.

Perhaps the most famous hand of fire case features a holy book called the Kada Codex. As recalled in a detailed account by Dr Ervin Bonkalo (*Fate*, June 1953), this curious episode began in April 1696, when, for several nights, the monks at the Calasantine monastery in Privigye, North Hungary, were disturbed by strange noises, disruption of their belongings by an unseen presence, and other signs of poltergeist-like activity.

Seeking an answer to this mysterious invasion of their retreat, Father Franciscus Hanacius finally succeeded in confronting the invisible presence in his cell, where, on a small table, he had placed a valuable book of Bible stories. The unseen presence turned the pages of

*Nickell's photograph of his self-prepared "hand of fire" image, as featured in his book* Looking For A Miracle.

the book, stopping at page 100. When visiting Father Hanacius a second time a few nights later, it identified itself as the late Stephen Kada, Bishop of Erdely and North Hungary, who had often rested at Hanacius's monastery, and had died in 1695. Kada stated that his soul had since been burning for 100 days in Purgatory – a realm of temporary punishment where the souls of the departed suffer until purged of their sin, according to certain schools of religious belief – and besought Hanacius to celebrate a Holy Mass over his grave at the town of Nagyszombat, and to pray for the release of his soul from Purgatory.

Hanacius, however, desired proof that the unseen presence was truly Bishop Kada, and not some evil entity impersonating his voice. In response, the presence reminded Hanacius that the devil has no power over sacred books, then commanded him to look at the book of Bible

stories on the table. Hanacius looked, and as he did so, he saw smoke and smelt the stench of burning leather rising up from the book, which now bore the scorched impression of a man's hand burnt through the book's leather cover and its first hundred pages. Remarkably, however, there was no trace of burning on page 101, which was on the opposite side of the sheet of paper bearing page 100. Convinced of the presence's veracity, Hanacius did as it had requested, celebrating Holy Mass over Bishop Kada's grave on 13 April.

All of this could be discounted as a fanciful myth of long ago, were it not for the fact that the hand-scorched book, subsequently dubbed the Kada Codex, really did exist – until as recently as 1952, when, ironically, it was destroyed by a fire, at the convent of Cinta in Portugal where it had been transferred with other relics in 1947.

Prior to its destruction, however, the Kada Codex had inspired many years of extensive research by historian Dr E. Friedreich, one of several participants at the first official investigation of this enigmatic relic, in 1903, a year after the codex had initially come to public attention. Scientific authorities attending the 1903 meeting included an anthropologist, a paper expert and various archaeologists. This engendered sufficient interest for Friedreich to stage a second meeting, in 1913, composed of historians, library experts and clergymen, but none was able to explain how one side of a paper sheet could bear a scorched hand impression while the other side of the same sheet remained unmarked. And confirming that the Kada Codex had not always borne the fiery handprint, Leopold Kollonits from Vienna had revealed in 1903 that this book had been presented to the monks at Privigye in 1667, for use in their school, and had been described in a letter from that period as being brand new.

Further investigations of the Kada Codex were planned, but were shelved indefinitely when World War I began in 1914. Nevertheless, in 1938, Dr Friedreich convened a meeting at which many of the original 1903 committee members were invited, as well as Dr Bonkalo, and he revealed the codex's above-recounted history, as pieced together by him during his own private, continuing studies. Tragically, this book's destruction just over a decade later has prevented further researches, but other hand-of-fire cases are also on record, including several discussed in a more recent *Fate* article (June 1981), by Georg Siegmund.

In a church in Germany's Saarland is a missal containing scorched fingermarks, said to have been made by the soul of a deceased priest in order to mark out selected passages during celebration of a Mass for that priest. The library of the dean of Hall in the Tyrol contains a sixteenth-century book of sermons bearing a sharp fiery thumbprint that has scorched through the book's leather cover and its first 64 pages. And maintained behind a protective grille in the chapel of St Romedius in the castle of Thaur, Austria, is a wooden box containing paper flowers, at the bottom of which is the charred impression of a hand.

This image supposedly appeared one evening in October 1659, in response to the chapel's hermit hearing the ghostly lamentations of his late colleague, Father Georg Meringer, priest of Thaur, and asking for confirmation that the voice was genuine. During his life, Father Meringer had forgotten to celebrate two Masses that had been paid for and his soul was now suffering in Purgatory, but when the hermit learnt this from Meringer's voice he celebrated the two Masses and Meringer appeared to him, confirming that his soul had been delivered.

An oddly shaped hand of fire occurred in a small eighteenth-century prayer book owned by a Czech family, the Hackenbergs, whose scorched impression begins on page 18 and penetrates through the 10 previous, intervening sheets to the front cover. According to an old account preserved by the family, this hand of fire manifested itself after a Hackenberg returned from a pilgrimage that he had promised his late father he would undertake. Falling asleep afterwards during his morning prayers, he dreamed a dream in which his dead father joyfully informed him that his pilgrimage had delivered him from Purgatory and that as a sign of his deliverance he would leave a scorched handprint in his son's prayer book. When the son awoke, he saw that a scorched handprint had indeed appeared in his book – at the precise location of the morning prayer.

In his absorbing, eye-opening book *Looking For A Miracle* (1993), former stage magician Dr Joe Nickell investigated the prosaic reality that may lie behind many supposed miracles and religious marvels. Turning his attention to the hand-of-fire phenomenon, he pointed out various inconsistencies present within the histories of some of the most famous examples.

In the Hackenberg case, Nickell notes that although the scorched handprint was supposed to have been produced by the soul of an adult man, the print itself was no larger than a child's hand, which was necessary if the handprint were to fit the prayer book as the latter was only very small. In Nickell's view: "The scaling of the size of the hand to fit the page is a detail that points to an amateurish forger; so is the crudeness of the anatomy ... since both the thumb and little finger appear proportionately too long." Indeed, the handprint's fingers give the appearance of being composed solely of bones, which, as Nickell explained, "would be consistent with a hot cast-metal 'hand' which, unlike a real human hand, failed to flatten slightly when pressed, instead remaining rigid so that a lesser surface area imprinted".

Indeed, in testing how easily a hand of fire print could be created artificially, Nickell produced a very eyecatching example himself by tracing a child's hand on to a sheet of brass, cutting it out, heating it on a stove, and then placing it on to a page within a book.

Dismissing as a fake for obvious reasons a German cloth bearing a fiery handprint containing six fingers, Nickell also viewed with scepticism the scorched missal from Saarland – rightly questioning why only the selected passages were burnt, when the margins of the book, which the Purgatory-inflamed soul of the priest would need to have touched in order to turn to the required pages, remained entirely unscathed.

As with many other alleged wonders and miracles, hoaxing is likely to be responsible for at least some of the hand-of-fire examples on record. But what of the Kada Codex, in which one side of a single paper sheet bore the scorched handprint and the opposite side of the same sheet bore nothing? Nickell does not mention this particular case in his coverage of the hand-of-fire phenomenon, which is a great pity, because of all the examples on file, this one offers the greatest challenge to researchers seeking mundane explanations.

# THE NEPHILIM

## A BIBLICAL MYSTERY OF GIANT PROPORTIONS

SOMETIMES TERMED "THE SONS OF GOD", AND SAID TO HAVE MATED WITH "THE DAUGHTERS OF MAN", WHO – OR WHAT – WERE THE NEPHILIM, AND WERE THEY TRULY ONE AND THE SAME AS THE SONS OF GOD?

One of the most mystifying passages of the Bible appears in the Book of Genesis (6:1–4), and reads in the Revised Standard Version (RSV) as follows:

*When men began to multiply on the face of the ground, and daughters were born to them,*

*the sons of God saw that the daughters of men were fair; and they took to wife such of them as they chose.*

*Then the Lord said, "My spirit shall not abide in man for ever, for he is flesh, but his days shall be a hundred and twenty years."*

*The Nephilim were on the earth in those days, and also afterward, when the*

*sons of God came in to the daughters of men, and they bore children to them. These were the mighty men that were of old, the men of renown.*

As will be seen, several different identities have been offered during centuries of profound theological controversy and discussion regarding the Nephilim and the sons of God.

Before we can entertain any thoughts concerning these identities, however, it is important to examine the origin and meaning of this problematical Genesis passage (hereafter referred to for convenience as the Nephilim Passage).

Notwithstanding the tradition that Moses wrote the entire Pentateuch (the first five books

of the Old Testament), most modern-day biblical scholars believe, as noted by N.H. Snaith in *The Century Bible* (1967), that this quintet is a compilation of at least five different sources. The earliest is the Jehovist (Yahwist) document (designated as J), dating back to c.850 BC, of southern origin, and split by later scholars into $J^1$ and $J^2$. Next is the Elohist document (E), dating back to c.750 BC, of northern origin, and combined in c.700 BC with J to yield the JE document. They are the documents most relevant to the subject of the Nephilim.

In addition, there are numerous different translations of these, which means that the

---

*"Ascension of Enoch" – a detail from the Verdun Altar of 1181 in Neuberg Monastery, Lower Austria.*

# SAINTLY TALENTS

DOWN THROUGH THE CENTURIES, MANY SAINTS HAVE BEEN ACCREDITED OR ASSOCIATED WITH SEEMINGLY INEXPLICABLE, MIRACULOUS FEATS. SOME OF THESE, SUCH AS SEEING VISIONS, INCORRUPTIBILITY AFTER DEATH, LEVITATION, EXUDING THE ODOUR OF SANCTITY AND DEVELOPING STIGMATA, ARE WELL KNOWN AND HAVE BEEN EXTENSIVELY DOCUMENTED (SEE MY BOOK "THE UNEXPLAINED" FOR VARIOUS CASES). OTHERS, CONVERSELY, SUCH AS THOSE SURVEYED HERE, ARE FAR LESS FAMILIAR, BUT NO LESS EXTRAORDINARY.

## I HAVE NO FEAR OF THE FLAME AND THE FIRE

St Polycarp of Smyrna, St Francis of Paola, St Catherine of Siena and Anne of Jesus among others shared a remarkable gift – for according to traditional lore, all of these devout figures were inexplicably immune to the scorching, death-dealing power of fire.

St Polycarp was Bishop of Smyrna in Turkey during the second century AD, but in 155 AD he was sentenced to death for denying the divinity of the Roman emperor ruling Smyrna at that time. The elderly bishop was tied to a stake and set alight by his captors, but reputedly remained entirely unscathed by the roaring flames encompassing him. Tragically, however, not even his fiery immunity could save St Polycarp from the wrath of the emperor, who instructed the executioner to stab him to death instead.

St Francis of Paola, who was born during the 1400s and canonized in 1519, achieved great fame on account of his incredible ability to handle red-hot or fiery objects with total impunity. On one occasion, he held a large chunk of red-hot iron in his hands in order, so he claimed, to warm himself. On another occasion, he prevented the

*St Catherine of Siena was one of several devout Christians who were allegedly immune to the effects of fire.*

spread of flames by using his bare feet to keep them at bay. And he provided a breathtaking demonstration of his astonishing power when tested by two church dignitaries – by plunging his hands into the heart of a blazing fire and pulling out some fiery coals and burning sticks.

Once, during the fourteenth century, it seemed as if St Catherine of Siena had come to an untimely end, because while experiencing a bout of religious ecstasy she inadvertently fell into a blazing fire in her convent's kitchen. When one of the other nuns came in and found St Catherine lying upon the fire's burning coals, she was horrified, fearing that she must surely be dead. Yet when she pulled St Catherine's body from the flames, she was delighted but astounded to find that neither her body nor even her clothes were in any way burnt.

Saints are not the only examples on record of "human salamanders". As recalled by John Michell and Robert J.M. Rickard in *Phenomena* (1977), a young woman called Lily White, from Liberta in the Caribbean island of Antigua, featured in American newspaper reports during the 1920s. This was due to the alarming but frequent tendency of her clothes to burst unexpectedly into flames and burn to cinders in seconds, leaving a highly embarrassed Ms White totally naked but always completely unharmed.

During the early 1920s, a 13-year-old boy and his mother were hounded from their home in Budapest, Hungary, by frightened neighbours. This was because they feared the boy's very presence after having watched in horror as flames appeared from nowhere while he slept, flickered all over his body, and burnt his bedclothes, but left him totally unharmed. And New York medical physician Dr K.R. Wissen unveiled a veritable modern-day St Francis of Paola, when he wrote about a backwoods boy encountered by him in Tennessee in 1927 who was able to pick up red-hot firebrands in his bare hands without suffering the slightest injury.

Such cases as these are instantly reminiscent of present-day feats of fire-walking, a technique

that seems to rely very heavily upon a person's mental state as well as his physical capabilities. For even experienced firewalkers can apparently burn their feet if they have failed to psyche themselves up sufficiently before taking their strolls across the coals. Clearly, then, they do not possess the "asbestos skin" that many would have us believe!

And in cases featuring persons emitting flames but without burning themselves, this may conceivably be associated with abnormally high levels of static electricity generated by their bodies. Similarly, some people are notorious for shorting any electrical equipment that they touch, or even approach. The mystery of why the flames that they generate can burn their clothes but do not burn their flesh, however, remains unanswered. Intriguingly, this literally constitutes a precisely converse phenomenon to that of spontaneous human combustion, in which a person mystifyingly bursts into flames and is utterly consumed, whereas his clothes often remain untouched by the flames.

## THE FIRE OF LOVE, AND THE DIVINE LIGHT

St Stanislaus Kostka and St Philip Neri were two sixteenth-century saints who displayed an equally anomalous heat-related condition, termed incendium amoris, or the fire of love.

Filled with such profound religious love for their Saviour that their body temperature soared as if fever-ridden, they were often obliged to apply cloths soaked in icy water to their bodies, or even to walk bare-chested on snowy days, in order to quench their internal furnace. Sometimes they would faint from the intensity of this incendium amoris, and even on the coldest of winter nights the windows of St Philip Neri's room were left open and his bed made cool in order for him to sleep.

An analogous phenomenon occurs with Tibetan lamas undergoing tumo, whereby they are able to raise their body temperature dramatically by will-power alone in order to sit

naked all night on a freezing mountain lake wrapped in a robe that has been dipped in the lake's chilling water. They can even dry this robe several times using their elevated body warmth.

St Lydwina of Schiedam, who died in 1433 AD, was frequently engulfed too, though not by fire but by divine light. Often, according to biographer Thomas à Kempis:

> *... she was discovered by her companions to be surrounded by so great a divine brightness that, seeing the splendour and struck with exceeding fear, they dared not approach nigh to her. And although she always lay in darkness and material light was unbearable to her eyes, nevertheless, the divine light was very agreeable to her, whereby her cell was often so wondrously flooded by night that to the beholders the cell itself appeared full of material lamps or fires.*

Another famous example of a holy human glow-worm was Father Bernardino Realino, who died in 1616. Many people averred that

*Moses's face was said to radiate light when he descended from Mount Sinai. (Woodcut after drawing by Gustave Doré.)*

they had seen his face glow so brightly that they had been forced to turn away in order to shield their eyes from its radiance (a scenario recalling Moses's glowing face when returning to the Israelites after speaking with God on Mount Sinai). Some also claimed to have seen sparks shooting forth from all over his body.

Again, many secular examples, including some from modern times, of this remarkable phenomenon of human radiance are also on record. Theories offered as explanations have included the emission of electromagnetic radiation by certain compounds in the glowing person's skin, and even the presence of luminous bacteria feeding on nutrients in sweat.

## SIGHTS FOR SORE EYES – AND SORE HEADS?

Owing to the fact that her name translates as "light", St Clare of Assisi is the patron saint of people with sore eyes. Bearing in mind that she lived over 700 years ago, however, it may not appear immediately obvious to everyone why, in 1958, Pope Pius XII also declared her to be the patron saint of television.

The explanation lies in her visionary abilities, and, in particular, with regard to the marvellous vision that she experienced one Christmas Eve as she lay ill in bed at her convent. For suddenly she experienced a vivid vision, in which she witnessed – with extraordinary accuracy, as later confirmed – the Christmas Mass taking place at a church situated at the opposite side of Assisi from where, in her own convent, she was lying. Indeed, it was almost as if she had been viewing the Mass on television – thereby explaining Pope Pius XII's decision to install her as patroness of this modern-day source of visions.

And speaking of visions: there are innumerable recorded accounts of saints, other holy persons and ordinary people alike experiencing visions of Jesus, angels and other religious figures. However, the most astonishing visions of all must surely be those of Hildegarde of Bingen, a German mystic from the twelfth

*A sixteenth-century Flemish roundel in St John's Church, Rownhams, Hampshire, depicting St Clare of Assisi.*

*Hildegarde of Bingen claimed to have experienced blinding visions that gave her remarkable mental powers.*

century AD. During her remarkable life, Hildegarde claimed to have experienced breathtaking visions of Heaven itself, whose blinding light flowed through her entire brain, instantly elucidating for her the writings of philosophers and seers, and enabling her to write extensively upon the most esoteric scientific and moral matters, compose music of extraordinary beauty, and become a valued advisor to popes and rulers.

And of especial note is that whereas most visionaries enter a trance in order to perceive their visions, Hildegarde saw hers while fully awake.

However, her heavenly visions, often featuring what she termed "stars and flaming eyes", were invariably accompanied by extreme physical debilitation. This has led some modern-day medical specialists to suggest a rather more prosaic explanation for them. Namely, the products of migraine, with her "stars and flaming eyes" possibly comprising the flashes of light (phosphenes) seen even with the eyes closed during severe headaches.

## BILOCATION: HOW TO BE IN TWO PLACES AT ONCE

According to the Catholic tradition, saints and other devout persons can possess the consciously controlled ability to be physically present in two widely separate locations simultaneously – a thoroughly baffling phenomenon known as bilocation.

In 1742, for instance, the Catholic Church formally confirmed that St Martin de Porres (1579–1639) had made "impossible" appearances in countries as far-distant from Europe as China and Japan. This declaration was based upon many reports that a mysterious figure, a dark friar matching St Martin's appearance, had often been seen working in these lands. Of course, sceptics may claim that there was no conclusive proof that this dark friar was truly St Martin, and they do have a valid point.

Far less easy to dismiss, conversely, is the evidence for possibly the most famous exponent of bilocation – a seventeenth-century Spanish Franciscan nun called Sister Maria Coronel de Ágreda. For although she spent her whole life within her Spanish convent, she was also reported more than 500 times in North and Central America, where the Spanish Catholic Church was expanding its missionary work. Described by eyewitnesses there as a "lady in blue", she appeared during the day and taught Christianity to the Jumano Indians of New Mexico, but always vanished again at night.

While working at the Isolita Mission in New Mexico, Father Alonzo de Benavides had collected many such stories, which so greatly perplexed him that he sought out Sister Maria

when in 1630 he returned to Spain. To his even greater surprise, he discovered not only that she freely admitted visiting this region of the New World via bilocation, but also that she was inexplicably knowledgeable concerning the area. She was even well-versed in the local names of places and people there – all of which were entirely unknown to people outside the Americas at that time. Most amazing of all, however, as also exposed by Father Benavides, was that a chalice used at Mass by Jumano Indians claiming to have been converted by the mysterious "lady in blue" had indeed come from Sister Maria's convent in Ágreda!

Another saint seemingly gifted with the power of bilocation was St Antony of Padua. During Easter 1226 in Limoges, France, St Antony performed the incredible feat of kneeling in prayer in full view of his parishioners in the Church of St Pierre du Queyroix while *simultaneously* reading a lesson in the presence of the monks in a monastery also situated in Limoges, but some distance further away.

Francisco Zurbaran's painting "St Anthony of Padua worshipping the baby Jesus", c.1627–30.

Padre Pio became known for his stigmata, but he was also allegedly capable of bilocation.

More recently, the Italian Capuchin monk Padre Pio of Pietrelcina (1887–1968) gained worldwide renown as a healer and stigmatic, but was apparently able to bilocate too. For he reputedly made a number of unexpected appearances around the world while simultaneously remaining at the monastery of San Giovanni Rotondo at Foggia in south-eastern Italy.

As with St Martin de Porres, sceptics suggest that some cases of bilocation may involve mistaken identity, trickery or, in early cases, distorted documentation or exaggeration of the facts. When, however, during a conversation with Dr Sanguinetti, the medical doctor of the hospital at the monastery of San Giovanni Rotondo, Padre Pio was asked his opinion as to the likely nature of the mechanism facilitating bilocation, he offered a unique insight.

Padro Pio stated that a person sent by God to another place via bilocation is consciously aware of the transference and is genuinely in two places at the same time, and that the transference occurs via "a prolongation of his personality".

# SERPENTINE SURPRISES

SINCE THE EARLIEST OF TIMES, HUMANS HAVE BEEN IRRESISTIBLY FASCINATED BY SNAKES, A FASCINATION EXEMPLIFIED BY THE ANCIENT PRACTICE OF OPHIOLATREIA OR SERPENT WORSHIP, PERFORMED DOWN THROUGH HISTORY BY HUMAN CULTURES ALL OVER THE WORLD. CONSEQUENTLY, IT SHOULD COME AS NO SURPRISE TO DISCOVER THAT THERE ARE MANY SNAKE-RELATED RELIGIOUS MYSTERIES AND ANOMALIES ON FILE, INCLUDING THE LITTLE-PUBLICIZED SELECTION PRESENTED HERE.

## THE VIRGIN MARY SNAKES OF CEPHALONIA

With an area of roughly 300 square miles (nearly 78,000 hectares) the largely mountainous Cephalonia is the biggest of the Ionian Islands. At the small village of Markopoulo (claimed in legend to be the birthplace of Marco Polo's ancestors), it hosts an annual Marian celebration, on 16 August, known as the Feast of the Assumption of Our Lady (the Virgin Mary).

As I learnt from Cephalonia chronicler Victor J. Kean and herpetology enthusiast Susan R. Stebbing, almost every year for more than two centuries, during the fortnight or so prior to the festival, large numbers of snakes mysteriously appear close to Markopoulo's Church of Our Lady, and just as mysteriously disappear again once the festival is over. This has earned these reptiles, which all seem to belong to a single species, the local names "Virgin Mary snakes" and "Our Lady's snakes" – a religious association heightened by the small black cruciform mark that they allegedly bear on their heads, and also at the forked tip of their tongues.

In 1991, I wrote to Victor Kean, requesting further details. In reply, he conceded that he did not know the snakes' precise species, but recalled that they are reputed to have "skin like silk", are non-poisonous, and are also credited with thaumaturgic (miracle-working) powers. One plausible candidate is the four-striped snake *Elaphe quatuorlineata*, a non-poisonous constricting species of colubrid, native to Cephalonia, whose head can bear a variety of dark markings, especially in its juvenile form. Herpetologist Dr Klaus-Dieter Schulz has noted the link this species

---

*The four-striped snake* Elaphe quatuorlineata *is found from Greece eastwards to the Aral Sea.*

has to Christian traditions within southern Europe, such as the annual snake procession at Cucullo, Italy, in honour of St Dominic.

During the mid-1990s, Alistair Underwood visited Markopoulo on the day of its annual Marian festival and saw the Virgin Mary snakes congregate outside the church, where they were freely handled by the local villagers, who drape them around their necks without fear. The snakes were also allowed to enter the church and to make their way towards a large silver icon of the Virgin Mary. In *Summertime Customs* (1981), Professor Dimitris Loukatos, an expert in folk traditions, recalled a visit of his own to this festival:

> *When we entered the church it was all lit up and full of people. Two, three, five, seven, many snakes wriggled up and down the gold-painted wood-carved reliefs of the chancel screen, the pillars and the side doors; I looked at them bewildered for a long time. Every now and then the snakes would open their mouths and poke out their thread-like tongues.*

Cephalonian researcher Spyros Tassis Bekatoros claims that the only years in which the Virgin Mary snakes have not made an appearance at Markopoulo's Marian festival are those during the German occupation of Cephalonia in World War II, and 1953, when much of the island was devastated by an earthquake.

Snakes, although usually deaf to sounds (i.e. airborne vibrations), are very responsive to groundborne vibrations. Alistair Underwood wondered if the reason why the Virgin Mary snakes' appearance coincides with the Marian festival and preparations for it is increased human activity at this time. If so, the exceptional terrestrial reverberations accompanying the 1953 earthquake would have greatly disturbed the snakes, disrupting their normal behaviour and overriding the vibrational stimuli produced by human activity at the Marian festival that year.

Victor Kean, conversely, offers a rather more wry solution to this serpentine mystery:

"I suspect that the local 'papa' gathers up the snakes at the end of the festival ... in order to release them the following year!"

## ST PAUL AND THE MALTESE MYSTERY VIPER

As recorded in the Acts of the Apostles (28:3–6) in the Bible's New Testament, when a ship transporting St Paul and other prisoners to Rome was shipwrecked on the island of Melita (known now as Malta) St Paul was bitten by a venomous viper:

> *And when Paul had gathered a bundle of sticks, and laid them on the fire, there came a viper out of the heat, and fastened on his hand.*

> *And when the barbarians saw the venomous beast hang on his hand, they said among themselves, No doubt this man is a murderer, whom, though he hath escaped the sea, yet vengeance suffereth not to live.*

> *And he shook off the beast into the fire, and felt no harm.*

> *Howbeit they looked when he should have swollen, or fallen down dead suddenly: but after they had looked a great while, and saw no harm come to him, they changed their minds, and said that he was a god.*

There is a notable problem with this account: no known species of viper exists today on Malta. So what could St Paul's viperine attacker have been?

*This twelfth-century fresco in Canterbury Cathedral shows St Paul and the viper.*

One of my American colleagues, Chad Arment, has combined his appreciable knowledge of herpetology, cryptozoology and Scripture to great effect in order to provide me with a considerable quantity of information and suggestions about this very intriguing yet little-known mystery.

Some authors, such as Charles W. Carter and Ralph Earle in their biblical commentary *The Acts of the Apostles* (1959), suggest that the absence of vipers on Malta today does not necessarily mean that there were none in St Paul's day; perhaps the increase in this island's human population since then has caused their extinction. As Chad noted, however, there is no physical evidence to suggest that vipers ever existed here, and the viper family's zoogeographical distribution offers little support for such a notion.

Chad favours as a more likely candidate for the identity of Malta's mystery "viper" a species of venomous rear-fanged colubrid known as the cat snake *Telescopus fallax*, which usually measures up to 2.5 feet (76 cm) long and is native to Malta. As its mouth is too small for its fangs to be used effectively when biting humans (which it will sometimes do if handled), the cat snake is not normally deemed to be dangerous. Given that its preferred habitat includes dry stony areas overgrown with low shrubs in which it can climb, this fairly small, lithe snake could easily be picked up with a bundle of sticks (unlike bulkier vipers).

All of this assumes, of course, that the snake which bit St Paul was venomous – but was it? Perhaps St Luke, author of the Acts of the Apostles, and/or the native Maltese islanders mistakenly assumed that it was, when in fact it was harmless. After all, in many parts of the world all manner of totally innocuous, non-venomous species of snake (and even certain lizards) are erroneously considered to be poisonous by their human neighbours. Accordingly, some authors of biblical commentaries have nominated the smooth snake *Coronella austriaca* as a plausible candidate, for although it is non-venomous, it will readily bite if handled. Yet as this species is no more native to Malta than any of Europe's vipers,

surely it would be preferable, as wisely suggested by Chad, to look for a candidate among those snakes that are.

Another theory offering a misinterpretation as a solution concerns Luke's description of St Paul's serpentine aggressor as fastening on to then hanging from St Paul's hand. Could this mean that the snake did not actually bite his hand, but merely coiled around it? Did St Luke and the other observers assume that it had bitten when it had not? There is no statement anywhere in the verses dealing with this incident in the Acts of the Apostles which claims that St Paul was

*The cat snake inhabits rocky ground with shrubby vegetation where it is well camoflaged.*

miraculously cured of snakebite – only an assumption by St Luke and the others that he had been bitten.

It seems unlikely that the incident of St Paul and the Maltese viper featured a true viper, and there may have been a medically inexplicable snakebite cure. As Chad concludes: "I would suggest that this passage should not be relegated to the 'saints picking up deadly snakes and scorpions' file, but should instead be looked at from another perspective – the islanders were consumed with fear and superstition."

## CATALEPTIC COBRAS?

One of the most miraculous, and mystifying, incidents in the life of Moses occurred when he and his brother Aaron confronted Pharaoh, in

order for Aaron to tell him to send the children of Israel out of Egypt. As the Bible reveals in the Book of Exodus (7:8–12):

> *And the Lord spake unto Moses and unto Aaron, saying,*
>
> *When Pharaoh shall speak unto you, saying, Shew a miracle for you: then thou shalt say unto Aaron, Take thy rod, and cast it before Pharaoh, and it shall become a serpent.*
>
> *And Moses and Aaron went in unto Pharaoh, and they did so as the Lord had commanded: and Aaron cast down his rod before Pharaoh, and before his servants, and it became a serpent.*
>
> *Then Pharaoh also called the wise men and the sorcerers: now the magicians of Egypt, they also did in like manner with their enchantments.*
>
> *For they cast down every man his rod, and they became serpents: but Aaron's rod swallowed up their rods.*

A possible zoological explanation for this has been mooted for many years within herpetological circles: if an Egyptian cobra *Naja haje* is held by pressing the nape of its neck in a certain manner, it will become stiff and immobile, suspended in a cataleptic state until the pressure is removed. One herpetologist has recently reported how a cobra became rigid as a defence mechanism.

Could these occurrences truly explain the interconversion of snakes and rods as performed by Aaron and the Egyptian magicians? Initially, it does seem plausible – someone skilled in handling cobras could surely "create" a stiff "rod" in this way. However, supporters of this solution seem to have ignored an earlier passage in Exodus (4:2–5), in which God revealed to Moses a miracle that would prove to the children of Israel that He, the Lord, had indeed appeared to him:

> *And the Lord said unto him, What is that in thine hand? And he said, A rod.*
>
> *And he said, Cast it on the ground. And*

*Van Dyck's painting "The Raising of the Iron Snake" shows Moses and Aaron changing rods into snakes.*

*he cast it on the ground, and it became a serpent; and Moses fled from before it.*

*And the Lord said unto Moses, Put forth thine hand, and take it by the tail. And he put forth his hand, and caught it, and it became a rod in his hand.*

*That they may believe that the Lord God of their fathers, the God of Abraham, the God of Isaac, and the God of Jacob, hath appeared unto thee.*

Moses picked up the serpent not by its neck but by its tail – hardly the likeliest way of inducing it to enter a cataleptic state. Unless one assumes that the account given in Exodus is metaphorical rather than literal, the proposal of catalepsy inducement as the answer to the "serpents and rods" transformation is not a tenable theory.

## THE PRE-CURSED SERPENT IN EDEN

Earlier in the Bible is one of the classic serpentine sources of theological speculation and controversy.

When God learnt that the serpent in the Garden of Eden had successfully tempted Adam and Eve to eat the fruit from the Tree of Knowledge of Good and Evil, He cursed the serpent (Genesis 3:14–15):

*And the Lord God said unto the serpent, Because thou hast done this, thou art cursed above all cattle, and above every beast of the field; upon thy belly shalt thou go, and dust shalt thou eat all the days of thy life:*

*And I will put enmity between thee and the woman, and between thy seed and her seed; it shall bruise thy head, and thou shalt bruise his heel.*

According to this account, the serpent only acquired its present-day form, as a limbless creature slithering upon its undersurface, *after* it had been cursed – which begs the oft-posed theological question: "What did it look like *before*?"

The Bible itself offers little in the way of clues. Apart from revealing that it could converse directly with Adam and Eve, the only reference to

the pre-cursed serpent (Genesis 3:1) states: "Now the serpent was more subtil [sic] than any beast of the field which the Lord God had made." Even so, theologians and artists have offered many putative answers.

Some theologians have been in no doubt that the serpent was physically transformed by God's curse. Thus, in their *Biblical Commentary on the Old Testament, Vol. 1* (1866), Carl F. Keil and Franz Delitzsch unequivocally stated:

*The punishment of the serpent corresponded to the crime. It had exalted itself above the man; therefore upon its belly it should go, and dust it should eat all the days of its life. If these words are not to be robbed of their entire meaning, they cannot be understood in any other way than as denoting that the form and movements of the serpent were altered, and that its present repulsive shape is the effect of the curse pronounced upon it, though we cannot form any accurate idea of its original appearance. Going upon the belly (= creeping, Lev. xi. 42) was a mark of the deepest degradation; also the eating of dust, which is not to be understood as meaning that dust was to be its only food, but that while crawling in the dust it would also swallow dust.*

Rabbinical tradition, however, formulated various ideas regarding the serpent's appearance before it received God's curse. According to the Zohar (Book of Splendour), which provides a vast commentary upon the Pentateuch, in its pre-cursed form it had stood upright on two hind legs, just like humans, and was as tall as a camel. Similarly, certain ancient Egyptian carvings depict the pre-cursed serpent as an exceedingly slender biped with a long neck and tail, a pair of lengthy arms, and standing slightly taller than a human

*A seventeenth-century interpretation of the Fall.*

on two elongate hind legs, offering Adam a fruit with one of its paws. When it was cursed, however, God cut off its arms and legs, thereby yielding the limbless snake known today, and took away its power of human speech by splitting its tongue, so that it could only hiss thereafter.

Another school of thought favoured the idea that the pre-cursed serpent was a winged snake. In his *Commentary Upon the Whole Bible* (1708–10), Matthew Henry opined:

> Perhaps it was a flying serpent, which seemed to come from on high as a messenger from the upper world, one of the seraphim;

for the fiery serpents were flying, Isa. xiv. 29. Many a dangerous temptation comes to us in gay fine colours that are but skin-deep, and seems to come from above; for Satan can seem an angel of light.

Other scholars have speculated that the serpent's transformation may not have been physical at all, but merely figurative. In his *Commentaries on the First Book of Moses Called Genesis* (1948), John Calvin suggested that there is:

> ... no absurdity in supposing, that the serpent was again consigned to that former

condition, to which he was already naturally subject. For thus he, who had exalted himself against the image of God, was to be thrust back into his proper rank; ... he is recalled from his insolent motions to his accustomed mode of going, in such a way as to be, at the same time, condemned to perpetual infamy. To eat dust is the sign of a vile and sordid nature. This (in my opinion) is the simple meaning of the passage.

And Frank E. Gaebelein, editing *The Expositor's Bible Commentary* (1990), opined:

> This curse does not necessarily suggest that the snake had previously walked with feet and legs as the other land animals. The point is rather that for the rest of his life, as a result of the curse, when the snake crawls on his belly, as snakes do, he will "eat dust." The emphasis lies in the snake's "eating dust," an expression that elsewhere carries the meaning of "total defeat" (cf. Isa 65:25, Mic 7:17).

Another theologically contentious facet of this biblical event is whether the serpent was merely a reptile, i.e. a corporeal animal, or whether it was Satan in the guise of a snake, or even a snake controlled by Satan. Was God's curse therefore imposed upon the serpent, or was it actually imposed upon Satan? Quoting theologian Winterbotham:

> 1. I lay down the position that no punishment in the way of physical degradation was inflicted by God in His sentence upon the serpent tribe.
>
> 2. I lay down the position, which I think no one will seriously dispute, that the real tempter was not the serpent at all, but the devil.
>
> 3. I conclude from the foregoing positions, and conclude with confidence, that the serpent was not really cursed at all, while the devil was.

Artistic representations of the serpent reveal a similar diversity of views. As already noted, early Egyptian carvings portrayed an erect, bipedal being, whereas early European painters tended to depict a normal, limbless snake coiled around the Tree of Knowledge. By the twelfth century AD, however, European artists had begun portraying a somewhat more humanoid version – often with a snake's body but the head (and sometimes also the arms) of a woman – a trend that crossed from art into literature. This hybrid monster also gained its own name, the draconopides, and was sometimes utilized by artists depicting Lilith.

Rabbinical lore claims that Adam's first wife was not Eve, but Lilith, made by God from dust like Adam (rather than from one of Adam's ribs, like Eve), and who therefore refused to be subjugated by Adam. Instead, she deserted him, becoming an evil demon, and in some texts she is made synonymous with the serpent – tempting Adam and his new wife, Eve, with the fruit from the Tree of Knowledge, thereby causing humanity's Fall.

By the fifteenth century, some painters had created even more complex, elaborate serpents. François Fouquet's "Le Péché Originel" depicts the serpent with a typically elongate anguiniform lower body, wrapped around the tree, with the upper body, arms and head of a woman, and a pair of extended bat-like wings. More striking still is the portrayal of the serpent in "The Temptation" by fifteenth-century Flemish painter Hugo van der Goes. Depicted is a bipedal, web-footed lizard with a long tail and a woman's head, whose hair is plaited into horns, leaning against the Tree of Knowledge alongside Adam and Eve.

Before Darwin's explanation of snakes' limblessness – as a natural, advantageous evolutionary progression from limbed ancestors – was accepted by the scientific community, naturalists offered their own input into the discussion about the pre-cursed serpent's likely morphology. One of the most memorable suggestions came from enthusiastic amateur naturalist Frank Buckland, who was intrigued that boas and pythons possess vestiges of hind legs beneath their skin, as well as two hook-like claws near their tail. In his book *Curiosities of Natural History* (1858), he explained these as follows:

*Supposing, then, the pre-Adamite [i.e. pre-cursed] snake to have gone on four legs, we might explain the passage by saying that after the curse the legs were struck off, but that the undeveloped legs were left (concealed, however, from casual observers) as evidence of what it formerly had been, and a type of its fallen condition.*

In other words, these were remnants of earlier, fully formed limbs, exactly as postulated by evolution – thus providing an example of science and Scripture in full agreement.

*Van der Goes's interpretation of the Fall portrays the serpent as a curious amalgam of various different species.*

# TEMPORAL LOBE
# HALLUCINATIONS

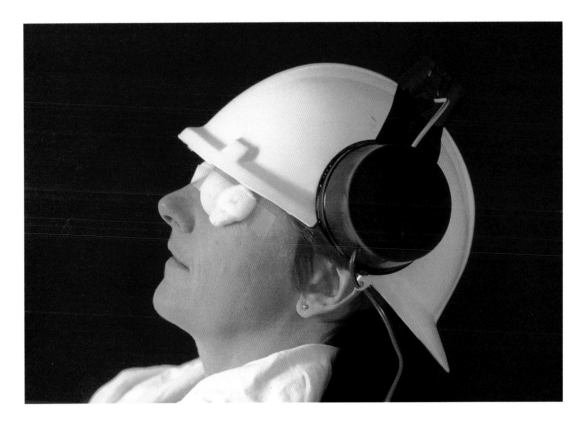

IN RECENT YEARS, CERTAIN MEDICAL RESEARCHERS HAVE COME OUT IN SUPPORT OF A VERY THOUGHT-PROVOKING SCIENTIFIC THEORY WHICH CLAIMS THAT RELIGIOUS VISIONS, AS WELL AS GHOSTS, ALIENS AND OTHER REPUTEDLY PARANORMAL IMAGES, ARE ACTUALLY COMPLEX HALLUCINATIONS ENGENDERED BY A MYSTERIOUS PAIRED REGION OF THE HUMAN BRAIN, KNOWN AS THE TEMPORAL LOBES.

Comprising a pair of evaginations (outgrowths) arising from the cerebral hemispheres (the most anterior and largest portions of the human brain) and situated laterally and below the frontal and occipital lobes, the temporal lobes contain auditory receptive areas and are associated with speech and thought. During early 1998, moreover, a research team at the University of California in San Diego claimed their investigations indicated that the regions of the brain dealing with religious experiences are the temporal lobes. Together with certain other structures, including the hippocampus, hypothalamus and amygdala, they also comprise a specific component of the brain known as the limbic system. And according to Dr Rhawn Joseph, writing in *Neuropsychiatry, Neuropsychology and Clinical Neuroscience* (1996): "... the amygdala, hippocampus and temporal lobe are richly interconnected and appear to act in concert in regard to mystical experience, including the generation and experience of dream states and complex auditory and visual hallucinations."

In addition, certain people suffer from a form of epilepsy known as temporal lobe epilepsy (TLE), a brain disorder that can be caused by a number of factors, including brain tumours, strokes and physical brain damage, yielding neuroelectrical aberrations that occur

---

*Dr Blackmore wearing a helmet like the one used to transmit magnetic pulses to the brain's temporal lobes.*

within these twin lobes. And as confirmed by Dr Tim Betts, from Birmingham's Queen Elizabeth Hospital in the West Midlands, England, who has many case histories on file, during a TLE seizure a sufferer often experiences bizarre but extremely vivid, vision-like hallucinations, which can include encountering weird, unearthly entities. A distinct medical condition but one that can also cause high temporal lobe instability is temporal lobe lability (TLL).

Two leading scientists who consider that many supposed paranormal experiences may simply be due to seizures within the temporal lobes engendering hallucinations are Laurentian University neurophysiologist Dr Michael Persinger, and psychologist Dr Susan Blackmore from the University of the West of England. As described by leading Fortean chronicler Joe McNally in a fascinating status report dealing with TLE (*Fortean Times*, March 1998), Persinger has even invented an electromagnetic helmet designed to test the effects of temporal lobe stimulation. Containing powerful solenoids that fit over the portions of the skull directly above the temporal lobes, the helmet is placed upon the head of a volunteer, and when magnetic pulses are transmitted to the lobes via this apparatus the resulting electrical activity often produces extremely vivid visual, aural and even tactile hallucinations.

Although such results are certainly very noteworthy, sceptics of this psychological explanation for visions, ghosts, alien abductions and the like have voiced a number of objections. Some critics, for example, feel that Persinger has sought to explain too diverse a range of apparent paranormal phenomena via his TLE theory.

Moreover, Persinger has claimed that sufferers of TLE or with high TLL tend to display a marked interest in paranormal phenomena anyway, which he believes would make them predisposed to interpreting strange events in this way. However, eminent ufologists such as Jerome Clark deny that UFO experiencers, for instance, are any more prone

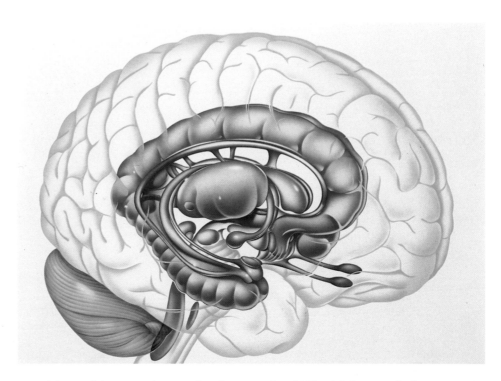

to applying such interpretations to what they see than anyone else would be.

Most intriguing of all are cases whereby, instead of engendering hallucinations that a sufferer has mistaken for genuine paranormal experiences, a TLE seizure seems to have actually facilitated the experiencing of bona fide extrasensory, paranormal phenomena by a sufferer. One of the most remarkable cases of this type took place in 1969, and featured a lady with TLE who was a patient at that time of Scottish psychiatrist Dr James McHarg.

On the day in question, the lady had been sitting in the kitchen of a friend when she suffered a TLE seizure. Abruptly, her surroundings felt "unreal" to her (a phenomenon commonly reported by persons undergoing a supposed paranormal experience and dubbed "the Oz Factor" by psychical researcher Jenny Randles), and an unfamiliar woman appeared, standing by a cooker that had not been there before. This strange scene lasted only a few moments before everything returned to normal. However, when she told her friend about it, her friend became very interested, because she knew that many years earlier a cooker had indeed stood in the precise location

where McHarg's lady patient had seen it appear.

But the greatest surprise concerning this lady's TLE vision was still to come. The unfamiliar woman that she had seen was subsequently identified conclusively from a photo as one of two sisters who had lived long ago in the house now owned by the lady's friend. Yet the lady had not seen a ghost – because the sister was still alive. Accordingly, McHarg concluded that his patient's TLE seizure must have somehow rendered her receptive to extrasensory influences, yielding a brief but authentic vision of an earlier period in the history of her friend's home.

So are angels, BVM visions, ghosts, aliens and other enigmatic entities merely in the brain of the beholder? Judging from what is already known about the temporal lobes, this could well be true in some cases. Nevertheless, it may also be true that under certain abnormal conditions these same portions of the brain can offer us, albeit only briefly, an insight of what lies beyond the normal detection range of our senses.

*The limbic system of the brain, shown in blue: in the centre is the oval-shaped thalamus and to the right of it are two lobes of the candate nucleus.*

# MYSTERIES OF THE
# VANISHED
# WORLD

*Nothing changes more constantly than the past; for the past that influences our lives does not consist of what actually happened, but of what men believe happened.*

Gerald White Johnson

T O DESTROY A PEOPLE'S FUTURE, IT IS NECESSARY ONLY TO ERADICATE THEIR PAST. ALL TOO OFTEN, THEREFORE, DURING HUMANITY'S TENURE OF PLANET EARTH, WHEN ONE CIVILIZATION, ETHNIC RACE OR RELIGION HAS BEEN STRIVING TO SUPERSEDE ANOTHER, IT HAS PURPOSEFULLY SOUGHT TO ERASE EVERY POSSIBLE TRACE OF ITS RIVAL'S ERSTWHILE PRESENCE. HOWEVER, THERE IS A NOTABLE AND INTRIGUING ARRAY OF CHRONOLOGICAL AND ARCHAEOLOGICAL ANOMALIES, MYSTERIES AND CONTROVERSIES PRESENTLY ON FILE AND STILL AWAITING A SATISFACTORY RESOLUTION THAT MAY PROVIDE TANTALIZING, ENIGMATIC CLUES REGARDING THE ONE-TIME REALITY OF SEVERAL HITHERTO-UNSUSPECTED BYGONE CULTURES.

## CHAPTER FIVE

## LONG AGO AND FAR AWAY

# LINGERING MYSTERIES

## IN LONG-BYGONE HISTORIES

IN HISTORY IS MYSTERY, AND THE FURTHER ONE TRAVELS BACK IN HISTORY, THE GREATER IS THE DIVERSITY OF MYSTERY UNFURLED, AS READILY UNDERLINED BY THOSE ENIGMAS FROM PAST AGES SURVEYED HERE.

## MARCO POLO AND XANADU

During the thirteenth century, the famous Venetian explorer Marco Polo spent several years in China, in the service of the Mongol emperor Kubla Khan – or did he?

After all, as pointed out by Dr Frances Wood, head of the British Library's Chinese Department, in her very thought-provoking book *Did Marco Polo Go To China?* (1995), if Polo really did spend time here it is exceedingly strange that such quintessentially Sinian items as tea, porcelain, Chinese pictograms, women with bound feet,

*A fifteenth-century portrait of Marco Polo – a woodcut from a German edition of travel writings.*

and, above all else, the Great Wall, are not mentioned in his celebrated travel writings. Equally mystifying is why Polo's sojourn in China is not referred to in any Chinese chronicles covering this period – unless, of course, it never happened, except in Polo's vivid imagination.

As for Xanadu, it is widely but erroneously assumed that this resplendent city is wholly fictitious, entirely confined to Samuel Taylor Coleridge's magnificent, incomplete poem, *Kubla Khan*. In reality, however, Xanadu was Shang Tu (= Shangdu), the Upper Capital and summer capital of Kubla Khan, located in what is now the Zhenglan Banner of the Autonomous Republic of Inner Mongolia, in north-eastern China.

According to legend, and immortalized in Coleridge's poem (see Chapter 3), Kubla Khan built in Xanadu an enormous gilded palace, encompassed by a vast garden of delights, containing a hedonistic "pleasure dome". Here, drugged soldiers were lain, and were told upon awakening that they were in Paradise – so that they would happily fight to the death in their emperor's battles, in the tragically mistaken belief that they would then return to this dome of decadence forever. Whether such an edifice truly existed is a matter for conjecture, as much of Kubla Khan's life is enshrouded in myth.

Nevertheless, the remains of his palace complex in Xanadu still exist, laid out in the form of three squares, one inside the other – as revealed in Caroline Alexander's absorbing travelogue *The Way To Xanadu* (1993), which documents her journey to Shangdu during the early 1990s to discover whether any vestige of this fabled city still survived.

## THE JESUS PAPYRUS

Comprising three tiny fragments bearing verses in Greek from the Gospel of St Matthew, the Jesus Papyrus had been virtually forgotten by scholars since October 1901 – until rediscovered in the library at Magdalen College, Oxford, by papyrus expert Carsten Thiede in 1994. First uncovered at Luxor, Egypt, by the Reverend Charles Bousfield Huleatt, what makes these fragments so significant is Thiede's revelation that they date back to at least 65 AD – not the third century AD, as thought by Huleatt.

This in turn means not only that they are the oldest remains of a Christian book ever found, but also that they may constitute actual eyewitness proof that Jesus lived – physical evidence confirming that the New Testament was written by contemporaries of Jesus, and thereby supporting its contents' accuracy and reliability.

## AMETHYST SKULLS AND A CRYSTAL MASK

The past few years have witnessed the public appearance of a number of crystal skulls, supplementing the two most famous, mysterious examples, documented in my book *The Unexplained* (1996) and elsewhere. Exhibiting varying degrees of complexity and workmanship, these visually alluring artefacts are usually carved from transparent quartz.

Perhaps the most spectacular crystal skull of all, however, is a full-sized violet-hued specimen carved from amethyst and weighing about 8 lb (3.6 kg). Bearing thin white striations, this exceptionally beautiful example was reputedly uncovered in Mexico during the early 1900s, among a cache of Mayan artefacts, and has been on display in Japan in recent times. In 1982, the

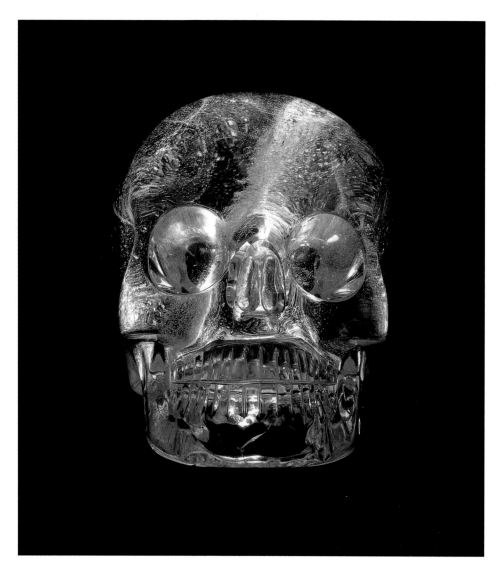

*One of the beautiful amethyst skulls whose origins remain a mystery.*

amethyst crystal skull was brought to the USA by an agent of a Mayan priest claiming ownership of it, who hoped to sell it, and in February 1983 it was examined by F.R. "Nick" Nocerino, the founder and director of The Society of Crystal Skulls, International. According to crystal-skull researcher Steve Mehler, who examined this specimen for four days in 1980, the Hewlett-Packard research laboratories have also seen it, and allegedly stated that they were uncertain how it could have been created, even if advanced technology were involved.

Another amethyst skull is the so-called Marin skull, weighing 5–6 lb (2.3–2.7 kg), possessing stylized teeth, and currently in a private collection within the San Francisco Bay area. Also privately owned is "Icabod", a cantaloupe-melon-sized crystal skull hewn from chevron amethyst.

No less exotic than amethyst skulls, but much less familiar, is an extraordinary crystal mask, hailing from Tibet, which was formally documented in January 1927 by H.C. Beasley in the anthropological periodical *Man*. Carved from rock crystal, with ivory eyes (including a third eye in the centre of the brow), other facial features applied in gilt bronze, and teeth that are probably of human origin, the mask represents the terrifying corpse-devouring, blood-quaffing goddess Palden Lhamo, whose Hindu counterpart is Kali, goddess of death.

## JOAN – OR SHOULD THAT BE JOHN? – OF ARC

According to a thought-provoking theory first aired by Georgia endocrinologist Robert Greenblatt in 1982, Joan of Arc, the celebrated Maid of Orleans who was eventually canonized, may have been a secret male. More specifically, she, or he, could conceivably have been a male suffering from testicular feminization – a curious medical syndrome in which cells are prevented from receiving the male hormone testosterone. The confusing outcome is a person who looks and thinks like a female, but is genetically a male.

After examining records relating to Joan's physical state, Greenblatt discovered that whereas she exhibited excellent breast development, she lacked pubic hair and romantic inclinations, she did not menstruate, and possessed unusually soft, unblemished skin – a combination of features characterizing testicular feminization.

## PHARAOHS DOWN UNDER?

Did the seafaring ancient Egyptians ever visit Australia? The discovery of various enigmatic objects Down Under indicates that this notion may not be as unlikely as it initially seems.

In 1976, for instance, at Gympie in Queensland, a workman dug up an Egyptian scarab – the symbol of Khepri, the ancient Egyptian god of rebirth and the rising sun – carved out of chert. This is just one of several Egyptian-style artefacts that have been uncovered here.

Similarly, in 1910 Andrew Henderson discovered near Barron Falls, again in

*Above: An ancient Eygptian pectoral showing two maidens praying to a scarab, the symbol of Khepri. Top: "Jeanne d'Arc outside Castle Chinon" from a fifteenth-century German tapestry.*

Queensland, a bronze Ptolemy IV coin. Dating from 221–204 BC, its head displayed the horned Zeus of Omon, and its reverse side bore a Ptolemaic insignia – an eagle riding a thunderbolt.

## A CRYPTOZOOLOGICAL CAVE PAINTING?

In 1985, while diving in the Mediterranean Sea near Marseilles, Henri Cosquer discovered a grotto with an entrance 120 feet (36.5 metres) beneath sea level. Six years later, it was found to lead to a huge underground gallery above sea level, whose walls were covered with extraordinary paintings dated at 26,000–16,000 BC, and including the enigmatic example depicted here.

Some scientists feel that this painting depicts a great auk *Alca impennis* – a large flightless relative of the razorbills and puffins, which became extinct in 1844 due to over-hunting by

man. However, great auk authority Errol Fuller is not entirely convinced by this identity. Others have likened it to a penguin, but as penguins are primarily southern hemisphere species that have never been native to this part of the world, that seems a rather implausible prospect too.

Intriguingly, French ichthyologist and cryptozoologist Dr François de Sarre has recently proposed in a number of periodicals that it might be a Palaeolithic artist's rendition of a sea monster, specifically of the long-necked sea serpent type, and he suggested that

it could be some form of long-necked seal. I personally do not subscribe to the long-necked seal identity as a satisfactory explanation for the long-necked type of sea serpent. Yet, whatever the creature depicted by the cave painting is, it does not seem to correspond closely to any animal currently recognized by science, and is therefore yet another of the many iconographical oddities on file within the chronicles of cryptozoology.

## A HORSE OF WHITE FROM THE AGE OF BRONZE?

Measuring 300 feet (91 metres) long, deemed by some to be a dragon rather than a horse, and carved into Oxfordshire's chalk hillsides near Wantage, the famous White Horse of Uffington was first recorded in the twelfth century. It was

once believed to have been carved by Saxons celebrating King Alfred the Great's victory over the Danes in 871 AD, but was reassessed more recently as the work of the Belgae, a Celtic tribe, serving as an offering to a dead leader.

In February 1995, however, Oxford University's Archaeological Research Laboratory announced that optical dating tests on soil samples taken from it indicated that the Uffington White Horse was first laid out as long ago as 1400 BC, thus dating back to the Late Bronze Age, i.e. a thousand years earlier than previously thought. Its purpose is still a mystery.

---

Above: *The great auk, from an engraving – a possible contender for the cave painting's identity.*
Left: *The mysterious cave painting, dating back to 16,000 BC or more, found in an underwater grotto near Marseilles.*

# GABRIEL'S FEATHER

PHYSICAL RELICS OF ANGELS ARE NOT THE MOST ABUNDANT COMMODITIES – WHICH IS WHY A CERTAIN EXCEPTIONALLY BEAUTIFUL PLUME SAID TO RESIDE IN ONE OF THE 515 RELIQUARIES AT THE RESPLENDENT EL ESCORIAL PALACE IN MADRID, SPAIN, IS SO NOTEWORTHY. FOR ACCORDING TO TRADITION, THIS MYSTERIOUS, SCARCELY KNOWN WONDER CAME FROM ONE OF THE WINGS OF THE ARCHANGEL GABRIEL!

A few centuries ago, this extraordinary relic was a celebrated sacred treasure, famous throughout Europe, but today its existence – if indeed it still exists, as I shall discuss later – has largely been forgotten. Perhaps its best-known observer was an exceedingly wealthy English author-traveller, William T. Beckford, who undertook several extensive forays around Europe, visiting religious sites and edifices. In 1787, Beckford arrived at El Escorial, where, on 19 December, he was privileged to be shown Gabriel's feather, which he documented as follows, within volume 2 of his travelogue *Italy, With Sketches of Spain and Portugal* (1834):

*The Prior, who is not easily pleased, seemed to have suspicions that the seriousness of my demeanour was not entirely orthodox; I overheard him saying to Roxas, "Shall I*

*A detail from Lippi's painting "The Annunciation to Mary" showing the Archangel Gabriel.*

*show him the Angel's feather? you know
we do not display this our most valued,
incomparable relic to everybody, nor unless
upon special occasions." – "The occasion is
sufficiently special," answered my partial
friend; "the letters I brought to you are
your warrant, and I beseech your reverence
to let us look at this gift of Heaven, which I
am extremely anxious myself to adore and
venerate."*

*Forth stalked the Prior, and drawing
out from a remarkably large cabinet an
equally capacious sliding shelf· – (the
source, I conjecture, of the potent odour I
complained of [a strong perfume of musk
and ambergris]) – displayed, lying
stretched out· upon a quilted silken
mattress, the most glorious specimen of
plumage ever beheld in terrestrial regions –
a feather from the wing of the Archangel
Gabriel, full three feet long, and of a
blushing hue more soft and delicate than
that of the loveliest rose. I longed to ask at
what precise moment this treasure beyond
price had been dropped – whether from the
air – on the open ground, or within the
walls of the humble tenement at Nazareth;
but I repressed all questions of an
indiscreet tendency – the why and
wherefore, the when and how, for what and
to whom such a palpable manifestation of
archangelic beauty and wingedness˙ had
been vouchsafed.*

*We all knelt in silence ... [then] we
rose up, after the holy feather had been
again deposited in its perfumed lurking-
place.*

Not surprisingly, this spectacular feather
attracted a great deal of interest not only from
theologians, but also from ornithologists, who
hoped to reconcile its origin with some known
species of bird.

One of the most popular candidates was the
quetzal *Pharomachrus mocino*, native to Central

*A model of the head of the Aztecs' sky god,
Quetzalcoatl, portrayed as a feathered serpent.*

America, particularly Mexico and Guatemala,
where the Aztecs associated it with their sky
god, Quetzalcoatl, often portrayed as a feathered
serpent. This is because the male quetzal during
the breeding season grows four exceedingly
lengthy tail feathers, each up to 3 feet (0.9
metre) long (its body, by comparison, measures
a mere 18 inches or 0.45 metre), and when it
flies through the air these extremely elongate
plumes undulate in a deceptively serpentine
manner.

When the Spanish conquistadors returned
home to Europe from Mexico during the 1500s,
they may well have brought back some
feathered skins of this magnificent species. And
if a stray tail plume from a male quetzal in
breeding plumage happened to reach El Escorial,
whose construction took place from 1563 to
1584 under the supervision of King Philip II, its
wholly    unfamiliar    but    incomparably
resplendent appearance might well have led
non-zoological theological scholars to assume
that it was of divine origin.

A very compelling theory – but one that,
sadly, possesses a serious flaw, which˙readily
dismisses the gorgeous quetzal from further
consideration as the origin of the Gabriel
feather. As noted above by Beckford, the latter
plume was a blushing rosy hue, whereas the tail
feathers of the quetzal are emerald green.

The quetzal was not scientifically described
until 1832. A year earlier, when the eminent
French zoologist Baron Georges Cuvier had first

*Count Raggi's bird of paradise – the origin of the "Gabriel feather"?*

read an account of the exquisite tail feathers sported by this species' breeding males, he could not believe that they were real. Instead, he claimed that they must surely be fakes – fraudulently created by skilfully combining several smaller feathers together to yield larger, composite plumes. Interestingly, some scholars in the past have also offered this notion as an explanation of the Gabriel feather.

In my opinion, however, there is a much more convincing identity for this mystifying specimen – and one which, if not truly divine, does at least sound heavenly. It was in 1522 that New Guinea's extravagantly plumed birds of paradise first came to western attention, when the survivors of Portuguese explorer Ferdinand Magellan's once-mighty fleet returned home to Europe, docking in Seville, Spain. On board were many delicate feathery skins from these incredibly beautiful birds, purchased from New Guinea tribesmen, but preserved minus their feet. As a result, for over 300 years ornithologists erroneously assumed that these avian wonders really were footless – spending their entire lives in unending sylph-like flight amid the empyrean, cloud-dappled realm of the sky, sinking earthward only to die.

During the mating season, the males of some of the larger species sprout forth gaudy flourishes of long gauzy plumes that cascade in eyecatching fountains of colour from beneath their wings and tail. One of the most spectacular of these species is Count Raggi's bird of paradise *Paradisea raggiana*, whose breeding males possess billowing sprays of blushing rose-suffused plumes – just like the Gabriel feather.

Perhaps, therefore, that is the true identity of El Escorial's enigmatic plume – a lone feather derived from a skin of this species brought back from New Guinea to Spain by Magellan's fleet a mere four decades before work commenced upon El Escorial's construction. Certainly, it would be singularly appropriate if a feather once thought to be from an archangel of Heaven ultimately proved to be from a bird of paradise.

Of course, one might imagine that such an identification could be readily tested, merely by an ornithologist visiting El Escorial and receiving permission to observe Gabriel's feather. As I discovered when investigating this relic, however, in practice it would not be so simple – for one very good reason. On 12 January 1998, I wrote to the monastery of San Lorenzo, housed within El Escorial, requesting information and sight of any existing photographs of the Gabriel feather. On 21 January, I received the following, somewhat perplexing response from the monastery's Keeper of National Heritage, Carmen Garcia-Frias Checa:

*I am sorry to inform you that there is no such thing as an archangel feather in the reliquaries of this monastery. Neither is there any bird feather or holy object which might be of ornithological interest.*

*I do not know where you got the information about the existence of the said feather but I can assure you it is not mentioned by the most important chroniclers of El Escorial (among them Fray José de Sigüenza who made an account of the monastery in his 1605 book* The Foundation of the Monastery of El Escorial. *[NB: according to my researches, this work was first published in 1598.]*

*Perhaps you could find some information about the Gabriel feather in the "Books of Donations", which contain a detailed account of all the objects donated to this monastery during the reign of King Philip II. They consist of eight handwritten volumes which are housed in the Archives of the Royal Palace in Madrid. The section of the "Books of Donations" dealing with relics has never been transcribed.*

The last line of Garcia-Frias's letter may well be the key to this "mystery within a mystery". As the Gabriel feather is not mentioned in de Sigüenza's book, we could assume that it was

donated to the monastery after this book's publication. Having said that, much of the latter work is concerned with church ceremonies and art works rather than holy relics anyway. However, details concerning the feather might indeed be found in the relics section of the Books of Donations – an avenue of investigation that I am currently pursuing.

In the meantime, Garcia-Frias's lack of knowledge regarding the Gabriel feather suggests that although (as confirmed by Beckford's account and those of others on record) this relic was once housed at El Escorial, it is no longer there today – unless, perhaps, it is present not in the monastery but elsewhere here? Certainly there are countless locations where such an object could be stored. For in addition to the monastery, El Escorial's massive complex also contains the Basilica of San Lorenzo el Real, the sacristy, the college, the Royal Palace of the Bourbons, a library, a throne room, a picture gallery, and several other edifices.

In a highly intriguing parallel to this curious case of the missing archangel feather, on 25 October 1998 a Spanish correspondent, Isabela Herranz, e-mailed me with news that she had learnt of an angel feather preserved in a small convent at Navarra, and would be seeking further details for me. In a later communication, however, she informed me that the convent claimed to have no knowledge of any such feather!

Should we really be so surprised? The cynic may say that our mundane mortal world is incapable of retaining for any length of time such fragrant, divine traces as the plumes of angels. In reality, of course, we must acknowledge that the concept of angels bearing feathery avian wings is a relatively recent one, nurtured principally by Renaissance artists and hence dating back only a few centuries, with no foundation in early theological lore.

Even so, it felt somewhat comforting to know that a few relics with claims to angelic fame (justified or not) existed on earth – which is surely now a little sadder for their absence.

# PARADOX OF THE
# PICTISH BEAST

THE PICTS ("PAINTED PEOPLE", AFTER THEIR BODY TATTOOS), WHO INHABITED NORTH-EASTERN
SCOTLAND IN C.300–850 AD BEFORE BEING UNITED WITH THE CELTIC SCOTS UNDER KENNETH I, ARE
MOST FAMOUS FROM AN ARCHAEOLOGICAL STANDPOINT FOR THEIR SYMBOL STONES – ORNATELY
CARVED WITH ALL MANNER OF CREATURES, OBJECTS AND OTHER DEPICTIONS.

These stones have been categorized into three classes. Class I stones date from around the sixth century and are usually unshaped slabs with at least one flat face bearing line-incised symbols. Class II stones, of

*Known as the Rodney Stone, this sandstone slab bears a carving of the unidentified Pictish beast.*

somewhat later date, bear more elaborate, intricate designs, often carved in low relief. And Class III stones, dating from when Christianity reached the Picts, depict Christian symbols, largely replacing the earlier Pictish ones, and are often sculpted into large ornate crosses.

Many types of animal are depicted on Class I and II stones, and are carved so realistically

that there is little problem in identifying them – with one very notable exception. Known as the Pictish beast, this extraordinary creature appears on many Pictish symbol stones (approximately 29 Class I stones, and 22 Class II stones). Perhaps the most famous example is a 6-foot- (1.8-metre) tall cross-slab of grey sandstone called the Rodney or Rodney's Stone.

As recorded in Elizabeth Sutherland's *Guide to the Pictish Stones* (1997), this Class II stone was originally found in the graveyard of the old church of Dyke and Moy, but was later moved to the Grampian village of Dyke to commemorate the victory of Admiral Rodney, and today stands on the left side of the avenue leading to Brodie Castle. Other symbol stones depicting the Pictish beast include a cross-slab on the Brough of Birsay at the north-western corner of Mainland, Orkney; the Dunfallandy Stone (Class II) in Tayside; the ninth-century, 10-foot- (3-metre) tall Maiden Stone near Pitcaple in Aberdeenshire; a carved stone in Grampian's Port Elphinstone Henge near Inverurie (the henge itself is considerably older than the carvings); and one of the Rhynie Pict Stones in Aberdeenshire. Perhaps the least stylized, most "natural" portrayal of the Pictish beast can be found upon a spectacular Class II stone at Tayside's Meigle Museum, which is adorned with carvings of horse-riders

and a tail-biting serpent as well as the Pictish beast, plus the customary Pictish V-rod and crescent symbols.

An alternative name that has been given to the Pictish beast is the "swimming elephant", and for good reason. As can be seen from the Rodney stone illustrated here, this bizarre creature sports a dolphin-like head with a lengthy beak, legs that curl beneath its body, an elongate curl-tipped tail, and a long slender horn or trunk-like projection sprouting from the top of its head and curving over its back. On the Meigle Museum stone, however, the legs are less fantastic, with only the paws curling backwards.

As the Pictish beast bears no resemblance to any known type of animal, it is little wonder that its putative identity has incited considerable speculation among archaeologists and other historians. Based upon its vaguely delphinoid head, some scholars have suggested that it may represent a dolphin or porpoise, and it has occurred to me that perhaps its anomalous

*Close-up of the blowhole on a dolphin's head.*

"trunk" might actually be a representation of a spout of water spurting upwards when the dolphin exhales through its blowhole (conjoined, modified nostrils), which is indeed situated on the top of this marine mammal's head. However, the Pictish beast's leg-like limbs and elongate, non-fluked tail cannot be easily reconciled with the flippers and fluked tail of cetaceans.

A bona fide elephant or even an unknown species of secondarily aquatic elephant has also been considered (albeit not seriously, for obvious reasons!). Of course, the Pictish beast could simply be a wholly imaginary beast, though in view of its abundant portrayals it clearly embodied some notable symbolic significance for the Picts. Indeed, as postulated by Elizabeth Sutherland among others, it might conceivably represent the mythical kelpie or Scottish water-horse. Certainly, one of the three famous

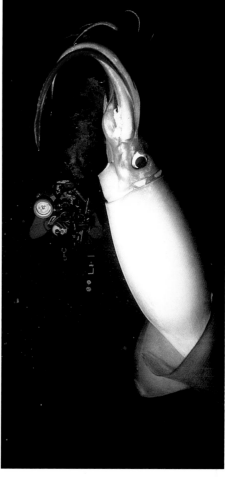

Above: *One identity proposed for the Pictish beast is a type of squid, like this large squid seen in the Sea of Cortez.*

Left: *Is the Loch Ness monster one and the same as the Pictish beast?*

Right: *Tony Shiels's drawing of the elephant squid (named by him* Elephanteuthis nnidnidi*), which he believes may be living in Loch Ness.*

Aberlemno symbol stones in Tayside depicts a pair of interlaced horse-headed, elongate aquatic monsters that some scholars believe may constitute a more sophisticated version of the Pictish beast.

Leading on from this is the fascinating possibility, as aired by Janet and Colin Bord in *Ancient Mysteries of Britain* (1986), that the Pictish beast is actually one and the same as the elusive water monsters reputedly inhabiting various of Scotland's lochs, with its trunk being

responsible for the famous "head and neck" images frequently reported and even photographed by Nessie eyewitnesses over the years. As the Bords rightly point out:

*Since a whole range of animals and birds is accurately depicted on the symbol stones – wolf, bull, cow, stag, horse, eagle, goose – perhaps these were the creatures most familiar to the Picts in their everyday world, and "monsters" were also*

*familiar to them, being more often seen in the lakes than they are today, and accepted as part of the natural world just like eagles and stags.*

This very thought-provoking hypothesis leads us to perhaps the most intriguing identity of all for the Pictish beast, which was proposed by Tony "Doc" Shiels in a *Fortean Times* article (autumn 1984) and also in his book *Monstrum! A Wizard's Tale* (1990). Shiels, who describes himself as a monster-hunter, stage magician, surrealist artist, and shaman of the western world (among other things), postulates that the Pictish beast may indeed be a representation of the unidentified Scottish water monsters, and that the zoological identity of these latter mystery beasts could in turn be a highly novel, specialized form of squid.

As conceived by Shiels, the most striking feature of his hypothetical species is a long, flexible, prey-capturing proboscis-like structure (the trunk of the Pictish beast), on account of which he has dubbed this creature the elephant squid. If held out of the water, its proboscis could resemble a long neck, which Shiels believes may explain the familiar "long-neck" images of Nessie and her kin. He also provides his elephant squid with inflatable dorsal airsacs as part of its buoyancy mechanism (which could yield the varying shape and number of humps reported for Nessie), six short tentacles, and a pair of longer curling arms (the Pictish beast's curling front legs), as well as a muscular tail bearing two horizontal lobes.

In his accounts, Shiels proposes that this remarkable mollusc may even be able to emerge briefly on to land, which might therefore explain why certain Nessie eyewitnesses (such as the Spicers, who claimed to have spied this mystery beast on land in 1933) have likened it to an enormous, hideous snail. Quite apart from the profound morphological modifications necessary for a beast corresponding to Shiels's elephant squid to have evolved from known cephalopod (squid and octopus) stock, however, a fundamental obstacle to this hypothetical creature's plausibility is that all known species of modern-day cephalopod are exclusively marine. There is not a single species of freshwater squid or octopus on record, and for one to evolve would require drastic tissue modifications relating to osmoregulatory ability.

Following Shiels's original speculation concerning his proposed elephant squid in his *Fortean Times* article, summaries appeared in a number of publications by other writers, most of whom erroneously stated that he had formally named this hypothetical species *Dinoteuthis proboscideus*. Unfortunately, however, this is not true. As Shiels subsequently pointed out in his book *Monstrum!*, that name had actually been given by Irish zoologist A.G. More to a huge specimen of squid washed ashore at Dingle in County Kerry, Ireland, during a severe storm in October 1673. Instead, Shiels suggested that an apt name for his own, wholly conjectural cephalopod would be *Elephanteuthis nnidnidi* – a name that needs no explanation for anyone acquainted with Shiels's experiments with psychic automatism.

In contrast, the Pictish beast remains resolutely unexplained; the subject of several worthy interpretations, but no satisfactory solutions – unless the answer lurks not among its petroglyphic portrayals but within the secretive depths of the lochs forming a major, familiar part of the landscape once inhabited by the painted people of Scotland's distant past.

# ANOMALOUS AILMENTS

TWO OF THE WORLD'S MOST MYSTIFYING AILMENTS ARE THE ENGLISH SWEAT AND PHTHIRIASIS, PLACED UNDER THE MEDICAL MICROSCOPE HERE IN SEARCH OF EXPLANATIONS FOR THESE "LONG-LOST" DISEASES.

## WORKING UP A LETHAL SWEAT IN TUDOR TIMES

The English sweat, or sudor anglicus, was well-named, as its two major characteristics were its predominantly English occurrence and the profuse sweating suffered by its victims. The first known outbreak of this mystery illness took place at the close of the Battle of Bosworth Field in August 1485, which ended the Wars of the Roses and saw the English crown pass from the House of York to the House of Tudor. However, Henry Tudor's victory was

*Cardinal Wolsey, who survived the sweat three times.*

overshadowed by the rapid deaths of many of his soldiers and also those of the fallen King Richard III from a deadly disease that often killed its victims in just a few hours. Symptoms were numerous and acute, including intense headaches, severe pain in the shoulders, back, arms and legs, gastric and hepatic maladies, extreme thirst, palpitations, and such elevated body temperature and profound sweating that sufferers felt as if they were literally on fire.

When Bosworth Field's infected soldiers struggled back to London from the battlefield, the English sweat duly began decimating the English capital – and to the horror of the

nobility present at court, it besieged not only the poor but also the rich. Indeed, it actually seemed to "favour" the aristocracy, who died in great numbers from this mystifying contagion, whereas its effects seemed less dramatic within the habitually disease-ridden hovels where those shackled by poverty dwelt. This suggests that the latter may have already acquired a degree of immunity to a variety of ailments and were thus shielded to some extent.

Meanwhile, Henry Tudor had no option but to postpone his coronation, at which he would be crowned as King Henry VII of England, and flee London in advance of the English sweat's expanding distribution. When it reached Oxford, it killed so many people that the university was closed down, and scores of students fled the city seeking sanctuary from certain death.

Then, in the late autumn of 1485, just as abruptly as it had appeared, the English sweat vanished again – and not for just a few weeks or months. Nothing more would be seen or heard of this extraordinary epidemic for another 23 years. During summer 1508, however, it suddenly resurfaced, annihilating so many victims so swiftly that Henry VII was forced once more to flee London, and stay beyond its baleful zone of influence until at last, in autumn of the same year, it disappeared again.

In 1517, Henry VIII discovered at close hand the very real horror that was the English sweat when this perplexing plague made the third of its unheralded visitations, and counted among its numerous victims his chancellor, Cardinal Wolsey. Evidently of uncommonly sound constitution, however, Wolsey survived – despite contracting it on three separate occasions!

The worst outbreak of all occurred during the sweat's fourth appearance, in June 1528. This time, not content with laying waste to the English population, and including Henry VIII's future second wife, Anne Boleyn, among its countless sufferers (though, like Wolsey, she survived), this virulent killer actually crossed the Channel, carried by infected persons hoping to escape its curse by fleeing to the continent. After reaching Europe, it claimed vast numbers of victims in Germany in 1529, and spread onward into Scandinavia and Central Europe to leave many more deaths in its febrile wake before finally petering out.

In 1551, the English sweat reappeared in London, and the all-too-familiar scene of rapid, agonizing, abundant deaths was played out once more before it vanished again – but this time for good, because the English sweat has never been recorded anywhere since then. In 1718, a

*Anne Boleyn survived the English sweat, but not the wrath of Henry VIII: "Anne Boleyn in the Tower after her arrest", Edouard Cibot, 1835.*

superficially similar sweating disease nowadays termed the Picardy sweat erupted in France, but the mortality rate was much lower, and it has since been linked fairly persuasively by some physicians to a disease of the sweat glands called miliary fever.

Conversely, with no physical evidence to examine, only the documented accounts in centuries-old works such as Dr John Caius's *A Boke, or counseill against the disease commonly called the Sweate, or sweatying sicknesse* (1551), modern-day medical researchers have been unable to offer any conclusive identity or explanation for the English sweat. Scarlet fever, bubonic plague, an unknown strain of influenza

(currently the most popular theory), malaria, typhus, meningitis, relapsing fever, and even various combinations of some of these ailments have all been suggested, but none can offer a comprehensive solution.

Yet whatever it was, the English sweat could evidently lie dormant for years before being somehow triggered or revived. And once activated, it spread even more rapidly than bubonic plague – responsible for Europe's infamous Black Death epidemic in the 1300s.

Little wonder that in 1995, Peter Rowan, a medical consultant for *The Guinness Book of Records*, said that the English sweat "has a claim to be the fastest, deadliest killer disease of all time".

## A LOUSY DISEASE – OR DELUSION?

Even more baffling than the English sweat is phthiriasis, also known as the lousy disease – from "morbus pedicularis", the term coined for it by the ancient scholar Antigonos Carystius in 240 BC. For as revealed by Dr Jan Bondeson in his delightful book *A Cabinet of Medical Curiosities* (1997), there is no confirmed evidence that this equally absent, but formerly greatly feared ailment ever actually existed!

Alleged cases of phthiriasis date back at least as far as the time of Aristotle (fourth century BC), who documented this disease in his famous *History of Animals*, and were still appearing in medical treatises little more than a century ago. For the most part, descriptions of phthiriasis were notably consistent. Sufferers developed inflamed swellings or tumours on their skin, which sometimes attained a considerable size, and if these swellings were cut open, they were found to contain great numbers of small lice or mite-like creatures, but no pus.

According to various scholars, many historical figures reputedly died from this revolting malady, after their bodies had quite literally rotted from these subcutaneous infestations – including Herod the Great, Herod Agrippa, and the Syrian king Antiochus IV Epiphanes, as well as an assortment of European royalty and nobility. However, as it was once commonly thought that phthiriasis was inflicted as a divine punishment, puritanical historians were swift to denounce almost any unpopular monarch as having died from this accursed ailment.

But how did lice come to be living beneath these sufferers' skin anyway? For centuries, the popular conviction was that they had simply arisen by spontaneous generation, from bad tissue ("corrupted humours") or sweat. By the eighteenth century, however, belief in spontaneous generation was fading, in the light of new advances in entomological knowledge concerning lice, which deemed it unlikely that these air-breathing insects could survive beneath the skin and lay eggs there. Instead, opinion regarding the agent responsible for phthiriasis leaned towards a species of mite (tiny parasitic arachnid). British entomologists William Kirby and William Spence even suggested that an unknown species of mite may be involved.

In 1865, however, following an exhaustive study of the literature dealing with phthiriasis, the eminent Viennese dermatologist Professor Ferdinand von Hebra published an extensive, serialized paper in the *Wiener Medizinische Presse*, in which he concluded that no such disease existed, and that all supposed cases of it were based solely upon superstition and inflamed imagination. Although this incited considerable scientific discussion for months afterwards, Hebra's informed opinion ultimately prevailed, and phthiriasis thereafter vanished from the medical textbooks – discounted as an unscientific delusion.

However, Bondeson considers that this conclusion may be a little premature – thanks to the findings of a detailed study into the history of phthiriasis published in 1940 by Dutch zoologist Professor A.C. Oudemans, within the journal *Zeitschrift für Parasitenkunde*. As aficionados of biological mysteries will realize, this was not the first time that Oudemans had entered the realms of zoological controversy. He had already published a tome dealing with the great sea serpent, and had also documented his belief that representatives of the flightless dodo may have persisted long after 1681, this bird's official date of extinction.

Professionally, however, Oudemans was a highly experienced acarologist (mite expert), and

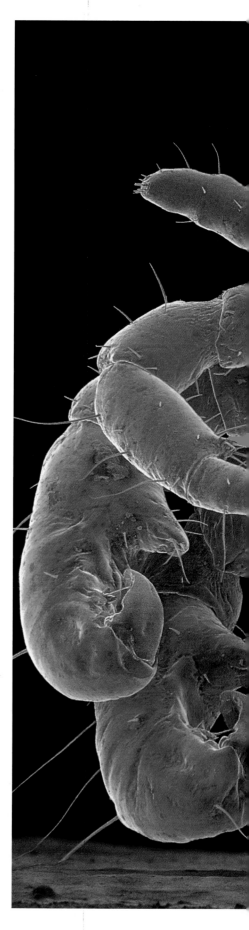

*The crab louse (magnification x 40), a parasite held responsible for various unspecified diseases.*

in his phthiriasis paper he not only argued compellingly that this officially fictitious disease may once have existed after all, but also nominated a certain species of mite as a plausible identity for the "lice" supposedly responsible. The mite in question is *Harpyrhynchus tabescentium*, which is the only mite capable of burrowing beneath the entire skin, where it thrives in large numbers, made up of individuals of varying age and size. Moreover, because of the size that tumours containing these arachnids can attain, they may sometimes kill their unfortunate host – but if the tumours are lanced, great quantities of mites will swarm out, though rarely if ever accompanied by pus. In short, an infestation of *H. tabescentium* certainly does correspond very closely indeed with the classic description of phthiriasis.

There is, however, a notable problem with this proposed solution: *H. tabescentium* infestations have never been confirmed from humans. They occur principally in birds, though they have occasionally also been documented from cats, squirrels and even snakes – but not humans. Nevertheless, some modern-day acarologists have conceded that human infestation with this mite could also occur. Equally worthy of note is that reports of phthiriasis corresponding very closely with one another have been documented in previous centuries from regions as geographically discrete as Scandinavia and China.

Thus, after assessing all of the above points, in his book Bondeson concludes that the dreaded lousy disease, even if no longer extant, may indeed have formerly existed, but rather than featuring genuine lice could have been caused by the mite *H. tabescentium*. Yet if this is true, and as this species of mite is still very much alive today, who can say with certainty, therefore, that humanity has definitely experienced its last contact with what is, even if not zoologically then at least metaphorically, the truly lousy disease of phthiriasis?

# MYSTERY OF THE
# MINARET SKULL

ONE DAY IN AUGUST 1965, WHILE BACKPACKING IN THE VICINITY OF CALIFORNIA'S MINARET MOUNTAINS, RETIRED PHYSICIAN DR ROBERT W. DENTON FROM BISHOP, CALIFORNIA, ASSISTED A MEXICAN FARM WORKER IN HAULING HIS MULE OUT OF A MUDDY BOG AT HEMLOCK CROSSING NEAR THE BANK OF THE SAN JOAQUIN RIVER, AND AS THE MULE STRUGGLED FREE ITS FLAILING HOOVES UNCOVERED A LARGE BOWL-SHAPED OBJECT IN THE MUD.

When Denton examined it, he found that it was a calvarium – the top and rear portion of a skull – which looked humanoid, but unusual in shape and size. Dr Denton forwarded this odd calvarium to pathologist Dr Gerald K. Ridge at Ventura County General Hospital for examination. On 29 September 1965, Ridge replied, noting:

*[The calvarium] ... turned into a rather interesting specimen largely by virtue of the unusual length of the skull as well as a very unusual development of the nuchal*

*ridge [a bony cranial ridge or crest to which the jaw muscles are attached] in the occipital zone. This latter fact for a time had me thinking this must be the skull of some anthropoid species other than human, inasmuch as this amount of nuchal ridge development had not been observed by me.*

In his letter, Ridge also revealed that he had shown the calvarium to two colleagues – Drs Jack Prost and Herman Bleibtreul (spelt "Bleibtreu" in some accounts) – in the Department of Anthropology at UCLA (University of California, Los Angeles campus). Both researchers were similarly surprised by the extent of nuchal ridge development exhibited by the calvarium. Nevertheless:

*Their conclusions were quite definitely that this is the calvarium of a young human, but that it represents that of an Indian [male], the remains very probably having been in the matrix or adjacent area for many, many years ... with no indications of any medico-legal import.*

Ridge had allowed Bleibtreul to retain the calvarium, but was given a receipt for it, and informed Denton that the two anthropologists had expressed an interest in ascertaining its precise provenance, in case it was an area that had not been investigated archaeologically in recent years. On 10 December 1965, Denton duly forwarded a map of the locality to Ridge – after which the promising case of the Minaret skull came to an abrupt, mystifying end.

In August 1973, while researching for his forthcoming book, *Bigfoot* (co-authored with B. Ann Slate), bigfoot investigator Alan Berry met Denton. Learning about the Minaret calvarium, he was both intrigued that Ridge had entertained the notion of it being from some form of

Left: *William M. Rebsamen's painting interpreting the bigfoot (sasquatch) as* Gigantopithecus.

anthropoid, and very surprised to hear that Denton had never received any reply or further information after posting off his map to Ridge almost eight years earlier. Was it conceivable that this strange cranial portion had been part of a bona fide bigfoot skull?

Anxious to find out more, Berry elected to pursue the case himself, and began by contacting Ridge, but he too had not heard anything more about it. Moreover, enquiries made directly, as well as via an anthropologist colleague, to UCLA regarding the calvarium's current whereabouts also drew a complete blank. Clay A. Singer, a technician at the museum of UCLA's Department of Anthropology, attempted a thorough search of the records and collections for any clues, but again without success. As for Bleibtreul and Prost (both of whom had left UCLA by then), according to Berry's documentation of this very curious affair in *Bigfoot* (1976), neither of them claimed to have any memory of the calvarium.

After Berry mentioned to Bleibtreul that Ridge had obtained a receipt from him after leaving the calvarium with him back in September 1965, however, Bleibtreul was able to recollect it, and revealed that although a search had been planned at the site of its discovery for further relics, it had never actually taken place. As for the calvarium itself, Bleibtreul was convinced that it had indeed been catalogued and retained in UCLA's collections, and he promised to investigate the matter, but when he spoke with Berry again in May 1974 he announced that he had not succeeded in locating it.

Matt Moneymaker of the Bigfoot Field Researchers Organization (BFRO) is also interested in the peculiar history of the Minaret skull, after first learning about it in 1988 while attending UCLA as a student, and he raises some salient points regarding it on his website. Bleibtreul had revealed to Berry that although he and Prost believed the calvarium to be from an ancient native American, they were puzzled that it did not correspond with any known population from that area. Moreover, while conversing with

Berry, Ridge had described this anomalous specimen as "a rather massive piece of bone of peculiar shaping".

Yet when Moneymaker queried UCLA anthropologist Professor Ted Rasmusen concerning how ancient native Americans and modern Americans compared, Professor Rasmusen revealed that for dietary reasons the former are normally smaller than the latter. He added: "It's possible for an ancient Indian to have a skull larger than a modern, six-foot- [1.8-metre] tall, Anglo Saxon male, but it's uncommon ... not unknown, but very uncommon."

In view of this, the conclusion by Bleibtreul and Prost that the calvarium was from a young ancient Indian is somewhat mystifying – as is the calvarium's pronounced nuchal ridge. In any event, as Rasmusen also noted, it would be very difficult to ascertain an individual's race merely from a calvarium; such identifications normally require facial bones and teeth.

And what of the biggest mystery of all – the Minaret skull's current whereabouts? After speaking with a friend who had been a graduate student in UCLA's History Department and who had spent one summer working in the off-campus museum annexe building at Chatsworth, California, Moneymaker considers this huge specimen-packed warehouse to be the likeliest locality for the cryptic calvarium. However, he concedes that it would be no easy task to persuade anyone to search through such an extensive array of material specifically for it.

Yet even if a portion of a bigfoot skull really does lurk unrecognized and uncatalogued within the museum collections of UCLA, it would certainly not be unprecedented. As I revealed in my book *The Lost Ark* (1993), there are many case histories on record of a major new species having been "discovered" not in the field but in some museum collection, following an alert, informed researcher's examination of a hitherto overlooked or misidentified specimen. Perhaps one day, therefore, history will repeat itself yet again, and divulge another zoological surprise.

# A PLENITUDE OF PYRAMIDS

WHEREAS PYRAMIDS ARE FAMOUS IN EGYPT AND MEXICO, FAR LESS FAMILIAR – AND MUCH MORE MYSTERIOUS – VERSIONS HAVE ALSO BEEN DISCOVERED IN CHINA, JAPAN, GREECE AND ELSEWHERE, AS REVEALED IN THIS EXAMINATION OF THESE LITTLE-KNOWN, LONG-NEGLECTED EDIFICES.

## A CHINESE CONUNDRUM

In 1994, German writer-researcher Hartwig Hausdorf published a remarkable book, *Die Weisse Pyramide* ("The White Pyramid"), subsequently translated into English as *The Chinese Roswell*, which concerns an equally

remarkable discovery in China. It all began one day in spring 1945, when, while flying his aeroplane over Qin-Ling-Shan's high valleys south-west of Xi'an City in central China's Shensi Province, US Air Force pilot James Gaussman spied (and photographed) an

extraordinary structure – a huge pyramid, resembling those of ancient Mexico! More photos, of more Chinese pyramids, some of

---

*The pyramids of ancient Eygpt may have been surpassed by even older structures elsewhere.*

depicts in great detail the events leading up to the Norman invasion of England and the Battle of Hastings in 1066, and as such it is a highly significant historical document. This is why, therefore, one of the birds portrayed in the rows of creatures decorating the tapestry's borders has attracted appreciable historical (as well as cryptozoological) attention – because it bears somewhat of a resemblance to a turkey. Yet accepted history dictates that turkeys did not reach European shores from the New World for almost another 500 years.

Some historians have sought to reconcile this chronological discrepancy by claiming that the bird in question is not an accurate portrait of a turkey but is merely a poor depiction of a peacock, which was certainly a popular dish, especially among the wealthy, in Europe at the time of the Bayeux Tapestry's creation (and for

several subsequent centuries too). Having closely scrutinized this controversial depiction, I too favour a peacock identity for it.

Others, conversely, have boldly suggested that if the Vikings did indeed reach North America during the early years of the eleventh century AD (i.e. several centuries before Christopher Columbus, not to mention the Spanish conquistadors), perhaps they returned to Europe with some turkeys. This would therefore explain how an exclusively New World bird could appear on the Bayeux Tapestry later that same century.

A further complication with the Bayeux case inadvertently stemmed from a short article by Maris Ross, published in the London *Daily Mail* on 31 August 1991, which briefly alluded to the turkey mystery. Accompanying Ross's article was a sketch prepared by one of the *Daily Mail*'s resident cartoonists, Haro, depicting in his own distinctive, readily recognizable style an eleventh-century man

with a turkey. Amusingly, albeit regrettably, Haro's sketch has since been reproduced in more than one account of the Bayeux turkey under the mistaken assumption that it is a direct representation of this bird as depicted in the tapestry!

Notwithstanding such unfortunate confusion, the Bayeux turkey remains a valid mystery, whereas the Schleswig turkey was ultimately exposed as a turkey (or canard?) in every sense of the word! The walls of Schleswig Cathedral in Germany are richly decorated with medieval murals. One of these, dating from around 1280, includes an unmistakable representation of a domestic turkey, complete with pendant facial wattle, upraised fanned tail feathers, and large broad wings. As with the Bayeux depiction, however, this would thus suggest that turkeys reached the Old World centuries before their official arrival here with the conquistadors.

Curiously, no one had noticed the turkey depiction in Schleswig Cathedral until after World War II, but during the early 1950s the reason for this odd oversight, and the even odder presence of the turkey depiction here, were sensationally revealed – during an art forgery trial. The accused was German painter Lother Malskat, who not only confessed to the charges brought against him, but also conceded that he was responsible for the Schleswig turkey! Apparently, he had been restoring some of the cathedral's murals just before World War II, and while doing so he had spotted an outline that reminded him of a turkey – so he skilfully painted one into the mural! With the onset of the war, no one had spotted Malskat's anachronistic addition straight away, so if it had not been for the forgery case, his turkey may still have been perplexing scholars of art and history even today.

# MONASTERY IMP

MANY PEOPLE WILL BE AT LEAST ACQUAINTED WITH THE FAMOUS STORY OF TWO STRANGE GREEN-SKINNED CHILDREN MYSTERIOUSLY APPEARING AT WOOLPIT IN SUFFOLK, ENGLAND, DURING THE TWELFTH CENTURY AD – AS DOCUMENTED, FOR INSTANCE, IN MY OWN BOOK "THE UNEXPLAINED" (1996). FAR LESS WELL KNOWN, CONVERSELY, EVEN TO DEVOTEES OF THE INEXPLICABLE, IS THE EQUALLY IF NOT MORE MYSTIFYING APPEARANCE IN 1138 AD – AND THE COMPARABLY DRAMATIC DISAPPEARANCE SOME MONTHS LATER – OF A TRULY BIZARRE EBONY-HUED ENTITY IN THE MONASTERY OF PRÜM IN TRÈVES, RHENISH PRUSSIA.

This monastery was founded by Pepin, father of Charlemagne the Great, and was dedicated to the apostles St Peter and St Paul. Today, we owe the amazing details of the following all-but-forgotten event associated with it to an account penned during the late twelfth century by a chronicler monk of Christ Church in Canterbury, England, called Gervaise. According to Gervaise, this extraordinary saga began one morning in 1138, when the keeper of the monastery's wine cellar discovered that during the previous night a cask had been emptied on the

*Woolpit, Suffolk, home of the strange green children.*

floor. He was very puzzled by this, because the cellar was always locked at night – and he was even more puzzled when history repeated itself on the next two mornings.

Greatly concerned, the wine keeper sought the advice of the monastery's abbot, who, after taking counsel with the senior monks, ordered that the bung-hole of every remaining full cask should be anointed with holy oil. The keeper duly complied; and when one of the monks was sent to the wine cellar at dawn on the following morning to see if anything strange had occurred there overnight, his eyes beheld an astonishing sight:

*[The monk], going into the cellar, found a marvellously little black boy, or dwarf clinging by the hands to one of the bungs. Hastily seizing him, he took him to the abbot and said: "My Lord, here is the urchin who has done all the damage in the cellar!" The abbot, astonished at the strange appearance of the boy, took counsel with the senior monks and ordered that the boy have a monk's dress prepared for him, and associate with the youths who were scholars of the monastery.*

*The strange boy lived with these scholars night and day but never took drink or food, never spoke, either in public or private, and while the others were sleeping at night or in noontide, he sat upon his bed and constantly moaned or deeply sighed. Meantime, the abbot of another monastery came to perform his devotions in the church. And with the scholars frequently passing before him as he sat with the abbot and the older monks, he saw the little boy stretch his hands towards him as if to ask a favour.*

*So often did the strange boy repeat this gesture that the abbot, noting his small stature, said to the monks who sat near him: "Why do you keep so little a boy in your convent?" They replied, smiling: "My Lord, he is not what you suppose!" They told him the story of the cellar, and the abbot groaned deeply and said: "Expel him at once! He is clearly a devil in human form; but, by the mercy of God and the merits of the saints, whose relics you have here, he has been held from doing you more injury." At the command of the abbot, the boy was at once brought before him, and while they were in the act of stripping off his monastic dress he vanished from their hands like smoke.*

It is hardly surprising to learn that such an entity was deemed an imp by medieval monks, but in the only modern-day contemplation of this remarkable event that I have seen, a very different, yet no less thought-provoking interpretation was considered. One of the explanations on offer for the green children of Woolpit is that they were somehow transported to our world from another dimension – possibly even an alternate universe. Similarly, in his book *Mysteries: Solved and Unsolved* (1959), Harold T. Wilkins, a veteran chronicler of inexplicabilia, reviewed a series of mystifying cases (including the green children and the monastery imp) that in his view supported such a notion.

Also postulated by various other psychical researchers, Wilkins's suggestion was that "holes in the wall" (i.e. interspatial, intertemporal "doors" or "windows") might exist through

which people, animals and objects may pass, albeit involuntarily and unexpectedly, from one region of the world to another, or even from one dimension to another. Regarding the monastery imp, he speculated: "The mysterious black and dwarfish boy had 'found the hole in the wall' and, as if he had been teleported to early medieval Germany from some tribe of Central African pigmies [sic], he had as mysteriously returned to that unknown bourne [region] whence he had come. Here, again, we have a story in part garbled by medieval monasticism."

Any concept along the lines of an African pygmy stumbling through some form of "cosmic doorway" and being transported instantaneously into another region of the world far-removed (in

*A Wambutti pygmy in the Congo – could one such person have slipped through an interspatial door to enter the monastery of Prüm?*

space, and perhaps also in time?) from his own sounds like the plot of a science-fiction movie. Yet unless this entire episode is fictitious, or tortuously distorted from beginning to end, it is so bewildering a tale that in the absence of further data to examine we can hardly expect proffered solutions to be any less so.

Perhaps, therefore, we should take heart from the following words of Nobel-Prize-winning physicist Professor Niels Bohr: "We all agree that your theory is mad. The problem that divides us is this: is it sufficiently crazy to be right?"

## CHAPTER SIX

## MORE THAN A LEGEND?
# THE DOBHAR-CHÚ TOMBSTONE

BOTH IN IRELAND AND IN SCOTLAND, THE TERM "DOBHAR-CHÚ" (ALSO SPELT "DOBARCU", AND PRONOUNCED "DURRA-GHOO") TRANSLATES AS "WATER-HOUND", AND HAS TWO VERY DIFFERENT USAGES. ONE IS SIMPLY AS AN ALTERNATIVE NAME FOR THE COMMON EUROPEAN OTTER *Lutra lutra*, BUT IS RARELY USED IN THIS CAPACITY NOWADAYS (HAVING BEEN SUPERSEDED BY THE TERM "MADA-UISGE"). ITS OTHER USAGE, WHICH IS MUCH MORE INTERESTING AND MYSTIFYING, IS AS THE NAME OF A SUPPOSEDLY MYTHICAL OTTER-LIKE BEAST, AND IS STILL WIDELY USED IN THIS CAPACITY WITHIN THE COUNTY LEITRIM REGION OF IRELAND.

According to Irish folklore, the mythical dobhar-chú originates as the seventh cub of a normal otter, and is therefore a very special, giant-sized otter that is also known as the master otter or king otter. Never sleeping and sometimes attended by a huge court of ordinary-sized otters, in some tales the dobhar-chú is claimed to be completely white, except for its black ear tips and a black cruciform mark upon its back. So magical is this handsome-looking creature that just an inch of its ermine-like pelt will prevent a man

Above: *The dobhar-chú carved on Grace Connolly's tombstone.*

from being wounded by gunshot, a ship from being wrecked, or a horse from being injured.

If this were all, the dobhar-chú, although undeniably memorable, would nevertheless be of scant interest outside Irish legend: but there is more – much more!

The most important dobhar-chú story dates back over 200 years, and tells of a man called Terence McGloughlan and his new bride, Grace Connolly (it was Gaelic custom for the bride to retain her maiden name). They lived in the townland of Creevelea at the north-west corner of Glenade Lake, just inside County Leitrim's border with County Sligo.

One morning in September 1722, Grace went to the lake to wash clothes (or to bathe, in some versions of the story), but she never returned. Greatly worried, her husband set out to look for her – but he did not have to look far. There at the lakeside was Grace's dead body, bloodstained and mauled – and lying across her prone form was her assassin, a dobhar-chú. Blind with fury, McGloughlan shot the savage creature dead with a single bullet, but not before it had emitted a shrill scream. Moments later, its call was answered from the depths of Glenade, and a second dobhar-chú surfaced – the dead beast's vengeful mate.

It made at once for McGloughlan, who mounted his steed and raced home, from where, accompanied by his loyal brother, he then set forth to flee the area, but the large, powerful dobhar-chú relentlessly pursued them. Eventually, the two men reached Castlegarden (Cashelgarren) Hill, where they dismounted, placed their horses lengthwise to block the path, and then concealed themselves, awaiting the arrival of their deadly pursuer. And when the dobhar-chú attempted to charge between their horses' legs, Terence McGloughlan jumped down from his hiding place and plunged his dagger into the startled creature, killing it. Of course, this could all be dismissed as just another fanciful folktale, were it not for the fact that, as documented in 1948 by Patrick Tohall in the *Journal of the Royal Society of Antiquaries of Ireland*, Grace Connolly's grave actually exists – and carved upon her tombstone is a detailed portrayal of her killer, the dobhar-chú. Her grave is in Congbháil (Conwall) Cemetery, in the town of Drumáin (Drummans), forming part of the approach to the Valley of Glenade from the coastal plain of north County Leitrim and south County Donegal, and not far from Bundoran. Part of the grave's inscription is still legible, and the names of Grace and her husband can be discerned.

In August 1997, two Irish colleagues of mine, Daev Walsh and Joe Harte, independently visited Conwall Cemetery to discover whether Grace's grave still existed. Not only were they both able to confirm that it did, but they also took some excellent photographs of it, which they kindly passed on to me. One of these is reproduced here. The tombstone is a recumbent flag of sandstone measuring approximately

*According to Irish legend, the master otter is predominantly white in colour and exceptionally large.*

4 feet 6 inches by 1 foot 10 inches (137 cm by 56 cm), and is dated 24 September 1722.

As can be seen, it depicts the dobhar-chú lying down, with its head and neck thrown backwards so as to lie flat along its back – presumably meant to represent it in its death-throes. A long weapon pierces through the base of the creature's neck, re-emerging below its body, and is gripped at its uppermost end by a human hand (which some observers have actually mistaken for the head of the dobhar-chú!). The carved dobhar-chú embodies an intriguing combination of morphological features. Whereas its long limbs and powerful thighs, deep-chested body, and lengthy curved tail (terminating in a conspicuous tuft) are all decidedly dog-like in

form, its notably large paws, long heavy neck, short head and tiny ears are those of an otter. Little wonder, then, that this beast is colloquially referred to both as a water-hound (dobhar-chú) and as an otter (master or king).

Having said that, however, it bears no direct resemblance to any type of animal known to zoology. This would not be a problem if the dobhar-chú could be discounted as wholly mythical, but the reality of Grace Connolly's grave shows that it would be rash to do this. Yet if Grace were indeed killed by such a creature, why are there no modern dobhar-chú reports? Surely the two animals that met their deaths in the Glenade episode recalled above were not the very last pair in existence? In fact, there is at least one notable episode on file that suggests that something tantalizingly similar to the

enigmatic dobhar-chú was still alive and well in Ireland as recently as 1 May 1968.

During that evening, two local men called John Cooney and Michael McNulty were driving home past a lake called Sraheens Lough on Achill Island, which is a small isle off the western coast of Mayo, the county immediately to the west of Sligo. Without warning, an unfamiliar-looking animal ran across the road just ahead of their vehicle, and disappeared into some undergrowth. As their headlights had illuminated the creature very effectively, their sighting of it, though brief, was sufficiently clear for them to be able to prepare a detailed description. Shiny dark-brown in colour, the animal had a long neck and a lengthy sturdy tail, four well-developed legs upon which it rocked from side to side as it ran, and a small head. The men estimated its total length to be 8–10 feet (2.4–3 metres), and its height at around 2 feet 6 inches (0.7 metre). A very similar beast emerging from the lake was reported a week later by teenager Gay Dever as he cycled past, and during this same period several other sightings were claimed too.

Cryptozoological sceptics have pointed out that Sraheens Lough is too small to support water monsters of this nature, as it has a circumference of only 1200 feet (365 metres). However, anything able to run across roads on four sturdy limbs is equally able to move from one lake to another, not residing permanently in any one body of water – which may resolve why sightings of monsters in this particular lake are sporadic rather than regular. In any event, the Sraheens Lough mystery beast certainly bears much more than a passing resemblance to the tombstone-depicted dobhar-chú, and Ireland has a longstanding tradition of elusive, unidentified water monsters. So is the dobhar-chú just a myth, or a living legend? Only Grace Connolly knew for sure, and she paid a terrible price for her knowledge

# THE GOLEM OF PRAGUE

IN JEWISH LORE, A GOLEM IS A STATUE OR FIGURE OF A MAN CREATED FROM MUD OR CLAY, BUT WHICH CAN BE BROUGHT TO LIFE WHEN CERTAIN HOLY WORDS, CARVED UPON THE GOLEM'S BROW OR HUNG AROUND ITS NECK, ARE SPOKEN BY A WISE RABBI SKILLED IN THE MYSTICAL ARTS OF THE QABALAH (KABBALAH). SIMILARLY, IF THESE WORDS ARE THEN MODIFIED ACCORDINGLY, THE LIVING GOLEM CAN BE RENDERED INANIMATE AGAIN, OR EVEN TRANSFORMED DIRECTLY BACK INTO CLAY OR DUST.

The most famous, and mysterious, example in history is the golem of Prague. According to Czech legend, in 1580 Rabbi Yehudah Loew ben Bezalel of Prague and two colleagues created a life-sized golem, which they

*Prague's legendary golem as depicted on the cover of* Fate *magazine.*

succeeded in animating by placing in its mouth a slip of parchment bearing the word "shem", which is a Qabalistic rendition of God's divine name. Under Rabbi Loew's control, the golem passively carried out menial labouring tasks that required great strength but little thought. And as the Jewish Sabbath is on Saturday, every Friday evening the Rabbi would remove the

parchment from the golem's mouth, thus rendering it inanimate again, so that it would not disturb their impending day of rest.

One Friday, however, the Rabbi forgot to remove the parchment, and while he was performing the Sabbath service the golem ran amok in a spate of destruction. When the Rabbi discovered what had happened, he immediately abandoned the service and set out in search of his wayward creation. When at last he came upon it, he succeeded in pulling the parchment out of the raging golem's mouth, and while it was once more immobile he and his colleagues carried it away, concealing its mighty form inside the attic of Prague's Old-New Synagogue.

From that day on, the Rabbi forbade everyone from entering the building and even removed the stairs leading up to the attic. Eventually, most people forgot about the golem, but even today no one is allowed inside this particular synagogue's attic, although free access is granted to those in the Czech Republic's other Jewish temples. Why is this? Could something – or someone – strange be hidden in the Old-New Synagogue's mysterious attic?

Certainly, this ban on entering the attic is very curious, especially as most scholars freely accept that the "history" of Prague's golem is entirely fictional – there is not a single historical Czech document from the period when Rabbi Loew lived that alludes to it. On the contrary, the story seems to have arisen as recently as the late 1700s or early 1800s, inspired by an earlier Polish version featuring Rabbi Elijah of Chelm. Yet if the entire history of the Prague golem is indeed fictitious, with no foundation whatsoever in truth, why, therefore, should the attic of Prague's Old-New Synagogue be out of bounds?

Someone who was determined to solve this riddle was Czech author-explorer Ivan Mackerle, who has documented his fascinating investigation in his book *Tajemství Praského Golema* (1992). After conducting meticulous bibliographical researches in Prague's archives, which confirmed that the story of an animated golem had no literal basis in fact, Mackerle formulated a very different, wholly original theory to explain the anomaly of the synagogue's sealed attic. He discovered that the word "golem" translates in Hebrew not only as "artificial man made with magic" but also as "fool". Accordingly, he proposed that the golem was neither an animated clay figure nor a

*Part of the interior of the Old-New Synagogue in Prague.*

mechanical figurine or automaton (as some previous researchers had speculated), but was merely a mentally deficient man, taken pity upon by Rabbi Loew, who cared for him and utilized him as a helper at the synagogue.

This identity might also explain an otherwise unexpected deviation from normal golem lore that featured in the legend of the Prague golem. This claimed that the Prague golem was controlled by placing the shem in its mouth, whereas in other golem accounts the shem is usually carved upon its brow or hung around its neck. If, however, the Prague golem was in reality a retarded man, then perhaps, as argued by Mackerle, the Rabbi supplied him with medicine in order to control fits or seizures from which the man suffered, which could have eventually given rise to a local legend whereby the Rabbi placed a shem into his mouth.

Continuing Mackerle's proposed elucidation of the Prague golem legend: when the Rabbi inadvertently forgot to give him his medicine on that fateful Friday evening, the man ran rampaging into the streets, having suffered a fit – from which he died when finally caught up with by the Rabbi. In fear of what might transpire if word escaped about the man's death, the Rabbi swiftly hid his body in the synagogue's attic, forbade everyone from entering it again, and thereby ensured that no news of this unfortunate incident was ever documented.

Only a dimly recalled, subsequently much-distorted memory lingered on within the local populace, which eventually metamorphosed into the grandiose myth of the Prague golem.

An interesting line of speculation, but was there any physical evidence to support it? There was only one way to find out. After weeks of lengthy negotiations with the Czech authorities, Mackerle was granted permission to enter the Old-New Synagogue's long-secluded attic, and in March 1984 he finally stepped inside its shadowy chamber. To his great disappointment, however, it was empty. As this synagogue is the oldest in Central Europe, dating back to the thirteenth century, Mackerle was not allowed to excavate the attic's floor, walls or columns, but he was permitted to use geophysical radar equipment, which would reveal any surprises that may be hidden there. Yet once again, nothing was found.

During his researches, however, Mackerle learnt that the synagogue had been renovated in 1883, and that if anything of human origin had been found there, it would have been buried in the Jewish cemetery. Perhaps, therefore, it is here, and not in the synagogue's mysterious attic after all, that the truth of Prague's golem may one day be uncovered.

# NOT JUST A MONSTROUS MYTH?

CENTAURS, SATYRS, GIANT ANTS, DRAGONS AND OTHER LEGENDARY FAUNA ARE WHOLLY FABULOUS,
IMAGINARY BEASTS – OR ARE THEY? AS REVEALED BY THE FOLLOWING SELECTION, THE
ZOOMYTHOLOGICAL LITERATURE CONTAINS SOME CURIOUS, PREVIOUSLY LITTLE-PUBLICIZED EVIDENCE
CLAIMING THAT CERTAIN "IMAGINARY" CREATURES HAVE A FIRMER BASIS IN REALITY THAN IS
GENERALLY SUSPECTED.

# Centaurs and Satyrs and Tritons, Oh My!

Phlegon of Tralles was a Greek freedman of the Roman Emperor Hadrian. He lived during the second century AD, but is still remembered today – thanks to his aptly titled *Book of Marvels*, which has been called "the earliest surviving work of pure sensationalism in Western literature". As suggested by this description, it is an enthralling collection of wonders and inexplicabilia, ranging from monstrous births and ghosts to abnormally rapid development in humans, births from males, and living specimens of supposedly mythical, fabulous beasts. Moreover, in 1996 Exeter University scholar William Hansen produced the first English translation of Phlegon's book, with a detailed commentary containing additional examples.

One of the many wonders documented therein by Phlegon was a reputed centaur (which he specified as a hippocentaur), captured alive in the Arabian city of Saune, and sent to Egypt as a gift. Sadly, however, it died, so its corpse was embalmed and sent to the Roman emperor, where it was initially exhibited in his palace, but later maintained in his storehouse. According to Phlegon's description, this incredible creature had hairy arms and fingers but the firm hooves of a horse, ribs that were connected to its stomach and its front legs, a face that was fiercer than a human's, and a tawny mane, stained darker by the embalming fluid.

Similarly, as noted by Hansen in his commentary, in 83 BC a sleeping satyr was allegedly captured in Nymphaion, Greece, by men belonging to the army of the Roman dictator Sulla, to whom the entity was brought. When spoken to by interpreters, however, the satyr merely uttered a harsh, unintelligible sound somewhat between that of a goat and a horse, and so was led away again. Its subsequent fate was not recorded.

Once ranked as one of the wonders of Rome was the preserved corpse of a triton – a merman-like entity. According to a description

*"The Satyr and the Peasant" by Jacob Jordaens, c.1620.*

of it by the second-century Greek geographer Pausanias, who had personally viewed it, this semi-human had hair upon its head but was otherwise covered in fine scales resembling the rough skin of sharks. It had greyish eyes, a human nose, a somewhat broad mouth with animal-like teeth, and gills beneath its ears. Its upper body sported a pair of arms with hands and fingers, but instead of legs its lower body terminated in a dolphin-like tail. Pausanias also saw a similar specimen displayed in Greece.

It is quite probable that these preserved tritons were in reality akin to the fake "stuffed mermaids" that wily mariners formerly created by skilfully sewing the posterior half of a fish on to the upper body of a monkey, or to the grotesque Jenny Hanivers and devil-fishes produced by deftly modifying the dried bodies of large skates and rays.

Having said that, however, as noted by Hansen it is exceedingly difficult when dealing with reports dating back as far as these to determine satisfactorily which of them were based upon deliberate frauds and which were

based upon misidentifications – especially when most people in those far-distant times readily accepted such specimens as these as genuine.

## Unmasking the Giant Ants of Herodotus

It has taken an age – literally – but one of mythology's oldest zoological mysteries has finally been solved. Almost 2,500 years ago, the Greek scholar Herodotus wrote in his *History* about a species of "giant ant", said to be the size of a small dog and covered in fur, which was

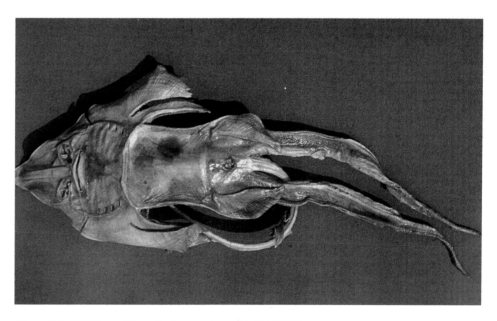

Above: *A devil-fish form of Jenny Haniver – masquerading as a triton?*
Left: *Franz von Stuck's painting "Spring" shows a centaur playing the flute.*

used by the Persians to locate and mine gold on behalf of what was then the vast Persian Empire! Not unreasonably, modern zoologists poured scorn upon this fanciful tale, but a team of Himalayan explorers recently confirmed that Herodotus was correct – in a sense.

In 1996, the team's leader Michel Peissel revealed that the creature in question does exist, is indeed covered with fur, and is the size of a (very) small dog. Furthermore, its Persian name translates as "mountain ant" – but it is not an ant. Instead, it is a species of marmot (ground squirrel), which, when burrowing, disturbs the top soil. This is then collected by the local people here, who duly extract deposits of gold from it using small sieves.

## THE CROCODILIAN DRAGON OF BRNO

According to a traditional, albeit many-versioned, Czech legend, long ago a savage dragon had terrorized Brno (formerly called Brünn), devouring children and livestock with great relish, until a particularly enterprising knight baited the creature using a calf skin filled with slaked lime. When the dragon greedily consumed it under the erroneous impression that it was a calf carcase, the lime imbued it with such a searing thirst that it raced at once to the nearby stream. Here, it quaffed the cooling waters feverishly, only for the water to react so violently with the lime in its stomach that the hapless monster ultimately exploded!

Quite evidently, however, there were some skilful dragon reconstructors in the vicinity – judging from the fact that its preserved corpse can still be seen today on display in Brno's town hall, suspended from the ceiling. In reality, however, this "dragon" is nothing more than a fairly large crocodile, seemingly coated in pitch. So was the Brno dragon merely an escapee crocodile, possibly from some menagerie, or was the story totally fictitious and the crocodile an unrelated specimen that somehow became

*The "dragon" of Brno – in reality a large, black-coated crocodile.*

linked to it? Countless notions, all conflicting with one another, have been aired regarding this crocodile's cryptic origin, but there seems good evidence for believing that irrespective of where it came from, it has been hanging in Brno's town hall since at least 1608.

## MEETING THE MIRRII DOGS

Among the least-known yet most interesting legendary animals are the mirrii dogs or mirriuula, featuring in the ancient lore of the Wiradjuri aboriginals from the central west of New South Wales, Australia. For despite their wholly separate ethnological origin, they bear an uncanny resemblance to the black dogs of British and North American traditions, and, again like these latter beasts, they seem to prowl the dim border between myth and reality.

Several stories concerning these canine entities can be found in *You Kids Count Your Shadows* (1990) – a fascinating book dealing with Wiradjuri folk traditions, by folklore researcher Frank Povah from Wollar in New South Wales. According to the Wiradjuri, when a mirrii dog is first seen it is only quite small, with red eyes and noticeably pointed ears – but the longer that someone looks at one of these beasts, the bigger it will grow. Indeed, it can sometimes attain the size of a calf or even a pony. Like certain British black dogs, mirriuula

are often associated with water, and some are actually referred to as water dogs, as revealed in the following testimony obtained from one of the Wiradjuri:

*They'll follow you and coax you away. They live in the river, in the water, and they've got real big eyes like saucers. The eyes is [sic] on the side of their face, like a fish ... I've heard a lot of stories about people being followed home at night by these big dogs. People just see em. Down the river fishin, a dog'll come out of the river, or a dog'll suddenly be behind em, followin em. Every time you look back, it's a bit bigger. Look back again and there's nothin there. We got a very special site called the Mirriigana and mirriigana means – well mirrii is a dog and gana is like ganya, place. Place where the water dog lives. It's one of our sacred sites.*

Several Wiradjuris recalled modern encounters with mirriuula in their conversations with Povah. For instance:

*They used to go to the pictures and when they'd come home this little dog used to follow them. He had pointy ears and red eyes. When they got to their house he used to disappear. Another one, too, you'd see a little dog in front of you about sundown, and as you get closer it'd get bigger and bigger. And it was hairy, real hairy. Oh yeh, it'd send you. It'd make you run, I'll tell you ... Goin' to Bushranger's Creek one night and this big, black Doberman lookin thing kept appearin and disappearin. You'd see it and then you wouldn't. Oh it was a scary lookin thing. Mirriuula they used to call em. Great big dogs that grow.*

Today, most scientists would dismiss tales of the mirrii dogs as mere folklore, discounting them as fanciful spirit beasts of the Dreamtime – belonging to an early age long since past.

*Somewhere between myth and reality, mirrii dogs are believed to live in water and appear and disappear at will.*

Unfortunately for science, however, just like their British and American counterparts the mirrii dogs do not appear to realize that they are not supposed to exist, and so they stubbornly continue to appear, at least to those who still know how to see them.

## IN THE PINK!

I am most grateful to cryptozoological researcher Richard Muirhead and *Fortean Studies* editor Steve Moore for providing me with details regarding this previously obscure quasi-mythical creature. In his book *The Vermilion Bird* (1967), concerning life in T'ang Dynasty China (618–907 AD), Edward H. Schafer referred to a highly distinctive type of elephant:

*One T'ang source* [namely, *Ch'ing I Lu*, by T'ao Ku] *tells of a race of black elephants with small pink tusks in Hsun and Lei* [corresponding to the Leizhou Peninsula and south-eastern Guangxi Province]. *Perhaps this describes the true Chinese race itself, whose furious representatives had been subdued by the agents of the kings of Shang* [the Chinese dynasty spanning c. sixteenth–eleventh centuries BC] ... *The naturally pink ivory of the local elephants was well favoured, indeed as equal to the ivory imported from overseas.*

Yet as such creatures do not appear to exist today, one might be forgiven for assuming that they owe more to local legend than zoological reality – which is why it came as such a surprise to discover that this elephantine enigma has actually been assigned its own official scientific name. In 1950, zoologist Dr P.E.P. Deraniyagala formally classified it as a discrete subspecies of the Asian elephant, dubbing it *Elephas maximus rubridens* ("pink-tusked").

Yet if there are no such elephants in existence any more, what did Deraniyagala use as his type specimen, upon which to base his formal description of this subspecies? Remarkably, he selected for this purpose an antique Chinese bronze statuette – or, to be precise, an illustration of this statuette – present within the collections of Chicago's Field Museum of Natural History. The illustration had been published in 1925 by B. Laufer, within one of the museum's own publications, an anthropology leaflet dealing with ivory in China.

Today, conversely, the name *Elephas maximus rubridens* is generally listed merely as a synonym of *Elephas maximus indicus*, so except for the museum's statuette it is as if the pink-tusked pachyderms with ebony hides never existed – and perhaps they never did!

# HERNE THE HUNTER

The setting is Windsor Great Park, bracing itself for a spectacular show of meteorological might. The storm clouds are gathering rapidly, darkening the sky like a baleful phalanx of demonic black crows as they hurl fiery javelins of lightning with wild, thunderous glee. Suddenly, from the shadowy depths of the forest, a great black horse appears, emitting an unearthly phosphorescent glow and accompanied by a pack of baying, slavering hounds with scorching eyes of living fire. Yet even the terror that these horrific apparitions incite is eclipsed by the bearded figure sitting astride the ebony steed.

Tall, of powerful, muscular build, and dressed in furs, he carries a large hunting horn in one hand, which he raises to his lips and blows. Its loud, resonant blast echoes even above the thunder's sonorous roar, and the strange figure throws his head back and laughs – a chilling, inhuman laugh. At that same moment, a bolt of lightning illuminates this eerie scene, and confirms that he is not human – at least, not entirely. Sprouting from his head is a huge pair of stag's antlers! The mystery rider's identity is a mystery no longer, for this is Herne – Windsor's horned, spectral huntsman, doomed to haunt its ancient park for all eternity.

The legend of Herne is one of the most exotic of all English folktales. Several different versions exist, set variously in the reign of Richard II (1377–99), Henry VII (1485–1509), Henry VIII (1509–47) and even Elizabeth I (1558–1603), and offering a number of conflicting narratives detailing Herne's crime and fate.

Perhaps the most widely accepted version identifies Herne as a royal deer keeper, who was accused (falsely, in some accounts) of practising the black arts, and was hung by order of the king from a great oak in the forest. A popular alternative storyline claims that Herne hung himself – driven mad either by despair after the king had defiled his daughter, or because he had

*Left: Herne's Oak after lightning tore its trunk apart and reputedly released the hunter from his doom.*

been betrayed by the king after valiantly saving him from being gored by a stag.

In any event, following his execution (or suicide), Herne reappeared in ghostly form, transformed into a frenzied, vengeful wraith with a pair of antlers growing forth from his head – a physical embodiment of his former allegiance to the king's deer herds.

Ever since, he has reputedly haunted the vicinity of the oak on which he was hung – popularly dubbed Herne's Oak – cursed forever to rampage through the forest on his glowing black steed with his pack of deathless hounds, blowing his horn with maniacal delight and ferociously pursuing anyone unlucky enough to encounter him.

Superstitious folk claimed that Herne had finally freed himself from his unending fate when, during a particularly violent thunderstorm in 1863, a spear of lightning struck Herne's Oak, blasting it apart. But even if so, Herne's release was short-lived, thanks to royal intervention. Anxious to perpetuate this traditional legend, Queen Victoria personally planted a young replacement oak on the site of Herne's original tree, and his legend duly survived.

So too, it would seem, has Herne. Not only have many reputed sightings of this horned phantom been reported in the past, a number have also been documented in modern times. In 1915, for example, British folklorist Dr Katharine Briggs was informed by one of her teachers that his father, a retired colonel with apartments at Windsor Castle, had sometimes observed Herne standing beneath his oak on moonlit nights. And he was also reported during the mid-1930s by a group of frightened workmen who were renovating the castle.

*The spectral figure of Herne the Hunter confronts Henry VIII as the shadows fall over Windsor Great Park.*

Some equally scared youths claimed in 1962 that after they had blown a large hunting horn, found lying on the ground in Windsor Park, a terrifying horned figure astride a huge black horse had abruptly appeared. Even more bizarre – and recent – is the testimony of a Coldstream Guard, who vehemently maintained that while on duty one evening in September 1976 at the East Terrace of Windsor Castle, he saw a statue in the Italian Garden come to life – and sprout a pair of antlers! The petrified guardsman was later found unconscious – but stone-cold sober – by a relief guard, and was revived, still in a very appreciable state of shock, at the garrison's medical centre.

As with all legends, however, facts have a tendency to desecrate these enjoyable fantasies. Some scholars aver that the real Herne's Oak was a very old specimen that was actually felled way back in 1796, and was not replaced until 29 January 1906, by Edward VII, whereas the oak that had been replaced by Victoria was an "imposter", situated elsewhere in the park.

Moreover, it is quite possible that the entire Herne legend is derived from a far earlier period in British history than the Middle Ages or Tudor times. A probable prototype for Herne occurred in ancient Celtic mythology – Cernunnos, whose name translates as "horned one". Often depicted with a club or with one or more ram-headed snakes, and a ruler's torque around his neck, Cernunnos was a Celtic lord of the animals, particularly of the stag and the bull, and was also associated with fertility and the Underworld. Other likely links with Herne include the longstanding tradition of the Wild Hunt, and Belatucadros – the horned war-god of the northern Celts.

# SEA NYMPHS
## AND
# STEAM DEVILS

IN HIS COMPILATION "TORNADOS, DARK DAYS, ANOMALOUS PRECIPITATION, AND RELATED WEATHER PHENOMENA" (1983), VETERAN ANOMALIES CHRONICLER WILLIAM R. CORLISS DEFINED STEAM DEVILS AS: "LONG FINGERS OR COLUMNS OF VAPOR RISING FROM A WATER SURFACE AND SWIRLING UPWARD INTO THE CLOUD DECK". RESULTING FROM THERMAL CONVECTION WHEN THE WATER IS MUCH WARMER THAN THE AIR, AND MOULDED INTO SHAPE BY AIR CURRENTS, STEAM DEVILS CAN SOMETIMES OCCUR IN LARGE ARRAYS AND YIELD GEOMETRICAL PATTERNS, BUT THE REASON FOR THEIR REMARKABLE STABILITY IS STILL A MYSTERY.

A classic observation of steam devils, which took place at New York's Canandaigua Lake, was recorded on 4 January 1912 in *Scientific American* by James S. Lee:

*The surface of the lake was covered by vapor caused by the difference in temperature between the cold air and the comparatively warm water. This vapor, white mist, gathered in spots in masses rising higher than the surrounding mist. As these masses of vapor reached a height of some twenty feet they appeared to take on a rotary motion and formed themselves into columns slowly rising until their apexes met the low-lying clouds, where they spread out in a funnel shape exactly as do water spouts. The columns varied from a foot to possibly ten feet in diameter; some of them ascending in a straight line and others bent into fantastic curves by the action of the wind. I saw a great number of these mist whirls during a drive of some two hours, covering a distance of ten miles along the lake shore, and as they formed and drifted slowly across the water, illuminated by the rays of the setting sun, they were a beautiful and to me a unique spectacle.*

*Left: "Faun and Nymph" by Franz von Stuck (1918); in Roman legend a faun was a deity of the forests, shown as a man with goat's horns, ears, hind legs and tail.*

In 1932, *Science News Letter*, another American periodical, published a report of a recent encounter with steam devils made by Professor Johannes Walther while voyaging in the waters around Greece during high waves and an impending snowstorm:

*The cold air striking the warm water caused numerous columns of white vapor to rise over the foamy caps of the waves. They hovered momentarily, then were caught up whirling by the wind, and as they spun away through the air it did not require any violent stretch of the imagination to see them as feminine figures dancing in filmy draperies.*

Faced with this magical scene, Walther proffered a very novel hypothesis, linking these enthralling meteorological creations with a certain company of maritime maidens from classical Greek mythology. He speculated that perhaps in ancient times, sightings by Greek sailors of diaphanous steam devils hovering at the surface of the sea may have given rise to legends of the Nereids. These beautiful sea nymphs were the fifty daughters of Nereus – an early thalassic shapeshifting deity who lived in a palace beneath the Aegean Sea – and would dance upon the waves, assisting endangered sailors.

I have not seen any subsequent commentary relating to this intriguing if somewhat poetic notion. Nevertheless, I have little doubt that if unexpectedly confronted by the type of surrealistic spectacle documented here, in bygone ages the human imagination may indeed have conferred some supernatural, divine identity upon the swirling steam devils – especially in a land like ancient Greece, where it was widely believed that every facet of nature was controlled or inhabited by its own designated deities. From such beliefs were legends born.

*"Glaucus and Scylla" by Bartholomaeus Spranger, c.1581; as a sea nymph, Scylla was able to live both beneath and upon the surface of the Aegean Sea.*

# BOVINE UNICORNS
## AND
# HORSES WITH HORNS

A SHAFT OF BRIGHT GOLDEN SUNBEAMS BROKE THROUGH THE LEAFY CANOPY OF THE FOREST, ILLUMINATING A CLEARING DEEP WITHIN ITS VERDANT, SECLUDED HEART – AND ALSO ILLUMINATING A WONDROUS CREATURE, STANDING SEDATELY LIKE A LIVING STATUE HEWN FROM SHIMMERING STARLIGHT. IT RESEMBLED AN ELEGANT SNOWY-HUED HORSE, BUT ITS NOBLE BROW BORE A SINGLE, CENTRAL HORN – LONG AND FINELY SPIRALLED, UPON WHICH THE SUNBEAMS JOYFULLY DANCED.

Here was the forest guardian, the very spirit of nature incarnate, for this was that most rare and fabulous of animals, the unicorn. Suddenly, however, the distant sound of a hunting horn pierced the stillness of this magical scene. Instantly alert, the unicorn raised its head, momentarily betraying flickers of alarm, and of sadness too, within its shining eyes. Then, as softly as the echo of a single heartbeat, it was gone, lost to human sight and knowledge within its woodland sanctuary.

Such is the elusive, magical unicorn of legend and lore. Conversely, ever since the damning words of eminent nineteenth-century French zoologist Baron Georges Cuvier, who denounced this mystical creature as a zoological impossibility – claiming that a single median horn could never develop from the paired frontal (brow) bones of a mammal's skull – it has received short shrift from science. Yet this attitude may be both unjust and unjustified.

To begin with, in 1934 Maine University biologist Dr William Franklin Dove successfully, and spectacularly, refuted Cuvier's claim concerning the growth of a single median horn from the frontal bones – by creating a bovine unicorn. He achieved this remarkable feat by removing the embryonic horn buds from a day-old Ayrshire bull calf, trimming their edges flat, then transplanting them side by side on to the centre of the calf's brow. Growing in close contact with one another, the transplanted buds yielded a massive single horn, which proved so successful a weapon that its owner soon became the undisputed leader of an entire herd of cattle. Yet despite his dominance, this unicorn bull was a very placid beast, thus resembling the legendary unicorn not only morphologically but also behaviourally. Just a coincidence?

Some researchers have since speculated that perhaps ancient people knew of this simple technique, and had created single-horned herd leaders, whose imposing appearance and noble temperament thereafter became incorporated into the evolving unicorn legend.

Thus, the development of a single median horn is not an impossibility after all – at least not in cattle, that is. Horses, however, must surely be a very different matter, bearing in mind that they do not even grow paired horns (let alone median ones) – or do they?

In fact, records of horned horses, though rare, are by no means unknown. In 1929, for instance, German zoologists P.P. Winogradow and A.L. Frolow published a short account within the journal *Anatomische Anzeiger* concerning a horse that had exhibited lateral horn development on its brow, accompanied by a photograph of the horse's skull. Even more intriguing, however, is the following excerpt, from South American explorer Felix de Azara's *Natural History of the Quadrupeds of Paraguay and the River La Plata* (1837):

*I have heard for a fact, that, a short time ago, a horse was born in Santa Fé de la Vera Cruz, which had two horns like a bull, four inches [10 cm] long, sharp and erect, growing close to the ears; and that another from Chili was brought to Don John Augustin Videla, a native of Buenos Ayres [sic], with strong horns, three inches [7.6 cm] high. This horse, they tell me, was remarkably gentle; but, when offended, he attacked like a bull. Videla sent the horse to some of his relatives in Mendoza, who gave it to an inhabitant of Cordova in Tucuman, who intended, as it was a stallion, to endeavour to form a race of horned horses. I am not aware of the results, which may probably have been favorable.*

Thus, if horses can occasionally develop paired frontal horns and a median horn can be induced to grow from the frontal bones of cattle, then surely in this unrivalled age of biological modification, where sophisticated techniques yielding cloned, transgenic, and other man-made life forms are already commonplace, it would not be difficult to conduct a slightly modified version of Dove's experiments – using equine-derived horn (or horn-substitute) tissue, and a foal, instead of a calf, as the recipient? It would make a fascinating project for any zoological team capable of ignoring the sound of Cuvier turning loudly in his grave, and, after all, it isn't every day that science is granted the opportunity to create a living legend.

*Giorgio Uccellini's painting of the mystical unicorn captures this legendary beast's alluring quality – a creature that may have existed in reality as well as in folklore.*

# IN THE
# FOOTSTEPS OF THE AMAZONS

According to classical historian Herodotus, writing in c.450 bc, while travelling through Scythia, north of the Black Sea between the Carpathian Mountains and the River Don, he had met a tribe of fierce woman warriors, which he referred to as Amazons. Long dismissed as legendary, it now seems possible that the Amazons had – and still have – a basis in fact.

In February 1997, Californian archaeologist Jeannine Davis-Kimball disclosed that during field work in the Russian steppes, she had found several weapon-containing female graves in burial mounds dating from 600–200 BC. The weapons, specially made with small hand-grips, included short daggers and long swords. Some researchers have speculated, therefore, that these weapons' long-deceased female owners may have been Herodotus's Amazons.

There might also be a modern-day tribe of Amazons, still awaiting formal scientific recognition, but in a remote locality far removed from Scythia. In April 1999, Lieutenant-Colonel

*Above: Modern-day Amazons may still exist. Left: Renowned for their warrior-like strength, the Amazons have also captured many an artistic imagination: "The Battle of the Amazons" by Rubens.*

Eddy Tejo, an Indonesian army colonel, announced that he was planning to set out in search of the elusive, highly dangerous, and ostensibly unique Bok tribe, which allegedly dwells amid the jungles fringing the Mamberano River, within the Jayapura district of Irian Jaya – the western, Indonesian half of New Guinea.

For many years, lurid but unconfirmed reports have emanated from this little-explored mountain region concerning the deadly Bok, because this cryptic tribe is reputedly composed entirely of women, believed to number at least 20 in total – whose favourite diet consists of men! According to local testimony, the Bok women lure men from other tribes away from their villages, after which they are led, at spearpoint, to a temporary Bok camp, where they are forced to mate with the Bok women. Once their male captives have fulfilled this task, however, these

veritable femmes fatales summarily kill them and devour their flesh. The same grisly fate also befalls any male children born to the Bok.

Not unexpectedly, anthropologists hearing such stories in the past have tended to give them short shrift, but Tejo has collected sufficient information from native sources to convince him that these tales may truly have a basis in fact. Similarly, Dorteis Asmuruf, the chief official of the Irian Jaya social affairs office, has taken Tejo's belief seriously enough to agree to send a team to accompany him on his mission of discovery.

Dietary considerations aside, it would certainly not be unthinkable for tribes still unrecorded to science to exist amid the vast verdant wildernesses of New Guinea. Indeed, as recently as June 1998 news emerged that two hitherto-unknown nomadic tribes had been discovered in Irian Jaya. Known respectively as the Aukedate and the Vahudate, they are tall, curly-haired, dark-skinned people, and communicate using sign language. They roam the regions between Waropen Atas sub-district, Yapen Waropen district, and – worth noting in view of the Bok reports – the edge of the River Mamberano. According to a preliminary survey, the Aukedate tribe consists of 33 families, and the Vahudate tribe of 20 families.

How extraordinary it would be if the ancient legends of the Amazons were finally vindicated, thousands of miles – and years – beyond their original setting.

And yet, we should not really be too amazed – just as we ought not to be overly surprised if any of the other mysteries and enigmas documented in this book are ultimately resolved via some equally unexpected disclosures. On the contrary, when investigating such matters we would do well to heed the words of the late Roald Dahl:

*Watch with glittering eyes the world around you, because the greatest secrets are always hidden in the most unlikely places. Those who don't believe in magic will never find it.*

# BIBLIOGRAPHY

Space considerations preclude my listing the many specialised scientific papers, magazine articles, and newspaper reports consulted by me during this book's preparation, but the following books and magazine runs were of particular worth:

Alexander, Caroline, *The Way To Xanadu*, Weidenfeld & Nicolson, London, 1993.

*Anomalist, The*, Jefferson Valley/San Antonio, vol. 1, 1993–present.

Azara, Felix de, *The Natural History of the Quadrupeds of Paraguay and the River La Plata*, London, 1837.

Beckford, William T., *Italy, With Sketches of Spain and Portugal*, vol. 2, Baudry's European Library, Paris, 1834.

Beebe, William, *Galapagos: World's End*, G.P. Putnam's Sons, London, 1924.

Beehler, Bruce M., *A Naturalist in New Guinea*, Texas University Press, Texas, 1991.

Bentley, James, *Restless Bones: The Story of Relics*, Constable, London, 1985.

Blackman, W. Haden, *The Field Guide to North American Monsters*, Three Rivers Press, New York, 1998.

Bondeson, Jan, *A Cabinet of Medical Curiosities*, I.B. Tauris, London, 1997.

Bord, Janet and Colin, *Alien Animals* (revised edition), Panther, London, 1985.

Bord, Janet and Colin, *Ancient Mysteries of Britain*, Grafton, London, 1986.

Bord, Janet and Colin, *The World of the Unexplained: An Illustrated Guide to the Paranormal*, Blandford, London, 1998.

Briggs, Katharine, *A Dictionary of Fairies*, Allen Lane, London, 1976.

Brookesmith, Peter (ed.), *The Unexplained: Mysteries of Mind, Space and Time*, 13 vols, Orbis, London, 1980-83.

Buckland, Francis T., *Curiosities of Natural History* (3rd edition), Richard Bentley, London, 1858.

Burne, Charlotte S., *Shropshire Folk-Lore*, Trübner, London, 1883.

Buttrick, George, *et al.* (eds), *The Interpreter's Bible*, Vol. I, Abingdon Press, New York, 1972.

Cable, Mary, *et al.*, *El Escorial*, Reader's Digest/Newsweek, London/New York, 1971.

Caldwell, Harry R., *Blue Tiger*, Duckworth, London, 1925.

Calvin, John, *Commentaries on the First Book of Moses Called Genesis*, William B. Eerdmans, Grand Rapids, 1948.

Caras, Roger, *Dangerous To Man* (revised edition), Holt, Reinhart & Winston, New York, 1975.

Carter, Charles W. and Earle, Ralph, *The Acts of the Apostles*, Oliphants, London, 1959.

Chapman, Robert, *Unidentified Flying Objects*, Granada, St Albans, 1968.

Clark, Jerome, *Unexplained!* (2nd edition), Visible Ink, Detroit, 1998.

Clark, Jerome and Coleman, Loren, *Creatures of the Outer Edge*, Warner, New York, 1978.

Clavijero, Francisco J., *Historia Antigua de Mexico*, Venice, 1780.

Cohen, John, *Human Robots in Myth and Science*, George Allen & Unwin, London, 1966.

Coleman, Loren and Clark, Jerome, *Cryptozoology A-Z: The Encyclopedia of Loch Monsters, Sasquatch, Chupacabras, and Other Authentic Mysteries of Nature*, Fireside Books, New York, 1999.

Constable, Trevor J., *Sky Creatures*, Pocket Books, New York, 1978.

Corliss, William R., *Handbook of Unusual Natural Phenomena*, Sourcebook Project, Glen Arm, 1977.

Corliss, William R., *Ancient Man: A Handbook of Puzzling Artifacts*, Sourcebook Project, Glen Arm, 1978.

Corliss, William R., *Incredible Life: A Handbook of Biological Mysteries*, Sourcebook Project, Glen Arm, 1981.

Corliss, William R., *Tornados, Dark Days, Anomalous Precipitation, and Related Weather Phenomena. A Catalog of Geophysical Anomalies*, Sourcebook Project, Glen Arm, 1983.

Corliss, William R., *Science Frontiers: Some Anomalies and Curiosities of Nature*, Sourcebook Project, Glen Arm, 1994.

Dailey, Timothy J., *Mysteries of the Bible: Exploring the Secrets of the Unexplained*, Publications International, Lincolnwood, 1998.

Dunne, John J., *Haunted Ireland*, Appletree, Dublin, 1977.

Emboden, William A., *Bizarre Plants: Magical, Monstrous, Mythical*, Studio Vista, London, 1974.

Evans, Hilary; Shuker, Karl P.N.; *et al.* (consultants), *Almanac of the Uncanny*, Reader's Digest, Surry Hills, 1995.

*Fate*, St Paul, Minnesota, No. 1, 1947–present.

Fitch, Eric L., *In Search of Herne the Hunter*, Capall Bann, Chieveley, 1994.

*Fortean Studies*, London, vol. 1, 1993–present.

*Fortean Times*, formerly *The News*, London, No. 1, 1973–present.

Freedman, David N.; Robinson, Thomas L.; *et al.* (consultants), *Mysteries of the Bible: The Enduring Questions of the Scriptures*, Reader's Digest, Pleasantville, 1988.

Gaebelein, Frank E. (ed.), *The Expositor's Bible Commentary*, Zondervan, Grand Rapids, 1990.

Gibbons, William J. and Hovind, Kent, *Claws, Jaws, and Dinosaurs*, CSE, Pensacola, 1999.

Gilroy, Rex, *Mysterious Australia*, Nexus, Mapleton, 1995.

Gooch, Stan, *Creatures From Inner Space*, Rider, London, 1984.

Gordon, Stuart, *The Paranormal: An Illustrated Encyclopedia*, Headline, London, 1992.

Gordon, Stuart, *The Book of Miracles: From Lazarus To Lourdes*, Headline, London, 1996.

Grant, John, *Unexplained Mysteries of the World*, Quintet, London, 1991.

Green, Andrew, *Our Haunted Kingdom*, Wolfe, London, 1973.

Guiley, Rosemary E., *Harper's Encyclopedia of Mystical and Paranormal Experience*, Harper, New York, 1991.

Hansen, William (translator), *Phlegon of Tralles' Book of Marvels*, University of Exeter Press, Exeter, 1996.

Harpur, Patrick, *Daimonic Reality: A Field Guide to the Otherworld*, Viking Arkana, London, 1994.

Hausdorf, Hartwig, *The Chinese Roswell*, New Paradigm Books, Boca Raton, 1998.

Henry, Matthew, *Commentary Upon the Whole Bible*, vol. 1, Fleming H. Revell, New York, 1708.

Hodson, Geoffrey, *Fairies at Work and at Play*, Theosophical Publishing House, London, 1925.

Joseph, Rhawn, *Neuropsychiatry, Neuropsychology and Clinical Neuroscience*, Williams & Wilkins, New York, 1996.

Keil, Carl F. and Delitzsch, Franz, *Biblical Commentary on the Old Testament*, vol. 1: *The Pentateuch*, William B. Eerdmans, Grand Rapids, 1866.

Kohn, George C. (ed.), *Encyclopedia of Plague and Pestilence*, Facts On File, London, 1995.

Legaut, François, *Voyage et Avantures de François Legaut et de Ses Compagnons en Deux Isles Désertes des Indes Orientales*, London, 1708.

Lloyd, E., *A Visit to the Antipodes*, Smith, Elder, London, 1846.

Low, Charles, *Great Asiatic Mysteries*, Stanley Paul, London, 1937.

McEwan, Graham J., *Mystery Animals of Britain and Ireland*, Robert Hale, London, 1986.

Mackal, Roy P., *Searching For Hidden Animals*, Doubleday, Garden City, 1980.

Mackerle, Ivan, *Tajemství Pražkého Golema*, Knížky Do Kapsy, Prague, 1992.

Marshall, Richard, *et al.*, *Mysteries of the Unexplained* (amended edition), Reader's Digest, Pleasantville, 1988.

Michell, John and Rickard, Robert J.M., *Phenomena: A Book of Wonders*, Thames & Hudson, London, 1977.

Michell, John and Rickard, Robert J.M., *Living Wonders: Mysteries and Curiosities of the Animal World*, Thames & Hudson, London, 1982.

Moran, Sarah, *Alien Art*, Bramley, Godalming, 1998.

Mullin, Redmond, *Miracles and Magic: The Miracles and Spells of Saints and Witches*, A.R. Mowbray, Oxford, 1978.

Myers, Allen C. (ed.), *The Eerdmans Bible Dictionary*, William B. Eerdmans, Grand Rapids, 1987.

Nickell, Joe, *Looking For A Miracle*, Prometheus, Amherst, 1993.

Nissenson, Marilyn and Jonas, Susan, *Snake Charm*, Harry N. Abrams, New York, 1995.

Pfeiffer, Pierre, *Bivouacs à Borneo*, Flammarion, Paris, 1963.

Picknett, Lynn, *The Encyclopaedia of the Paranormal: The Complete Guide to the Unexplained*, Macmillan, London, 1990.

Porter, Enid, *Cambridgeshire Customs and Folklore*, Routledge & Kegan Paul, London, 1969.

Povah, Frank, *You Kids Count Your Shadows: Hairymen and Other Aboriginal Folklore in New South Wales*, Frank Povah, Wollar, 1990.

Randles, Jenny, *Beyond Explanation?*, Robert Hale, London, 1985.

Randles, Jenny, *Mind Monsters: Invaders From Inner Space?*, Aquarian Press, Wellingborough, 1990.

Rogo, D. Scott and Clark, Jerome, *Earth's Secret Inhabitants*, Tempo, New York, 1979.

Rohl, David, *Legend: The Genesis of Civilisation*, Century, London, 1998.

Ronan, Margaret, *Strange Unsolved Mysteries*, Scholastic, New York, 1974.

Sanderson, Ivan T., *Caribbean Treasure*, Viking Press, New York, 1939.

Schafer, Edward H., *The Vermilion Bird: T'ang Images of the South*, University of California Press, Berkeley/Los Angeles, 1967.

Shiels, Tony 'Doc', *Monstrum! A Wizard's Tale*, Fortean Tomes, London, 1990.

Shuker, Karl P.N., *Mystery Cats of the World*, Robert Hale, London, 1989.

Shuker, Karl P.N., *Extraordinary Animals Worldwide*, Robert Hale, London, 1991.

Shuker, Karl P.N., *The Lost Ark: New and Rediscovered Animals of the 20th Century*, HarperCollins, London, 1993.

Shuker, Karl P.N., *Dragons: A Natural History*, Aurum Press, London, 1995.

Shuker, Karl P.N., *In Search of Prehistoric Survivors*, Blandford, London, 1995.

Shuker, Karl P.N., *The Unexplained: An Illustrated Guide To The World's Natural and Paranormal Mysteries*, Carlton, London, 1996.

Shuker, Karl P.N., *From Flying Toads To Snakes With Wings*, Llewellyn, St Paul, 1997.

Shuker, Karl P.N. (consultant), *Man and Beast*, Reader's Digest, Pleasantville, 1993.

Shuker, Karl P.N. (consultant), *Secrets of the Natural World*, Pleasantville, 1993.

Slate, B. Ann and Berry, Alan, *Bigfoot*, Bantam, New York, 1976.

Snaith, N.H., *The Century Bible* (new edition): *Leviticus and Numbers*, Thomas Nelson & Sons, London, 1967.

Speiser, E.A., *The Anchor Bible: Genesis*, Doubleday, Garden City, 1964.

Steiger, Brad, *Bizarre Cats*, Pan, London, 1993.

Stejneger, Leonhard, *Georg Wilhelm Steller*, Harvard University Press, Cambridge, 1936.

*Strange Magazine*, Rockville, Maryland, No. 1, 1987–present.

Sutherland, Elizabeth, *A Guide to the Pictish Stones*, Birlinn, Edinburgh, 1997.

Truzzi, Marcello (consultant), *Into The Unknown* (amended edition), Reader's Digest, Pleasantville, 1988.

Ullman, James R. (ed.), *Kingdom of Adventure, Everest*, Collins, London, 1948.

Underwood, Peter, *Dictionary of the Occult and Supernatural*, Fontana, London, 1979.

Usher, George, *A Dictionary of Plants Used By Man*, Constable, London, 1974.

Wilkins, Harold T., *Secret Cities of Old South America*, Library Publishers, New York, 1952.

Wilkins, Harold T., *Mysteries: Solved and Unsolved*, Odhams Press, London, 1959.

Wilson, Ian, *Holy Faces, Secret Places*, Doubleday, London, 1991.

Wood, Frances, *Did Marco Polo Go To China?*, Secker & Warburg, London, 1995.

*X Factor, The*, London, No. 1, 1997–present.

# INDEX
## OF MAIN ENTRIES

# ACKNOWLEDGEMENTS

I wish to thank most sincerely the following people and organisations for their greatly-appreciated encouragement and assistance during my preparation of this book.

Lorna Ainger, *All About Cats*, *All About Dogs*, Chad Arment, Dr Geoff Bailey, Endymion Beer, Trevor Beer, Matthew Bille, Birmingham Public Libraries, Janet and Colin Bord, British Library, British Museum (Natural History), Tim Brown, Carmen Garcia-Frias Checa, Mark Chorvinsky/Strange Bookshop/*Strange Magazine*, Loren Coleman, William R. Corliss, Paul Cropper, cz@onelist discussion group, Jonathan Downes/*Animals and Men*, Dudley Public Libraries, Dr John Ely, *Enigmas*, *Fate Magazine*, Angel Morant Fores, Fortean Picture Library, *Fortean Times*, Philippa Foster, Errol Fuller, Bill Gibbons, Etienne Gilfillan, Craig Gosling, Craig Harris, Joe Harte, David Heppell, Isabela Herranz, Dr Bernard Heuvelmans, *History For All*, *Hobart Mercury*, Victor J. Kean, Clinton Keeling, Nicky Knott, Brad LaGrange, Graham Law, Gerard van Leusden, Ivan Mackerle, Camilla MacWhannell, Dr Jaroslav Mares, Deborah Martin, Debbie Martyr, Dr Ralph Molnar, Steve Moore, Sarah Moran, Dr Robert W. Morrell, Dr Timothy Mowl, Richard Muirhead, Scott T. Norman, Carina Norris, Heather Norris, Richard O'Grady, Chris Orrick, Sally Parsons, Michael Playfair, Alan Pringle, Richard Pullen, Michel Raynal, William M. Rebsamen, Bob Rickard, the late Roy Robinson, Sandwell Public Libraries, Dr François de Sarre/*Bipedia*, Dr Robert M. Schoch, Phil Scott, Paul Screeton/*Folklore Frontiers*, Steven and Frances Shipp/Midnight Books, Mary D. Shuker, Paul Sieveking, Dr Lala Singh, Susan R. Stebbing, Richard Svensson, Lars Thomas, Dr Warren D. Thomas, Topics, Giorgio Uccellini, Walsall Public Libraries, Daev Walsh, *Wild About Animals*, Wolverhampton Public Libraries, the late Gerald L. Wood, *The X Factor*, YEC@onelist discussion group, Zoological Society of Glasgow and West of Scotland, Zoological Society of London.

Last, but certainly not least, I wish to offer my especial thanks to my agent, Mandy Little, of Watson, Little Ltd, and to my publisher, Carlton Books, for presenting me with this wonderful opportunity to share some of my favourite mysteries with you.

Unless otherwise stated, all biblical extracts are from the Authorized King James Version of the Bible.

# PICTURE CREDITS